In the Name of Pauk-Phaw

The **Institute of Southeast Asian Studies (ISEAS)** was established as an autonomous organization in 1968. It is a regional centre dedicated to the study of socio-political, security and economic trends and developments in Southeast Asia and its wider geostrategic and economic environment. The Institute's research programmes are the Regional Economic Studies (RES, including ASEAN and APEC), Regional Strategic and Political Studies (RSPS), and Regional Social and Cultural Studies (RSCS).

ISEAS Publishing, an established academic press, has issued more than 2,000 books and journals. It is the largest scholarly publisher of research about Southeast Asia from within the region. ISEAS Publishing works with many other academic and trade publishers and distributors to disseminate important research and analyses from and about Southeast Asia to the rest of the world.

In the Name of Pauk-Phaw

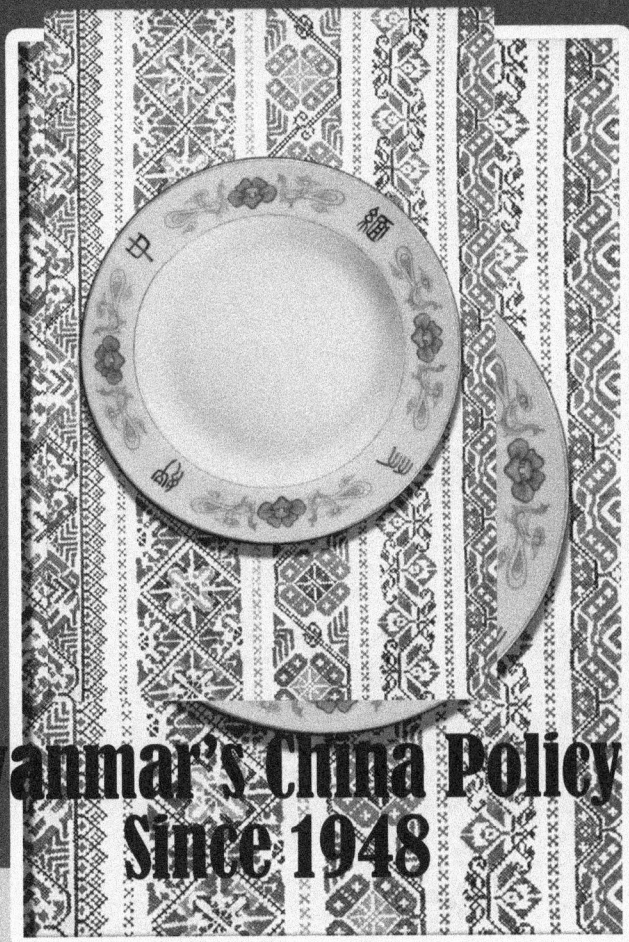

Myanmar's China Policy Since 1948

MAUNG AUNG MYOE

LSEAS

INSTITUTE OF SOUTHEAST ASIAN STUDIES
SINGAPORE

First published in Singapore in 2011 by
Institute of Southeast Asian Studies
30 Heng Mui Keng Terrace
Pasir Panjang
Singapore 119614

E-mail: publish@iseas.edu.sg
Website: <http://bookshop.iseas.edu.sg>

The responsibility for facts and opinions in this publication rests exclusively with the author and his interpretations do not necessarily reflect the views or the policy of the publisher or its supporters.

ISEAS Library Cataloguing-in-Publication Data

Aung Myoe, Maung.
   In the name of pauk-phaw : Myanmar's China policy since 1948.
   1. Burma—Foreign relations—China.
   2. China—Foreign relations—Burma.
   I. Title.
DS528.8 C5A92   2011

ISBN 978-981-4345-17-0 (soft cover)
ISBN 978-981-4345-18-7 (E-book, PDF)

Typeset by Superskill Graphics Pte Ltd
Printed in Singapore by Seng Lee Press Pte Ltd

This work is dedicated to the International Relations Programme (IRP) at the International University of Japan.

CONTENTS

ABOUT THE COVER

The pictures of the plate and the cloth that appear on the cover are gifts presented by the Chinese Government to the people of Myanmar in the early 1960s, after the successful completion of the demarcation of Sino-Myanmar boundary and the conclusion of the Treaty of Friendship and Mutual Non-Aggression. These items were commonly known in Myanmar as "loving kindness plate (မေတ္တာပန်းကန်ပြား) and loving kindness cloth (မေတ္တာပိတ်)". The Chinese characters printed on the plate (中緬友好) were ancient Chinese calligraphies written to mean "China-Myanmar Friendship" and they read as 中缅友好 (Zhong Mian Youhao). I should leave a note of thanks to Thone Thone from Green Book Store for helping me to design this cover.

ACKNOWLEDGEMENTS

I was fortunate to receive exceptional help from a number of people in Myanmar who deserve to be mentioned here but would prefer to remain anonymous. Without their kindness, support and encouragement, this book could not have been accomplished. They have my heartfelt gratitude and thanks. I am particularly grateful to Professor John Welfield for his various insightful comments and suggestions and his painstaking effort in reading through the manuscript. I am benefitted enormously from his wisdom and intellectual motivation. However, I alone take full responsibility for its content. I would like to express my deep appreciation to Asian Research Institute (ARI) and Professor Anthony Reid, former Director of ARI, for giving me an opportunity to work on this manuscript. I should also express my sincere thanks to the ISEAS library and the EAI library in Singapore. I am also grateful to Dr Geoff Wade who has helped me in many ways. Last, not the least, infinite gratitude and special thanks are owed to my family.

CHINESE NAMES

Buhe (布赫)
Cao Gangchuang (曹刚川)
Chen Bingde (陈炳德)
Chen Muhua (陈慕华)
Chen Yi (陈毅)
Chen Zaidao (陈再道)
Chi Haotian (迟浩田)
Deng Xiaoping (邓小平)
Deng Yingchao (邓颖超)
Feng Zhenglin (冯正霖)
Fu Quangyou (傅全有)
Ge Zhenfeng (葛振峰)
Geng Biao (耿飚)
Guo Boxiong (郭伯雄)
Guo Moruo (郭沫若)
He Long (贺龙)
He Qizong (何其宗)
Hu Jintao (胡锦涛)
Hu Yaobang (胡耀邦)
Hua Guofeng (华国锋)
Huang Hua (黄华)
Ismail Amat (司马义•艾买提)
Jiang Zemin (江泽民)
Keng Sheng (康生)
Li Changchun (李长春)

Li Jiulong (李九龙)
Li Mi (李弥)
Li Peng (李鹏)
Li Ruihuan (李瑞环)
Li Xiannian (李先念)
Li Zhaoxing (李肇星)
Liang Guanglie (梁光烈)
Lin Biao (林彪)
Liu Dongdong (劉冬冬)
Liu Shaoqi (刘少奇)
Liu Yalou (刘亚楼)
Lu Xuejian
Luo Gan (罗干)
Mao Zedong (毛泽东)
Peng Dehuai (彭德懷)
Peng Zhen (彭真)
Qian Qichen (钱其琛)
Qiao Shi (乔石)
Qin Jiwei (秦基伟)
Soong Ching Ling (宋庆龄)
Su Yu (粟裕)
Sun Yat-sen (孫逸仙)
Sun Zhiqiang (孙志强)
Tan Zhenlin (谭震林)
Tang Jiaxuan (唐家璇)
Wan Li (万里)
Wang Dongxing (汪东兴)
Wang Guangmei (王光美)
Wang Yi (王毅)
Wang Zhen (王震)
Wen Jiabao (温家宝)
Wu Bangguo (吴邦国)
Wu De (吴德)
Wu Xueqian (吴学谦)
Wu Yi (吴仪)
Xi Jinping (习近平)
Xiao Jingguang (萧劲光)
Xie Fuzhi (谢富治)
Xu Xin (徐信)
Yang Jiechi (杨洁篪)

Yang Shangkun (杨尚昆)
Yeo Wenyuan (姚文元)
Zhang Chunqiao (张春桥)
Zhang Gaoli (张高丽)
Zhang Li (张黎)
Zhang Qian (张茜)
Zhang Wannian (张万年)
Zhao Erlu (赵尔陆)
Zhao Ziyang (赵紫阳)
Zhou Enlai (周恩来)
Zhou Tienong (周铁农)
Zhu De (朱德)
Zhu Rongji (朱镕基)

1

INTRODUCTION

After a long period of anti-colonial struggles and movements for national liberation, Myanmar finally regained her independence on 4 January 1948. Many sacrifices were made in the name of sovereignty, national self determination, and territorial integrity. At the time of Independence, one immediate task for Myanmar was to become a member of the "family of nations"; thus it applied for the membership in the world body known as the United Nations. Myanmar became a member of the United Nations on 19 April 1948. For the people of Myanmar, this signified the recognition of their country as a sovereign state in the Westphalian international system. Successive Myanmar governments since independence have based their foreign policy on "non-alignment" or "neutralism" and highlighted their "independent" nature in the conduct of diplomacy. The Myanmar government expects that the principles of sovereign equality and non-interference in internal affairs should form the basis upon which a country's foreign relations should be regulated. It is in this context that Myanmar has formulated her China policy. Nevertheless her relations with China have never been easy and have been subjected to numerous strains over the years. Historically, China established Sinocentric world order of tributary relations with political entities near and far, which was regulated by rules, customs and rituals, not by treaties. This worldview, constructed primarily upon Confucian norms, was based on hierarchy rather than equality. Lesser political entities were obliged to send tribute and offer symbolic obeisance to the Chinese emperor. Although the Sinocentric world order of tributary relations did not necessarily involve any significant political control by China, it did require the lesser political entities to recognize a hierarchical structure with China at the apex. With this historical legacy, China entered into the world of twentieth century international politics based on the Westphalian model of the theoretical sovereign equality of nation-states. Whether China will ever really reconcile her own traditional worldview with Westphalian norms is a question that has often troubled Myanmar's leaders.

CONCEPTUAL FRAMEWORK

The foreign policy of a nation can be studied at various dimensions and levels. Analysis can be made on the basis of issues, actors, goals and strategies, and so on. In addition, the whole process of the conduct of foreign policy can be reviewed to assess the fundamental nature of a nation's foreign relations. The foreign policy of a nation is determined by a number of factors, all conceived in terms of national interest; these factors may include regime or state security, various geopolitical and geostrategic realities, historical memories, perceptions of ruling elites, and so on. This explains why different states, or the same state at different historical moments, have different policies, intentions, goals, and preferences toward the outside world. One important area of foreign policy study is foreign policy restructuring. According to K. J. Holsti, foreign policies can be classified into four broad categories: isolation, self-reliance, dependence, and non-alignment diversification. These classifications are based on levels of external involvement, policies regarding types and sources of external penetration, directions and patterns of external involvement, and military and diplomatic commitments. Nevertheless, nations restructure their foreign policy orientations in the context of changing international and domestic situations.[1]

Foreign policy study also involves levels of analysis. In the analysis of foreign policy, as in the case of explaining the dynamics of international politics, there are many schools of thought. For convenience sake, a foreign policy can be analysed from at least three levels. First, it can be explained at the individual level, on the basis of the actions and behaviour of individual statesmen. Their education, socialization, personalities, ideological beliefs, motivations, ideals, perceptions, values, or idiosyncrasies all influence the choice of foreign policy options. Their role in the societal and political system will also affect their choices. Beyond this individual level is the state level. One can explain the foreign policy behaviour of a state by reference to not only the impact of the external environment but also of domestic conditions, such as structure of government, the political system, the nature of society, national ideologies, public opinion, or economic and social needs. At the state level, foreign policy is not merely an output of reaction to the external environment. This level of analysis is also important in identifying the foreign policy behaviour. Next is the systemic level. The systemic level explanation of foreign policy focuses solely on the impact of the external environment on the individual political unit, in this case the state, and in term of the condition of whole system or the world order.

However, it is important to understand the true nature of international politics. It is a fact that nation-states have different levels or degrees of power in the international system which is characterized by anarchy. In every international system, as Stephen Krasner argues, there is a set of rules or norms that define actors and appropriate behaviours, but these are rarely obeyed in an automatic or rote fashion. Actors violate rules in practice without at the same time challenging their legitimacy. Krasner called this "organized hypocrisy".[2] This situation occurs because (1) states have different levels of power, (2) rulers in different political entities will be responsive to different domestic norms which may, or may not, be fully compatible with international norms, and (3) situations arise in which it is unclear what rule should apply since there is no authority structure that can resolve these differences in the international system of anarchy.[3] All political and social environments are characterized by the logic of expected consequences and the logic of appropriateness. The logic of expected consequences sees political actions and outcomes, including institutions, as the products of rational calculated behaviour designed to maximize a given set of unexplained preferences. The logic of appropriateness understands political action as a product of rules, roles and identities. Identities specify appropriate behaviour in given situations. The question is not: "How can I maximize my self interest?, but rather, given my role, "How should I act in this particular circumstance?"[4]

Stephen Krasner explains that in a well-established domestic polity, logics of appropriateness prevail and will usually, but not always, be consistent with logics of consequences, since doing "the right thing" is usually consistent with an actor's self-interest. Besides, any disagreement about contested rules can be resolved by institutions, such as the courts or the legislature, which all actors regard as authoritative. He points out, however, that in the international system, logics of appropriateness and logics of consequences will not always be compatible. Saying one thing but doing another, endorsing the logic of appropriateness while acting in ways consistent with logic of consequences, will be a more frequently observed phenomenon. This kind of "organized hypocrisy" will be inevitable unless one of the parties abandons, or is forced to give up, its normative architecture. The reasons for the prevalence of "organized hypocrisy" in international politics are power asymmetries and the absence of any universally recognized legitimate authority. The stronger states can pick and choose from among those norms that best suit their material interests, or ignore norms altogether, because they can impose their choices on weaker states in the absence of any legitimate institution that could constrain their coercion and take action against them.[5]

In the Westphalian norm based international system of sovereign equality and non-interference in the internal affairs of other states, logics of appropriateness should prevail over logics of consequences. Yet the international system is, in reality, an environment in which logics of consequences dominate the logics of appropriateness. This kind of explanation can be found in neorealist and neoliberal explanations of international politics. States are to refrain from interference in the affairs of other states but, at the same time, attempt to alter or influence the domestic institutional structures of those states. This is partly as a result of the asymmetric relations that exist between nation-states.

Asymmetric relations are not uncommon in world politics. Disparity of power does not necessarily mean that the more powerful dominate the less powerful. Brantly Womack explains that in an asymmetric bilateral relationship the two sides nurture different patterns of attention and status sensitivities. The stronger side will tend towards error of inattention in its behaviour, while the weaker side will be more tempted by error of overattention. These differences are the major causes of what Womack calls systemic misperception that can lead to conflict. However, systemic stability can be achieved by fulfilling the minimum expectations of both the more powerful and the less powerful. For the less powerful, the minimum expectation is acknowledgement of its autonomy by the more powerful. For the more powerful, the minimum expectation is deference on the part of the less powerful, which does not necessarily mean submission but simply pursuit of the latter's interest in a manner that corresponds to and is respectful of the superior status of the more powerful.[6]

Womack explains that there are four bilateral factors that moderate structural misperception in asymmetric relationships: (1) inclusive rhetoric (2) issue routinization (3) precedents, and (4) diplomatic ritual. The first two are considered as "inner dimensions" which help creation and expansion of a neutralized core of policy areas in the relationship that are buffered from bilateral confrontation. The last two are "outer dimensions" that aim at establishment of a sleeve for the relationship that makes increasingly radical misperceptions less plausible. In the case of the inner dimensions, neutralization of potential problem areas can be accomplished rhetorically through the use of discourse that articulates the vital interests of both sides or through the conversion of issue areas to 'low politics' through routinization and institutionalization. If both sides present their actions in mutually shared terms and values, that is "inclusive rhetoric", there is more chance of drawing them both into dialogue rather than confrontation. Likewise, "issue routinization", which leaves the direct involvement of central leadership, is less likely to produce confrontation and exacerbate misunderstanding. For the outer dimensions, structural misperception can be mitigated through the presentation of the continuum of historical precedents and the application of diplomatic rituals. "As long as precedent provides familiar ground for an asymmetric relationship, it provides a horizon of common sense that defines what is normal and implicitly places an increasing burden of proof on perceptions of the abnormal", Womack remarks. The practice of diplomatic rituals and exchanges of state visits provides occasions in which both sides can fulfil their minimum expectations, that is, the stronger side acknowledging the weaker side's autonomy and the weaker side deferring to the stronger side's superior position, without either prejudicing their cases on specific issues. While diplomatic ritual and inclusive rhetoric are designed to enhance a common mindset, historical precedents and issue routinization are intended to strengthen the institutional capacity of problem management.[7]

Womack also develops a typology of asymmetric relations. He presented nine different types of asymmetries, of which four are more relevant to modern nation-states. First, "distracted asymmetry" exists between two political entities in asymmetric relations when both of them have other more important relationships to worry about. Both sides will stand shoulder to shoulder in their relationship in facing others. The case of "dependent asymmetry" can be found when the weaker side is under the constraint of not having a feasible alternative to compliance with the preferences of the stronger. "Hostile asymmetry" occurs when one or both sides are perceived as denying minimal levels of autonomy or deference to the other. Finally, "normalized asymmetry" exists, although it is by no means a completely harmonious relationship, when both sides are confident of fulfilling their basic interests and expectations of mutual benefits, leading to the institutionalization of the bilateral relationship management.[8]

At times when bilateral relations are asymmetric, in favour of stronger power, the weaker power can also find appropriate strategies to deal with the stronger side, in addition to deference. Kenneth Waltz once argued that international politics is based on great powers.[9] However, small states do play a role in international politics too. Within the neorealist school of International Relations theory, a number of scholars provide conceptual insights as to how small states can adopt policies to preserve and advance their interests *vis-à-vis* great powers; balancing and bandwagoning are two prominent concepts in the literature. When confronted by a significant external threat, states may balance or bandwagon. Balancing is defined as allying with others against potentially threatening great power while bandwagoning refers to the strategy of alignment with the perceived source of danger.[10]

Traditional balance of power theory argues that states form alliances in order to prevent stronger powers from dominating them, since they see their survival at risk if they fail to curb a potential hegemon before it becomes too strong, or seek to increase their influence within such an alliance. To ally with the dominant power, it is believed, means placing one's trust in its continued benevolence, for it is the stronger state that threatens the weaker; it is therefore much safer for a weaker state to join with those that cannot readily dominate their allies. Thus, neorealists argue that weaker states, in response to a threat perception, will naturally ally among themselves against the more powerful state to preserve their security and try to affect the distribution of power. Subsequently, Stephen Walt refined this proposition to argue that "states balance against threats rather than against power alone". He called this the "balance of threat" theory. He went on to argue that "although the distribution of power is an extremely important factor, the level of threat is also affected by geographic proximity, offensive capabilities, and perceived intention".[11]

Weaker states are tempted to engage in bandwagoning — a less common pattern of behaviour, according to many neo-realists because the stronger state poses the greater threat or/and the weaker states are too small to influence the distribution of power, even if they choose to balance. Thus, in this context, the international system forces small states into bandwagoning as a security strategy; small states are helpless to resist "systemic pressure" and bandwagoning offers one road to survival in the anarchic world of great power rivalry. However, Randall Schweller contests this proposition and argues that small states adopt bandwagoning not simply because they are helpless in the face of an acute threat but rather as a carefully calculated policy option to exploit the great power's need for friends and allies, a course of action which can advance their political, economic and strategic interests. Thus, bandwagoning is not adopted out of fear and is not a response to threats. It provides a mixture of benefits and incentives. Schweller called this "bandwagoning for profit" and further explains that "balancing is driven by the desire to avoid losses; bandwagoning by the opportunity for gain".[12] In sum, small states also have strategies to deal with great powers and they can even gain political and economic benefit from them.

LITERATURE ON SINO-MYANMAR RELATIONS

There are a few scholarly works and journalistic writings that address the issue of Sino-Myanmar relations. In 1963, William C. Johnstone examined Sino-Myanmar relations in the context of a study of neutralism in Myanmar's foreign policy. Chi-shad Liang's "Burma's Foreign Relations: Neutralism in Theory and Practice" also examined Sino-Myanmar relations up to the late 1980s in a similar context. Liang devoted one chapter to the Sino-Myanmar relationship, but he was more interested in the developments of bilateral relations rather than in Myanmar's actual China policy. Ralph Pettman's "China in Burma's Foreign Policy" addressed the issue of the China factor in Myanmar foreign policy up to around 1973 but the primary purpose of this excellent piece of research was to question the arguments put forward by Johnstone and to reassess Myanmar's overall foreign policy of neutralism. Jurgen Haacke's "Myanmar's Foreign Policy: Domestic Influence and International Implications", as the title suggests, analysed the domestic factors that contributed to the country's foreign policy direction since 1988 and the international implications of this policy. More recently, there have been several articles that examine the Sino-Myanmar relationship; some of them have focused on the wider context of regional power politics and most of them have analyzed the Sino-Myanmar relationship since 1988.[13]

The more intimate Sino-Myanmar relationship that has developed since 1988, and its regional strategic and security implications, has attracted the attention of scholars and policymakers around the world. Chi-shad Liang, a China-watcher with a special interest in Myanmar, argues that the Sino-Myanmar relationship since 1988 has been marked by a shift from 'delicate friendship' to 'genuine cooperation'. He holds an optimistic view of this closer and more stable relationship between the two countries. Donald Seekins, another scholar specializing in Myanmar, views recent developments in Myanmar's relations with China as 'playing with fire'. Mohan Malik, who is concerned about Indian security interests in the Indian Ocean, raises a number of questions concerning Myanmar's regional role and asks whether the country has surrendered her traditional foreign policy of neutralism and has become a strategic pawn or pivot player for China. He concludes: "Myanmar is unlikely to play the role of an independent or pivotal player in regional security affairs, given its role in China's grand strategy for the next century". Mya Maung, a respectable Myanmar dissident scholar, also argues that Myanmar has been overwhelmed by China and is being "sinicized". Andrew Selth, a long term observer knowledgeable about Myanmar affairs, while accepting the thesis that the country has abandoned its neutralist foreign policy, offers a somewhat more optimistic view. He suggests that Myanmar's government can successfully manage her relations with China and "there is every indication that Myanmar will eventually attempt to draw back from China and try to find a more balanced position". A number of scholars identify three schools of thought on the Sino-Myanmar relationship. These are: (1) the "domination school", comprised mostly of "pessimists", who argue that Myanmar has abandoned her neutralist foreign policy and has become a pawn or client state of China, or is being subjected to so-called "sinicization"; (2) the "partnership school", represented by "optimists", who predict a closer, genuine and mutually supportive strategic relationship; and finally (3) the "rejectionist school", with "alarmists" at the very core, who believe that Myanmar can resist China's enormous strategic weight and remain independent but it might be playing with fire.[14] In recent years, some scholars have published articles on the Sino-Myanmar relations from Beijing's perspectives.[15] While all these academic papers do contribute to the better understanding of Sino-Myanmar relations, they do not adequately reflect the complexity and realities of the bilateral relationship and fail to examine Myanmar's China policy in the wider context of her overall foreign policy.

THEME AND ARGUMENTS

This empirically grounded work analyzes the historical development of Myanmar's China policy since 1948. It examines the whole process of Myanmar's relationship with China with an emphasis on goals and strategies and the factors that have shaped it. The study is divided into three historical periods: the Anti Fascist People's Freedom League (AFPFL) and the Union Party (UP) period (1948–62); the Revolutionary Council (RC) and the Burma Socialist Programme Party (BSPP) period (1962–88); and the State Law and Order Restoration Council (SLORC) and the State Peace and Development Council (SPDC) period (1988–). The Sino-Myanmar relationship has been described as "Pauk-Phaw (kinsfolk)" friendship. Myanmar reserves this term exclusively to describe her relations with China. China also accepts it. The Myanmar term "Pauk-Phaw", spelled in Myanmar as (ပေါက်ဖော်), is transcribed as (胞波) in Chinese.

This work argues that within the context of this "Pauk-Phaw" friendship, although the Sino-Myanmar relationship is an asymmetric one, tilted in favour of Beijing, Myanmar has skillfully played the "China card" and still enjoys considerable space in her conduct of foreign relations. Myanmar has constantly repositioned her relations with China to her best advantage. Myanmar's China policy has always been located somewhere between balancing and bandwagoning, and the juxtaposition of accommodating China's regional strategic interests and resisting Chinese influence and interference in Myanmar internal affairs has been a hallmark of Myanmar's China policy, and this will likely to remain unchanged. As long as it recognizes the legitimate strategic interests of China in Myanmar, the Myanmar government will be left to conduct her foreign relations within the context of its long established non-aligned policy. In addition, with the growing significance of Myanmar to China in geopolitical and geostrategic terms as well as in the context of its own drive for modernization and economic development, China will base its diplomacy on the good neighborliness policy, mutual benefit, and the Five Principles of Peaceful Co-existence. Myanmar will also continue to conduct her China policy in the context of the traditional "Pauk-Phaw" friendship that will allow Myanmar flexibility in her foreign relations. However, if Myanmar's engagement with China in the past decades offers any lesson for future reference, it is most likely that Myanmar will be very cautious in dealing with China, because Myanmar is thoroughly convinced that China, like all other countries, will determine its policies toward Myanmar according to the calculations of her own interests.

Notes

1. K. J. Holsti, *Why Nations Realign: Foreign Policy Restructuring in the Postwar World* (London: George Allen & Unwin, 1982).
2. Stephen D. Krasner, "Organized hypocrisy in nineteenth-century East Asia", *International Relations of the Asia-Pacific* (Vol. 1, 2001), pp. 173–197; Stephen D. Krasner, *Sovereignty: Organized Hypocrisy* (New Jersey: Princeton University Press, 1999), pp. 1–9.
3. *Ibid.*
4. *Ibid.*
5. *Ibid.*
6. Brantly Womack, "Asymmetry and Systemic Misperception: China, Vietnam and Cambodia", *The Journal of Strategic Studies* (Vol. 26, No. 2; June 2003), pp. 96–100; Brantly Womack, *China and Vietnam: The Politics of Asymmetry* (Cambridge: Cambridge University Press, 2006), pp. 77-92.
7. Brantly Womack, "Asymmetry and Systemic Misperception: China, Vietnam and Cambodia", *The Journal of Strategic Studies* (Vol. 26, No. 2; June 2003), pp. 103–106.
8. Brantly Womack, *China and Vietnam: The Politics of Asymmetry* (Cambridge: Cambridge University Press, 2006), pp. 240–147.
9. Kenneth Waltz, *Theories of International Politics* (Massachusetts: McGraw Hill, 1979), p. 73.

10. Stephen M. Walt, *The Origins of Alliance* (Ithaca: Cornell University Press, 1988), p. 17.

11. *Ibid*, p. 5.

12. Randall L. Schweller, "Bandwagoning for Profit: Bringing the Revisionist State back In", *International Security* (Vol. 19, No. 1: Summer 1994), p. 74.

13. Tin Maung Maung Than, "Myanmar and China: A Special Relationship?", *Southeast Asian Affairs 2003* (Singapore: ISEAS, 2003), pp. 189–210; Poon Kim Shee, "The Political economy of China-Myanmar Relations: Strategic and economic Dimensions", *Ritsumeikan Annual Review of International Studies* (Vol. 1, 2002), pp. 33–53; Wayne Bert, "Chinese Policy Toward Democratization Movements: Burma and the Philippines", *Asian Survey* (Vol. 30, No. 11; November 1990), pp. 1066–1083; Donald M. Seekins, "Burma-China Relations: Playing with Fire", *Asian Survey* (Vol. 37, No. 6; June 1997), pp. 525–539; Chishad Liang, "Burma's Relations with People's Republic of China: From Delicate Friendship to Genuine Co-operation", in Peter Carey (ed.), *Burma: the Challenge of Change in a Divided Society* (London: MacMillan Press, 1997), pp. 71–93; Andrew Selth, "Burma's China Connection and the Indian Ocean Region", *SDSC Working Paper No. 377* (Canberra: Australian National University, 2003); Baladas Ghoshal, "Trends in China-Burma Relations" in Verinder Grover (ed.), *Myanmar: Government and Politics* (New Delhi: Deep & Deep Publications Pvt. Ltd., 2000), pp. 504–522; J. Mohan Malik, "Myanmar's Role in Regional Security: Pawn or Pivot?, *Contemporary Southeast Asia* (Vol. 19, No. 1; June 1997), pp. 52–73; Wayne Bert, "Burma, China and the U.S.A", *Pacific Affairs* (Vol. 77, No. 2; Summer 2004), pp. 263–182.

14. See Poon Kim Shee, "The Political economy of China-Myanmar Relations: Strategic and Economic Dimensions", *Ritsumeikan Annual Review of International Studies* (Vol. 1, 2002), pp. 33–53; Andrew Selth, "Burma's China Connection and the Indian Ocean Region", *SDSC Working Paper No. 377* (Canberra: Australian National University, 2003).

15. Ian Holliday, "Beijing and the Myanmar Problem", *The Pacific Review* (Col. 22, No. 4; September 2009), pp. 479–500; Rak K. Lee, Gerald Chan and Lai-Ha Chan, "China's 'Realpolitik' Engagement with Myanmar", *China Security* (Vol. 5, No. 1; Winter 2009), pp. 101–123.

2

SINO-MYANMAR RELATIONS 1948–1962
The Years of Charting the Water

Ever since her independence in January 1948, Myanmar has been, inevitably, preoccupied with her relations with China. Political elites and policy makers in Myanmar are apparently concerned about Chinese intentions towards their country, and, understandably, they are worried about "Great Han Chauvinism", since they are fully aware of Chinese attempts to assert suzerainty over Myanmar in the pre-colonial era. The view that Myanmar lies within the Chinese sphere of influence has long been imbedded in the minds of Chinese rulers. Chinese leaders, both Nationalist and Communist, during much of the twentieth century, saw pre-colonial Myanmar as having been a vassal or tributary state. As far as Myanmar was concerned that had never been the case.[1] Myanmar's anxiety over the "Chinese imperial mentality" was proved justified when the country's first ambassador presented his credentials to the Chinese Head of State in 1949. Despite Myanmar's having been the first non-communist nation to recognize the People's Republic of China (PRC) led by Mao Zedong (毛泽东), when Ambassador U Myint Thein was about to present his credentials, he was advised that one of Mao's deputies would receive him. The Myanmar ambassador promptly refused to present his credentials, on the grounds that he brought them from one sovereign nation to another and could not present them to one of lesser dignity than the Head of State. Yangon subsequently instructed the ambassador that unless he could present his credentials to the Head of State he should return home. With this threat of withdrawing diplomatic recognition, Mao himself personally received the Myanmar ambassador.[2]

Taking all the relevant factors into consideration, the Myanmar government decided that it was in the interests of the newly independent state to adopt a neutralist foreign policy with a high degree of flexibility in deciding international issues. This, it was felt, would guarantee not only peace and stability but also the freedom from foreign interference which was imperative for national development. To a mass rally on 11 December 1949, U Nu declared:

> In regard to our foreign policy, we are convinced that the course we have adopted is the best in the circumstances of our country and we are therefore pursuing it steadfastly no matter how strongly it is criticized. Our circumstances demand that we follow an independent course and not ally ourselves with any power bloc. Any other course can only lead the Union to ruin... The only political programme which we should pursue is the one which we genuinely believe to be the most suitable for our Union, whatever course the British, the Americans, the Russians and the Chinese Communists might follow... Be friendly with all foreign countries. Our tiny nation cannot have the effrontery to quarrel with any power. If any country comes with an offer of a mutually beneficial enterprise, welcome it by all means... but... in laying down political programmes, do not forget to ensure that it is fully suited to the requirements of the Union.[3]

In this way, it was hoped, while maintaining amicable relations with countries near and far, Myanmar would be able to receive bilateral and multilateral assistance, so long as the donor countries did not violate its sovereignty. In a sense, Myanmar's neutralist foreign policy was designed to prevent, or at least to minimize, foreign intervention or interference in Myanmar's internal affairs, and this was particularly true in the case of her relations with China. With the principal objective of ensuring regime survival, which was seen as synonymous with state security, Sino-Myanmar relations were premised upon ensuring that there would be no excuse whatsoever for any adverse Chinese reaction to any possible development, and to this very end, successive Myanmar leaders repeatedly emphasized strict neutrality in their foreign policy while cultivating personal friendships with Chinese leaders.[4] However, initially, it was clear that China was not happy with Myanmar's neutralist foreign policy. As an ideologically committed Communist state with a profound interest in championing revolutionary forces on a global scale, the PRC under Mao Zedong took the militant position that there were only two camps in the world, the anti-imperialist democratic and the anti-democratic imperialist, that all countries must be in favour of either imperialism or socialism, and that "neutrality" was merely a camouflage. China considered that a third road simply did not exist. In November 1949, in Beijing, Liu Shaoqi (刘少奇) denounced the Myanmar Prime Minister, U Nu, along with Nehru and Sukarno, for being neutralist and sitting on the fence. On 16 November 1949, at the Beijing-sponsored World Federation of Trade Unions Conferences of Asian and Australian Countries, Liu Shaoqi asked delegates to support the so-called "war of national liberation" being carried out by the Burma Communist Party (BCP) against the imperialists and their lackeys in Myanmar. In addition, he recommended the BCP to follow the Maoist model of armed struggle in Myanmar.

Against this background, the issue of how to maintain friendly, stable and peaceful relations with China without compromising Myanmar's neutralist foreign policy was to become one of the main concerns for Yangon's decision-makers. In fact, understanding China and rationalizing China's place in regional and international politics has been an important policy-related exercise for the Myanmar government for several decades now. It was during the early 1950s that the Myanmar government first coined the term "Pauk-Phaw" (kinsfolk) to guide and denote her bilateral relationship with China. Living on the periphery of the PRC, the Myanmar government was understandably cautious in its relations with the authorities in Beijing. Myanmar leaders were worried that the PRC might interfere in their internal affairs because of the disparities in power and the geographical proximity of the two countries. With the benefit of hindsight, the events of the late 1960s proved that these fears were well-justified.

At the time of Myanmar's independence in January 1948, the Anti-Fascist People's Freedom League (AFPFL) formed a government which established diplomatic relations with China under the Kuomintang (KMT). Subsequently, on 18 December 1949, some weeks after the victory of the Chinese Communists in the civil war, Myanmar withdrew its diplomatic recognition from the KMT and recognized the newly established People's Republic of China (PRC) under the leadership of the Chinese Communist Party (CCP). Myanmar was the first non-Communist as well as the first Asian country to recognize the People's Republic of China. The primary reason for the change of recognition was "Myanmar's belief that recognition of a government carries with it no implied approval of the form of government or of the means by which the government came into power".[5] Dr. Maung Maung, a prominent political figure and a prolific author, argued that "the fear of aggression was at the back of the Union government's mind when it decided to be first to recognize the new Communist regime in China".[6] The Myanmar government was clearly cautious about the possibility that other countries might misinterpret this act since the then Myanmar foreign minister stated that recognition did not imply approbation.[7] Needless to say, in the context of China's communist internationalism and Mao's anti-neutralist policy, Beijing's initial response to Myanmar's begrudging behavior was predictable. In an article on "Diplomacy and Friendship" in *The People's Daily*, January 1950, it was noted that while the Soviet Union and other people's democracies had "immediately and without calculation of selfish interest" established diplomatic relations with China, it was only after three or more months that the governments of several other nations such as Myanmar and India had also decided to recognize the new republic. The article said, "As clearly indicated by the governments of these countries, the victory of the Chinese people has been so overwhelming and decisive that they are left with no alternative. It must be clearly borne in mind that genuine friendship is confined to the people of these countries only. Their governments are of a different frame of mind". Therefore, it was claimed, China would have to maintain an "attitude of unabated vigilance" towards these governments.[8]

Myanmar's China policy since her independence has been designed to prevent China from interfering in the country's internal affairs. In the early 1950s, the Myanmar government under the leadership of U Nu was able to convince the Beijing leadership, which was clearly and strictly following the "leftist strategy" endorsed by the Cominform in 1948, that Myanmar was truly independent and free from the control of the capitalist-imperialist camp. In other words, it was able to convince China that Myanmar was not an imperialist stooge or running dog. Since foreign policy in Myanmar itself was also an outcome of the ideological position of its leaders, who were profoundly influenced by socialist or more generally leftist ideology, Yangon was naturally sympathetic with leftist countries. Yet that was not good enough for Communist China. Since the early 1950s, the Myanmar government was certainly aware that China operationally pursued her foreign policy at three levels: state-to-state, people-to-people, and party-to-party. The Myanmar government realized that China, particularly the CCP, had maintained clandestine contacts with the BCP. Nevertheless, Beijing had yet to publicly endorse the BCP's armed struggle. With some outstanding issues, such as undemarcated boundaries and the presence of KMT remnants on Myanmar soil, the AFPFL government was worried that the PRC might make excuses to interfere in Myanmar's internal affairs, for there were various leverages, such as the overseas Chinese population, communist insurgents, and the aboveground leftist political opposition, to pressure the Myanmar government. Despite the Chinese rhetoric of Myanmar being an imperialist stooge, the Chinese government did not act beyond words. On her part, Myanmar has maintained the "One-China" policy — that Taiwan is part of Mainland China — consistently ever since her recognition of the PRC. As Doak Barnett rightly put it, "in some respects Burma's policy toward China might better be called one of non-provocative rather than neutralism".[9] Before going into state-to-state relations, it is important to examine people-to-people relations and party-to-party relations.

PEOPLE-TO-PEOPLE RELATIONS

According to Alexsandr Kaznacheev, who defected to the United States from the Soviet Embassy in Yangon in June 1959, China extended financial support to the communist dominated aboveground Burma Workers and Peasants Party (BWPP), commonly referred to as "Red Socialists", which in turn controlled the National United Front (NUF), a united front of left leaning political parties. In fact, both the Chinese and Soviet embassies had secretly financed the BWPP. The Myanmar government had knowledge of this fact even before the Soviet defector published his memoirs in 1962. In addition, the Myanmar government held a strong opinion that the Chinese embassy in Yangon and two PRC state-owned banks, the Bank of China and the Bank of Communications, were involved in financing a number of pro-Communist front organizations and activities, such as the Burma-China Friendship Association, the All Burma Peasant Union, the People's Democratic Youth League, the All Burma Peace Committee, the Burmese Asian-African Solidarity Committee, the All Burma Women Union and the All Burma Trade Union Congress. In 1951, the Chinese government invited a delegation from the Burma-China Friendship Association and the World Peace Committee. A seven-member delegation headed by Thakin Kodaw Hmaing and Thakin Lwin went to China to attend the second anniversary of the PRC Day. (This was the first Myanmar delegation to visit China since the diplomatic recognition.) According to the Soviet defector, China even made efforts to infiltrate the Myanmar government, army, other political parties and student organizations.[10]

　　China distributed its propaganda through two newspapers presumably established by the NUF itself or people close to it: *The Mirror* (in Yangon) and *Ludu* (in Mandalay). Radio Peking also broadcasted in Myanmar, in addition to the English and Chinese languages. Beijing's Foreign Language Press published books, pamphlets, and magazines in the Myanmar language and distributed them at low cost. The *Xinhwa* (New China) News Agency distributed films and documentaries. The Chinese Embassy in Yangon organized various cultural exhibitions and functions to promote China's national interest. Chinese language newspapers in Yangon, such as *China Commercial Times*, *New Rangoon Evening Pao*, *New China Pao-Zin*, and *Zin Min Pao*, were primary targets of Chinese propaganda to influence the political orientation and to win the political loyalty of the overseas Chinese community in Myanmar.

The Overseas Chinese Affairs Commission and the United Front Department under the Central Committee of the CCP were two major organizations responsible for organizing political work among the overseas Chinese in Myanmar. Moreover, the Chinese Democratic League was also influential among Chinese in Myanmar. However, the Chinese community in Myanmar was divided between mainland supporters and Taiwan supporters. Nevertheless, in 1950s and 1960s, through its cultural diplomacy, China maintained contacts with the Chinese community, promoting exchanges of visits in various fields. China also maintained a Chinese Communist Party (Burma Branch) and a Chinese Youth Organization in Myanmar. The Myanmar government was concerned with Chinese communist activities in Myanmar. In this regard, Johnstone remarked:

> Members of the government and particularly the top officers in the armed services have been quite aware that the presence of both Soviet and Chinese Communist Embassies in Rangoon, together with the easy access to Burma afforded citizens of Communist countries opportunities for Communist espionage, recruitment of Communist agents, and subversion of officials and political organizations within Burma... The Burmese government, quite naturally, has been more concerned about Chinese Communist operations.[11]

China tried every possible means to maintain close contacts with the Chinese community in Myanmar. According to Hugh Tinker,

> In every possible way the Chinese government ensures that its nationals in Burma are kept in touch with the homeland. Every variety of Chinese overseas organizations — Chamber of Commerce and other trade associations, trade unions, schools, temples even Christian churches — all have their quota of Communist rapporteurs. So long as Burma and China remain on friendly terms this creates no difficulty; but the Chinese in Burma do represent a potential fifth column, growing ever larger and more powerful.[12]

Financial support was perhaps the best instrument for the PRC to influence the Chinese community in Myanmar. To secure loans from PRC-owned banks, a Chinese had to comply with three basic conditions: (1) to send his or her children to a pro-PRC school and pledge loyalty to China, (2) to raise the PRC flag on special holidays, and (3) to employ only PRC sympathizers.[13] The Myanmar government was concerned with any possible political implication of Communist Chinese infiltration into Myanmar's overseas Chinese community. Although Chinese Premier Zhou Enlai (周恩来) publicly urged overseas Chinese to abide by the laws of the county in which they were residing, during his tour to Myanmar in June 1954, their allegiance to Myanmar had remained untested until late 1960s. According to one study, there were about sixty Chinese organizations in Myanmar and, among them, ten were prominent.[14] However, among the 400,000 overseas Chinese resident in Myanmar in the 1950s, majority were neither pro-PRC nor pro-Taiwan, in terms of their political orientation. Yet even the handful of organizations that worked for the Beijing cause could jeopardize the bilateral relationship if not properly handled.

PARTY-TO-PARTY RELATIONS

The party-to-party relationship between the Chinese Communist Party (CCP) and the Burma Communist Party (BCP) in the 1950s and the early 1960s was covert, and the former confined it mostly to the level of moral support. The CCP maintained its contacts with the BCP mainly through the International Liaison Department (ILD) which was directly answerable to the CCP Central Committee. In the early days of the BCP insurrection, in November 1949, Yebaw Aung Win, representing the All Burma Workers' Congress, went to China to attend the World Federation of Trade Unions Conference of Asian and Australian Countries. While he was there, Aung Win sought closer ties with the CCP. Thakin Tun Shein, on a scholarship from the BCP to study medicine in India, contacted Chinese communists during a World Peace Conference in China.[15] Since 1950, the BCP had planned to seek Chinese assistance in its armed struggle. BCP Chairman Thakin Than Tun officially proclaimed the policy of "Victory within Two Years" on 17 March 1950. However, the policy became defunct within a few months due to the government counterinsurgency campaigns. After the failure of this policy, the BCP reviewed the political and military situation of its armed struggle in September 1950 and the report recommended that the party should open base-camps along the Myanmar-China border and seek Chinese assistance.[16]

Subsequently, with the help of Tun Shein (alias Pe Nyein), Aung Win (alias Tin Aye), Aung Gyi and Than Shwe (alias Ho Kauk), who had already resided in China, the BCP adopted a new political and military line, on the advise of the Chinese Communists.[17] In 1951, it was reported that Liu Shaoqi had written a letter to Aung Gyi, in which he suggested that the BCP assume a more moderate attitude toward the AFPFL government and that the BCP declare its desire for peace, but prepare a stronger base for revolution. Liu suggested that the BCP should form a single united front of all revolutionary forces.[18] Although there was no concrete evidence of a link between Liu's letter and the BCP's new political strategy, at the BCP conference in Kyaukse district in March 1951, Than Tun did call for the formation of a united front against the AFPFL government. Six months later, at a Central Committee meeting held at Thazin Camp, the BCP adopted a new programme called the "Peace and Coalition Government Line".[19] The CCP leaders also pointed out that the BCP had failed to acknowledge the strategic significance of the Myanmar border and advised that, if the Myanmar revolution were to be successful, it was necessary to establish bases along the Chinese border and accept Chinese assistance. Without hesitation, the BCP drew up a new military strategy known as the Aung-Zeya Military Plan, while continuing to implement the "Peace and Coalition Government Line".[20]

According to the Aung-Zeya plan, bases were to be established in the border area between July 1951 and June 1952. The objective of the plan was "to expand the liberated area from Stalingrad (codename for a base area encompassing the northern part of the Kathar/Bhamo and Namtu/Kutkai areas) to the liberated area of Gyophyu (white dove — codename for China) to achieve territorial continuity, and then to liberate the whole of northern Burma". To carry out this plan, forces were reorganized and concentrated in the "3-M Area" (Mandalay, Meikhtila, Myingyan). However, the Aung-Zeya Military Plan was defeated by the Tatmadaw's military operations. The AFPFL government was aware of the two-pronged policy of the BCP: Peace and Coalition Government and the Aung-Zeya Military Plan. When a joint declaration was issued by the BCP and the People's Democratic Front on 15 March 1952, calling for the formation of a Peace and Coalition Government, the AFPFL government saw the move as intended to buy time for the communists, and, in a statement issued on 10 April 1952, the government officially rejected it.[21]

It was fairly obvious that since 1950 the CCP had become a mentor of the BCP. The CCP promised to provide training facilities in China. Under this arrangement, the BCP could send batches of trainees to China. In sending trainees, Thar Dun Aung from the Chinese Embassy in Yangon, whose background and official position was rather ambiguous, played a major role, according to Myanmar intelligence sources. The first batch of trainees left Pyinmana in November 1950 and crossed the Myanmar-China border via Bhamo-Nankhan on 2 July 1951. It was led by Bo Ba Phyu and Bo Ba Nyunt and the group included sixty-three trainees. The trainees were sent to staff college courses, armour and artillery courses, infantry courses, intelligence courses, naval and air force courses and signal intelligence courses.[22] The second batch, of about sixty trainees led by Thakin Ba Thein Tin, crossed the China border via the Bhamo-Myitkyina road on 5 June 1953.[23] Ko Han Kyi, a secret agent of the CCP from the Overseas Chinese Association in Yangon, served as liaison officer.[24] The third batch, comprising 24 trainees led by Bo Zeya, Thakin Pu and Thakin Than Myaing, used the same route and reached China on 16 December 1953. U Shwe Gae, Ko Maung Maung and Ko Ko Gyi, who were CCP trained wireless and cipher experts from the Overseas Chinese Association in Yangon, served as liaison officers.[25]

Some BCP trainees in China studied at the CCP Central Party School located in Beijing whereas others studied at the Yunnan Nationality Institute in Kunming and the Marxism-Leninism Institute in Chongqing. Elite members of the BCP, after completion of their political courses in Beijing, were transferred to a Military Academy in Sichuan. Subsequently they were assigned to the PLA 54th Corps to hold posts at divisional or regimental levels.[26] The CCP urged the BCP trainees to organize the BCP (Overseas) and a Central Committee in Beijing. With the consent of the CCP, the Central Committee (Overseas) maintained a liaison office in Beijing, established relations with communist parties in about fifty countries, and sent delegations to party congresses. According to one study,

> In every case where the identity of the BCP delegates to an International Communist meeting is known, it was a member of the Overseas BCP, that is, a Burmese Communist who was actually living in China. For instance, the BCP delegate to the meeting of Communist parties in Moscow in November 1960 was Thakin Ba Thein Tin himself. There is no evidence of the Burmese Communists who remained in Burma ever taking part in an international meeting. (In fact, there is no evidence that the Burmese Communist Party, that is, the Party in Burma, concerned itself with international affairs at all. Telegrams sent in the name of the BCP — for instance, the telegram congratulating the Albanians for their stand against the Soviets in early 1962 — were sent by Burmese Communists in China, no doubt at the direction of the Chinese.) At international Communist meetings, the Burmese Communists, who were invariably members of the Overseas BCP, always supported the Chinese position on issues in dispute in international Communist movement.[27]

Although the BCP (Overseas) was to provide liaison for its party headquarter (HQ) in Myanmar, it had practically become a CCP liaison for the BCP. The activities of the CC (Overseas) were in accordance with instructions from the CCP. The CCP asked the members of the CC (Overseas) to translate and publish the writings of Marx, Engels, Lenin and Stalin, and Mao Zedong, and collect data for propaganda. Other BCP cadres in China were allocated to different places. They had no contact with each other and were not even allowed to use their Myanmar names; they had now been provided with Chinese name. From 1960, the overseas BCP members, including the CC members, participated in the socialist construction of the PRC in accordance with the CCP's policy.[28] According to former members of the BCP:

> Although the BCP (Overseas) should have been under the control of the BCP, since it was obviously a branch of the latter, it acted in a superior way to its mother organization and relayed the directives the CCP had to give to the BCP. The latter had to comply with the orders of the CCP without any changes. The BCP had never formulated any plan or introduced any idea of its own; it took orders from the CCP and faithfully complied with them. The Central Committee of the CCP always formulated policies, plans and programmes for the BCP and sent them over wireless... The much-maligned '1955 line', adopted by the BCP's Central Committee in 1955, advocating an end to the civil war and the re-establishment of internal peace, was a directive sent to the BCP from Beijing over the wireless. At the Central Committee meeting, it was delivered under the label of 'the Resolution of the BCP Central Committee' ... After having laid down the programme to stop the civil war and re-establish internal peace, the CCP sent detailed instruction for implementation of that policy, also over the wireless.[29]

The BCP HQ had radio contacts with Beijing. Chinese-trained wireless experts were sent to Yangon with the assistance of the Overseas Chinese Association. The Chinese Embassy in Yangon also relayed messages from the CCP to the BCP. But the CCP maintained a public silence on its assistance to the BCP and when Myanmar leaders asked about the BCP trainees in China during their state visits to Beijing, their Chinese counterparts denied any knowledge of the matter.[30] Of course they were now known by Chinese names. Those BCP members stayed in Sichuan were later known as the Sichuan Group.

During his visit to China in December 1954, U Nu raised the issue of the BCP trainees there. Yet he did not receive a satisfactory answer. In this context, on 11 December 1954, Mao said: "Revolution cannot be exported. However, this does not mean that the revolution of a certain country will not be influenced by foreign countries." He further said: "What is non-interference in each other's internal affairs? It means that internal disputes of a certain country should be handled by that country itself and other countries should not bother about them or take advantage of them. A country can only recognize the government of another country chosen by the latter's people".[31] In addition, Mao said that "it is quite likely that those who are dissatisfied with their government might flee to the other country. We shall never utilize those who have fled over to harm the interests of the Burmese government. This is non-interference in each other's internal affairs and also mutual benefit". After Mao made these remarks, China shelved the Kachin group led by Naw Saing and the BCP group led by Thakin Ba Thein Tin, at least for the time being. The party-to-party relations between the CCP and the BCP did not resurface until the mid 1960s.

STATE-TO-STATE RELATIONS

On 8 June 1950, the very day Mao Zedong accepted the credentials from Myanmar's ambassador in Beijing, the two countries formally established diplomatic relations. Myanmar opened its embassy in Beijing on the same day. Twenty days later, the PRC opened its embassy in Yangon. Soon afterwards, in August 1950, the PRC sent its first ambassador, Yao Zhongming, to Yangon. He presented his credentials on 5 September 1950. Yet the contact between the two governments was limited. The first Myanmar government delegation to China was a 15-member cultural delegation led by Minister U Tun Pe in April 1952. The delegation arrived in China on 19 April 1952 and returned home on 6 June 1952. The second delegation was a four-member delegation led by the Minister of Land Nationalization to study China's land reform. It left for China in August 1952 and spent several days there. Later, in April 1953, Myanmar sent another delegation, this time to study workers' life in China. This delegation stayed in China for nearly two months. During the first three years of diplomatic relations, the trade between two countries remained at a low level. The first major state visit between the two countries took place in June 1954, when Premier Zhou Enlai stopped over in Myanmar, on his way back from the Geneva conference. Ever since, personal diplomacy has played an important role in bilateral relations.

Meanwhile, there were several interesting developments in the period between 1950 and 1954 which put Myanmar's foreign policy to the test. Among these were Myanmar's stand on China in the United Nations, the Korean War and the Tibet issue. As noted earlier, ever since its diplomatic recognition of the People's Republic, the Myanmar government has pursued a policy of "One China" and advocated the UN seat for the PRC. In 1951, U Myint Thein, at the UN General Assembly, said: "The stern fact ... is that the real China, one of the Big Five, is not represented in our midst... We have faced the facts of the Chinese situation, and I would urge the assembly to face the same facts... that the People's Republic of China is the effective and legitimate government of the Chinese people".[32] On 25 June 1950, the North Korean army invaded the south, beginning the Korean War. Myanmar supported the Security Council's action of 27 June to send troops to defend South Korea. In parliament U Nu explained Myanmar's position on the issue, comparing Myanmar with South Korea: "What was foremost in our thoughts was the expectation of United Nations assistance when our country is subjected to aggression by a stronger power. We have pinned our faith to the United Nations Organization on that score. With this advantage in view, we felt a reciprocal obligation to contribute our mite to the United Nations when that great organization tackles any aggression in any place at any time".[33] In October 1950, China entered into Korean War, crossing the Yalu river. On 1 February 1951, when the U.S. sponsored a General Assembly resolution branding China as the aggressor, the Myanmar government opposed it. When the UN General Assembly called for an embargo on the shipment of war material to China, though it abstained from voting, Myanmar announced its intention to comply with the request. With regard to the US sponsored resolution, U Nu explained that it would not contribute to peace since the problem extended far beyond a mere finding of whether or not Communist China had committed an act of aggression. In the case of the subjugation of Tibet by the Chinese government, the Myanmar government adopted a cautious approach. Information Secretary U Thant said in a radio broadcast: "Our country has not the least desire to take sides on the Sino-Tibetan affair, but Burma with its policy of abhorrence of aggression of any character is certainly not happy at the news... Burma believes in the settlement of differences by peaceful means".[34]

In retrospect, Sino-Myanmar relationship in the period between 1950 and 1954 was in a phase of uncertainty and caution. This was explained by U Nu in 1958: "Our relations with the new Chinese regime remained uncertain for a number of years... The new Chinese government seemed inclined to give our Communists their moral support, apparently regarding us as stooges of the west".[35] In the early 1950s, when the first military doctrine was promulgated by the Tatmadaw, it was premised on the assumption that Communist China was an immediate threat. The objective of this doctrine, based on the concept of strategic denial, was to contain an offensive of invading forces at the border for at least a couple of months, while waiting for the arrival of international forces. The doctrine required a massive injection of military hardware, such as tanks and armored carriers, and elaborate formations to meet conventional warfighting capabilities. The doctrine was never properly implemented, due to the high cost of a military buildup on such a scale and the cheaper alternative of diplomacy, although China remained a potential enemy [Athuya] in military exercises and war games at military training institutes throughout 1950s.

Several new developments in Myanmar helped China change its position on the Yangon government. On the domestic front, by early 1952, the Communist rebellion was clearly in decline. The BCP ultimately failed to establish a revolutionary base area in the Myanmar borderland which could have provided them a territorial connection with Communist China. The Myanmar communists did not seem likely to come to power in the near future. On the international front, China was busy with the Korean War, which came to an end with a ceasefire agreement only in July 1953. Myanmar's positions throughout the Korean War might have convinced the Chinese leadership that Yangon was not an imperialist stooge. In addition, Myanmar's cautious remark on the Tibet issue might also have positively contributed to the change of view among the Chinese leadership.

Anxious to convince China that it would not do anything detrimental to Beijing's strategic interest in Myanmar, the Yangon government promoted PRC's diplomatic image regionally and internationally. By early 1954, Yangon had convinced the Chinese leadership that it had much to gain from improved relations with neutralist Myanmar. This might have prompted Chinese policy-makers to pursue a flexible policy toward Myanmar in order to advance China's security interests. Myanmar was one of the first countries to adopt the "Five Principles of Peaceful Coexistence" with China. When Premier Zhou Enlai paid his first ever state visit to Myanmar in June 1954, at the invitation of Prime Minister U Nu, the two countries agreed to follow the principles: (1) mutual respect for each other's territorial integrity and sovereignty, (2) non-aggression, (3) non-interference in each other's internal affairs, (4) equality and mutual benefit, and (5) peaceful co-existence. This was the time China had entered a new era of diplomatic charm offensive and Myanmar was ready and willing to go along with it. In the joint communiqué issued on 29 June 1954, Zhou Enlai and U Nu affirmed the guiding principle that "the people of each nation should have the right to choose their own system and the way of life without interference from other nations".[36] More importantly, the communiqué declared: "Revolution cannot be exported; at the same time outside interference with the common will expressed by the people of any nation should not be permitted".[37] It was perhaps China's public assurance that it would not interfere in Myanmar's internal affairs, in the case of BCP's armed struggle, that paved a road for further improvement in bilateral relations.

To reciprocate Zhou Enlai's visit, U Nu led a delegation to China, via Vietnam, on 29 November 1954. The delegation stayed in China for 17 days and visited several places. U Nu was thoroughly impressed with the sincerity and determination of the Chinese leaders. Moreover, he was grateful for the hospitality they accorded him during his visit. When he met Chairman Mao Zedong on 1 December 1954, U Nu expressed his gratitude for China's understanding of Myanmar's position on the residual KMT troops issue. Nu said:

> The attitude of China toward Burma has been consistently correct. If the Chinese government had taken advantage of the presence of Kuomintang troops in Burma, that might face the Burmese government with many difficulties. But the Chinese government has never taken advantage of that and has instead shown sympathy with the difficulties of the Burmese government. On behalf of the government and people of Burma, I wish to express our thanks to the Chairman for this correct and friendly attitude of the Chinese government.... If the government of the People's Republic of China had not adopted an attitude of sympathy toward us, they might have led to a second Korea or a second Indochina. That was our worry in the past. However, thanks to the Chinese government's sympathetic attitude toward us, no dispute whatsoever has occurred.[38]

In his reply, Mao said:

> We understand your difficulties. We know that the continued presence of Kuomintang troops in Burma is because you have difficulties and not that you intentionally allow them to stay in Burma. We shall never use the Kuomintang troops' presence in Burma as an excuse to undermine the peaceful relations between our two countries.... The Kuomintang troops in Burma are not many. We are not afraid of them. The harassment they can make is rather limited... We have issued strict orders to our people in the border area to confine themselves to defensive measures and never take even one step across the boundary.[39]

Mao Zedong's assurance was certainly a relief for the Myanmar leadership. U Nu repeatedly expressed his gratitude toward China on several occasions. Zhou Enlai, in turn, praised Myanmar's China policy and said that China appreciated Myanmar's support at the Geneva Conference and at the Colombo Meeting for the termination of hostilities in Indochina. He also lauded Myanmar's decision to oppose the US-sponsored SEATO (Southeast Asia Treaty Organisation). U Nu also assured Zhou Enlai that Myanmar would not allow any foreign military base on its soil and would not become the stooge of any external power. At the end of the journey, seven members of the delegation authored a book titled "Record on Gandhalarit (China)", in which they portrayed the People's Republic and Sino-Myanmar relations very positively. One of the members of the delegation was Colonel Aung Gyi, Vice Chief-of-Staff from the War Office. During his meeting with General Su Yu (粟裕), Chief of the General Staff of the PLA, Aung Gyi explored the possibility of sending a Myanmar military delegation to China. The Chinese general was happy to extend an invitation and advised to the Myanmar come in September or October. (Later, the Chinese Minister for Defence invited General Ne Win.) Aung Gyi was impressed with General Su Yu and with the PLA soldiers.

U Nu's visit to China in 1954 also brought closer trade relations between the two countries. China agreed to buy 150,000 to 200,000 tons of rice annually from Myanmar for three years, from 1955 to 1957. In return, Myanmar would import "industrial installations and equipment as well as articles of daily use that China could supply".[40] The Chinese decision to purchase Myanmar rice saved the Yangon government from economic trouble. Rice exports were indispensable for Myanmar's economic prosperity since more than 80 per cent of its imports were paid for by rice exports. When the world rice price declined severely in 1953, after the Korean War, Myanmar was confronted with a critical shortage of foreign exchange. By 1954, unsold carry over rice stocks and continuously falling world rice prices had began to seriously alarm the Yangon government. World rice prices had dropped significantly from 80 pounds per ton in 1951 to just over 40 pounds in 1954. The carry-over rice stocks and a new exportable surplus of approximately 1.5 million tons in 1954 added up to 2.3 to 2.5 million tons for export. The Chinese government not only earned gratitude from the Myanmar government for this decision but also gained prestige in diplomacy. Show argued:

> It is apparent that the Chinese Communist government came to the aid of Burma in 1954 by agreeing to buy the Burmese surplus rice, chiefly because this move suited China's special interest to cultivate a more friendly connection with a non-aligned neighbor. Therefore, no matter what practical economic necessities might have prompted Communist China to engage in trading activities with Burma, this action had an unmistakably political overtone. And this assertion is borne out by the fact that during the following years, the Chinese Communists consistently harped on the same tune that the Sino-Burmese economic relations were conducted just between two equal parties, and were for mutual advantage.[41]

The Chinese government was indeed cautious in trying not to offend Myanmar's declared policy of non-alignment and neutralism and consistently claimed that its trade relations with Myanmar were founded on the basis of equality and mutual benefit. To implement the trade agreement, the Myanmar government immediately sent a delegation to China on 25 January 1955. The delegation signed a contract with Chinese authorities to sell 150,000 tons of rice at US$112 (K560) per ton, which was US$42 below the world market price. Myanmar received K84 million from the sale of rice to China and imported K26.6 million worth of textiles and steel from China, which were also below the world market price. This economic relationship was occasionally publicized by the Chinese government to demonstrate its goodwill and readiness to help the Myanmar government. On 4 January 1956, on Myanmar Independence Day, Zhou Enlai stated, "China is ready to render Burma every possible and technical assistance on the basis of equality and mutual benefit".[42] On 11 December 1956, Zhou again stated: "Our economic cooperation is cooperation between equals, mutually beneficial, with no terms attached and in full accordance with the five principles of peaceful coexistence".[43]

Another important issue during U Nu's China visit in 1954 was the status of the Chinese community in Myanmar. The joint communiqué issued on 12 December 1954 stated,

> With a view to improving the conditions under which nationals of one country reside in the other, the two Premiers agreed that each country would encourage its own nationals residing in the other country, i.e. Burmese nationals residing in China or Chinese nationals residing in Burma, to respect the laws and social customs of the country in which they reside and not to take part in the political activities of that country. Each government would be willing to protect the proper rights and interests of the nationals of the other country residing in its country. With regard to the question of the nationality of such residents, the two governments would, at the earliest opportunity, undertake negotiations through normal diplomatic channels.[44]

Apart from the issue of the Chinese community in Myanmar, U Nu had an opportunity to discuss border demarcation and reached an agreement to settle the issue in "a friendly spirit at an appropriate time through normal diplomatic channels".[45] In sum, the 1954 U Nu visit to China was a milestone in Sino-Myanmar relations.

This new development was also as a result of changing perceptions and political realities in China. By 1953, the PRC appeared to realize that its leftist strategy of supporting, at least in moral terms, so-called "national liberation movements" (in fact revolutionary armed struggles) in non-aligned or non-communist countries paid few political dividends and was even counterproductive. Moreover, China discovered that these countries were generally sympathetic toward China during the Korean War. In addition, China needed time to rebuild its economy, which had been devastated by wars for more than a decade, so that a stable regional and international political environment was desirable. In this context, increasingly confident about China's desire to forge close and friendly ties with non-communist countries, U Nu was willing to promote the Chinese image abroad. The first opportunity came with U Nu's attempt to bring Zhou Enlai to the Bandung Conference in 1955. Some countries opposed the invitation of China to this conference. But U Nu publicly declared that he would not come to Bandung unless Zhou Enlai were invited. In the end, China was invited to the conference. On his way back from Bandung, Zhou Enlai spent a few days in Yangon to celebrate the Myanmar New Year in April. By this time, Sino-Myanmar relations were based firmly on the Five Principles of Peaceful Coexistence and Bandung Spirit. The Sino-Myanmar relationship now transcended political, trade and cultural arenas and began to include military contacts between the two countries.

At the invitation of Marshal Peng Dehuai (彭德懷), the Minister for Defence, a high level Myanmar military delegation led by General Ne Win, the Commander-in-Chief of Defence Services, went to China on 21 September 1955. The 13-member delegation included the Vice Chief-of-Staff (Air Force) Brigadier Tommy Cliff, Adjutant General Brigadier Kyaw Win, the Commander of Northern Command Brigadier Kyaw Zaw, the Commander of Southern Command Brigadier D.A. Blake, the Commander of No. 6 Brigade Colonel Chit Myaing, the Director of Frontier Affairs Colonel Saw Myint, the Director of Armour and Artillery Colonel Khin Nyo, General Staff Officer Major Lwin (Intelligence), Lieutenant Commander Tin Thein Lu from the Office of the Vice Chief-of-Staff (Navy), and two captains from the Commander-in-Chief's Office. The delegation was received by Chinese dignitaries, such as Chairman Mao Zedong, Premier Zhou Enlai, Vice Premier Marshal Chen Yi (陈毅), Marshal Zhu De (朱德), Marshal Peng Dehuai (彭德懷), Marshal Lin Biao (林彪), Marshal He Long (贺龙), the Chief of the General Staff Senior General Su Yu (粟裕), the Chief of the PLA-Navy Senior General Xiao Jingguang (萧劲光), and the Chief of the PLA-Air Force General Liu Yalou (刘亚楼). In addition, the delegation met General Chen Zaidao (陈再道) in Wuhan and General Zhao Erlu (赵尔陆) in Nanjing. While General Ne Win, Brigadier Kyaw Win and

Ne Win's staff officer went back to Myanmar on 6 October, the rest of the delegation stayed in China until 18 November and visited several places that included military training schools, air force and naval bases, and weapons factories. On their return, the deputy leader of the delegation, Brigadier Cliff, prepared a 48-page confidential report, including details of places visited together with various observations. The delegation was apparently impressed with and, indeed, rather overwhelmed by the hospitality of the PLA's marshals (元帅), senior generals (大将), and generals (上将).[46]

In her capacity as Vice-Chairman of the Standing Committee of the National People's Congress, Soong Ching Ling (宋庆龄), otherwise known as Madame Sun Yat-sen (孫逸仙), visited Myanmar in January 1956, as part of her three-country tour that included India and Pakistan. During her 21 days in Myanmar, Soong Ching Ling emphasized the "close friendship on the basis of equality and mutual benefit" between the two countries on several occasions. She praised Myanmar for bringing into being the "Five Principles of Peaceful Coexistence" along with China and India. In her speech at Yangon University on 20 January 1956, Soong said: "More and more nations have adopted this set of principles which has now become the standard of international morality... Each and every citizen of India, Burma and China should indeed feel proud that our three nations have contributed towards this world force for peace".[47]

By early 1956, the new phase of the Sino-Myanmar relationship had been firmly consolidated. In the context of the Five Principles of Peaceful Coexistence, the Bandung spirit, and the Pauk-Phaw relationship, the Myanmar government tried to resolve the outstanding issues between the two countries, namely, the presence of PLA troops in Myanmar, the Kuomintang issue and, and the demarcation of boundaries.

THE PLA TROOPS IN MYANMAR

The PLA troops on Myanmar soil in the period between 1953 and 1956, a well-kept secret of the 1950s, constituted a major security problem for the newly independent nation. China stationed its troops on the land claimed by the PRC as its own, as China did not recognize the boundary line drawn by the British in 1941. While some would speculate Beijing's action as a pressure on the Myanmar government to resolve the KMT issue, there was no evidence to that effect. The Myanmar government decided not to make this issue public and simply engaged in quiet diplomacy so as not to jeopardize Sino-Myanmar relations which were now ceremoniously based on the so-called five principles of peaceful coexistence. It was also acutely aware of the complications and ineffectiveness of international bodies like the UN, especially after its disappointment with the KMT issue in 1953. Yangon feared that going public and confronting the PRC might invite the direct and unwelcome involvement of the world powers, turning Myanmar into a battleground. At the same time the KMT issue would certainly have become more complicated if the US had decided to openly intervene on the side of the Chinese nationalist remnant forces. Several reports about PLA incursions into Myanmar territory claimed by Beijing were made by field commanders to the War Office in Yangon. Moreover, Yangon was aware that some Chinese authorities were involved in fomenting secessionist sentiment among the national minorities in the border region, apparently in the hope that they would join autonomous areas established by the PRC state in the 1950s. In order to avoid clashes with the PLA troops, on 25 March 1953, General Ne Win instructed Colonel Chit Myaing, Commander of No. 6 Brigade at Lashio, not to send his troops across the Thanlwin River. Nevertheless, on 17 January 1955, with the approval of the War Office in Yangon, Colonel Chit Myaing sent out a 68-day flag march into the Wa sub-state to explore the situation there and nurture a good friendship with the local people. Meanwhile, in October 1954, the Myanmar government organized a secret mission, headed by Colonel Saw Myint, to find out, among other things, how many PLA troops were stationed on its territory and to investigate the Sino-Myanmar border stretching from the India-China-Myanmar trijunction to the Lao-Myanmar frontier. By early 1956, the PLA troops were said to occupy almost 1,000 square miles of Myanmar territory along the Sino-Myanmar border.

The issue of PLA troops in Myanmar became public when the *Nation* newspaper in Myanmar reported it for the first time on 31 July 1956. The *Nation's* report carried a full series of eyewitness accounts, maps and photographs. The background to this press reporting was a military clash between the Tatmadaw and the PLA in late 1955. As mentioned earlier, a Myanmar military delegation had gone to China in late 1955. Some members of the delegation had returned overland. Leaving Kunming on 14 November, the Myanmar military delegation, accompanied by two PLA generals, arrived at Lashio on 18 November. While the two PLA generals were in Lashio, Colonel Chit Myaing received a report of a PLA incursion and ordered his troops to engage the intruders while he filed a complaint with the visiting generals. This was on 20 November 1955. The incident was kept secret until July 1956 when the *Nation* newspaper revealed details of the PLA troops on Myanmar soil, as mentioned above. In this way, by late 1955, the overlapping territorial claims and the presence of PLA troops became immediate security issues for Myanmar. Chit Myaing explained that although relations between the two countries, based on the Five Principles of Peaceful Coexistence, seemed to be smooth at the official level, local tensions remained in the border area. There was, in fact, growing pressure and various provocations from the PRC in 1955 and 1956 in the border region. As a result, by way of exercising diplomatic pressure, a report of the incident of November 1955 was released to the press in July 1956, stating that the Tatmadaw had fought against the intruding PLA troops.[48] This incident was officially acknowledged on 7 August 1956.

Was the leak concerning the PLA troops in Myanmar intentional? Chit Myaing suggested that it was. Why? There were several developments in early 1956 that may have been connected. The first was the 1956 general election. U Nu was incensed by foreign interference in the national election process. Four days before the poll, on 23 April 1956, Nu said in general terms: "In the past, if a country wanted to have another country, it invariably launched war and conquered the country. Nowadays, however, military conquests are not as easy as in the past. Therefore, new tactics are employed whereby the interested country breeds stooges and pawns in the country in which it is interested. When the stooges and pawns are denied political power, the distant masters just incite them to unrest and insurrection. I need not tell who in our country are whose stooges. Their own words and actions are unmistakable evidence of the character of their allegiance". After the elections, on 2 May, at a press conference, the then Deputy Prime Minister U Ba Swe told the reporters that the left wing National United Front, commonly believed to be the aboveground communist party, received funding from outside. Asked where the opposition obtained its funds, Ba Swe said: "You know that source as well as I do." Pressed further for a more definite answer, he said: "I have reason to believe that the money came from the jungle. As to where it originated, your guess is as good as mine". A letter to the editor, which appeared in *The Nation* on 3 June, speculated that U Nu would not head the next government because of the "alleged failure of his neutralist policy and of his aspiration for establishment of friendly relations with all countries". According to the letter, U Nu was reported to have been disillusioned at the absence of a reciprocal attitude on the part of some countries whose friendship he had worked so assiduously to cultivate. Moreover, the letter said that U Nu was extremely disappointed at the way in which the Soviet and Chinese embassies operated in Myanmar. When U Nu held a press conference on 5 July, he confronted direct questions from the press on the foreign interference in Myanmar. He was asked a specific question: "What are your feelings about the Russian (Soviet) and Chinese embassies pouring money into the opposition, giving them aid and advice to subvert and overthrow the government which you head?" U Nu answered diplomatically: "I am in a different position from the press which can make accusations and get away with it. I am in the responsible position of having to maintain good international relations. Without proof it would be improper for me to make any such statement as you have made". However, his answer could not leave anyone in doubt that the charge was absolutely correct.

Second, more PLA troops had poured into the disputed border area. They built roads and other installations, undoubtedly signaling a longer or permanent stay on Myanmar soil to validate China's territorial claims. According to a report in *The Nation*, about 1,500 PLA troops had penetrated up to 60 miles into Myanmar in areas inhabited by Wa people. They maintained outposts on a permanent basis with full supplies of arms and ammunition, and established telephone lines from Kunming. In another report, about 3,000 PLA troops were said to be in Longseng area, Kachin State. According to *The Nation*, these troops had entered the area only on 21 July after destroying the boundary pillar at Namnilka. *The Nation* also reported that PLA troops had entered into Myanmar at Gamlanghka (point 16037), about 20 miles south-west of Namnilka on the Burma-Tibet border, and at Sharalika (point 11204), about 30 miles southwest of Namnilka on the Burma-Yunnan border. Another PLA deployment was in an area a few miles away from Sadon in Myitkyina district. These fresh deployments of PLA troops alarmed Myanmar authorities and finally led to the decision to publicize the whole issue.

These incidents were immediately perceived, throughout Myanmar, as constituting a serious national threat. The Myanmar press generated an atmosphere of national urgency in an effort to resolve the issue. The government was exceedingly reluctant to confirm the full extent of the PLA's presence in Myanmar. Yangon used diplomatic pressure and wooed various Asian countries, including India, Pakistan and Indonesia, in an effort to elicit their support. As Watson has explained, it was Myanmar policy to keep the frontier dispute secret, so as not to jeopardise good relations and its hopes of building a secure frontier.[49] U Nu went to China to discuss the issue and the PRC finally agreed to settle it peacefully. In the joint communiqué issued on 9 November 1956, it was said: "the Chinese and the Burmese governments have arrived at the understanding that starting from the end of November 1956, Chinese troops will withdraw from the area to the west of 1941 line and Burmese troops will withdraw from Hpimaw, Kangfang and Gawlum, the withdrawal to be completed before the end of the year 1956".[50] In order to avoid further clashes between the two armed forces, the PRC proposed that the forces of the two countries should maintain the status quo as agreed upon in the disputed areas pending a negotiated settlement. This issue was finally resolved when the Treaty of Friendship and Mutual Non-Aggression was signed in 1960 and the boundary was demarcated in 1961.

THE KUOMINTANG ISSUE

One of the first major security problems that the AFPFL government faced, in the context of Sino-Myanmar relations, was the presence of Kuomintang (KMT) troops on Myanmar soil, an issue also known as the "KMT Aggression". When the Chinese Communists came to power in 1949, the People's Liberation Army had ejected the KMT troops from China proper. Subsequently, in early 1950, remnants of the KMT troops and their families, under General Li Mi (李弥), moved into Myanmar and used the country's frontier region as a springboard for attacks against the PRC. These KMT soldiers were from 26th Army, 93rd Division and 8th Army of the Nationalist Chinese Army. The KMT forces were eventually placed under the command of General Li Mi, General Lu Kuo-chuan and Major General Mah Chao Yu. According to Myanmar government sources, about 200 KMT entered Kengtung State in early 1950 and established themselves in Mongyang. Later, in March, about 1,500 additional KMT, accompanied by 500 dependents, joined these forces. In June, the Military Force Commander of the Tatmadaw in Kengtung sent an ultimatum to the KMT forces to surrender together with their arms and to leave the Union territory. At the same time, he captured 200 KMT troops and sent them to Meikhtila for interrogation. However, on 8 June, the KMT commander in Kengtung demanded the release of the KMT soldiers and announced that he would attack if the Myanmar army pursued further attacks on the KMT. In the Myanmar government report,

> Their arrogance was demonstrated by their seizure of Tachilek and the fortification constructed along Kengtung/Tachilek road up to 81st mile. Furthermore, General Lai Iang of 26th Army had given a clear picture of the arrogant intention of KMT troops in Burma during his Press Interview in Thailand.[51]

The Myanmar army launched a military operation in the second week of June and succeeded in driving the KMT troops stationed along the Kengtung-Tachilek road away. The KMT soon regrouped and established a headquarters in Mong-hsat. By then, the KMT strength had increased to 2,500 men. By April 1951, it had reached the 4,000 level.[52] In January 1952, a report surfaced in the *New York Times* that well-armed KMT troops were moving daily from Formosa through Thailand to join General Li's army.[53]

Having realized the strategic significance of the Myanmar border area, the KMT planned to use the Shan State and the border areas as long term military bases.[54] As indicated earlier, their strength, about 2,000 soldiers in 1949, had increased six fold by 1952. Yangon was alarmed by the activities of the KMT, who had formed an alliance with two insurgent groups, the Karen National Defence Organization (KNDO) and the Mon National Defence Organization (MNDO), and were urging people in the border region to rise up against the Myanmar government.[55] Moreover, the KMT imposed taxes on the local people and forced them into military services when required. By the end of 1952, the KMT controlled a large portion of land on the eastern side of Thanlwin (Salween) river. They virtually controlled Kengtung, Manglun and Kokang states in the Shan State and had opened headquarters in Mongmao and Mong-Yang.

The Kuomintang forces were secretly armed by the US government. Indeed, the Central Intelligence Agency's first secret war in Southeast Asia was in Myanmar. The CIA's Office of Policy Coordination implemented "Operation Paper" to support the KMT. Under this operation, using aircrafts provided by General Claire Chennault's Civil Air Transport (CAT), and working through two CIA front organizations, the Far East Film Company and the Southeast Asia Defense Supplies Corporation, the CIA shipped American arms and supplies from Taiwan to Thailand and then airdropped them in Mong-hsat. The Thai authorities also assisted in the operation. According to some studies, if Western military bases had been established in territories bordering the southern frontiers of China, such as Myanmar, Communist China might have been tempted to use force against them.[56] In November 1950, an American officer from the "Sea Supply Co." in Bangkok, a CIA front organization, and some Thai representatives visited Mong-hsat, the KMT headquarters. At their instigation, the KMT, under the command of General Li Mi, initiated a counter-attack against Chinese People's Liberation Army (PLA) troops in Yunnan Province, in the Gengma and Xishuangbanna areas, in first week of May 1951, as a diversion to the war in Korea. This resulted in humiliating defeat for the KMT.[57] In October, General Li Mi and about 700 KMT soldiers were evacuated to Taiwan, leaving General Lu Kuo Chuan in command. However, General Li Mi returned to Mong-hsat after consultation with Taiwan authorities in January 1953. According to a Myanmar government report:

> It was observed from reports that General Lu Kuo Chuan had concentrated on the organization, recruiting and training of his forces while they were centralized at Monghsat. The early part of his command saw the rapid construction of airdrop zones in various sectors of Kengtung

State, besides the reconstruction and formalizing of Mong-hsat airstrip into an air base. In February 1952, the airfield became a terminus for regular air traffic between KMT troops in Burma and KMT HQ in Taiwan. A regular plane service of two flights a week between Taiwan and Monghsat was reported. These C-46 and C-47 transport planes were reported to have brought in arms and ammunition and medical supplies and carried opium on their outward flight. With the supply of arms and ammunition by air, the new recruits were equipped and trained with the aim of launching another counter-offensive on Yunnan after occupying strategic bases in Northern Burma.[58]

The Myanmar government was apparently worried that China might misunderstand its position on the KMT issue, which not only posed a external security threat but also created domestic instability.

General Ne Win was concerned about possible PLA infiltration into Myanmar in the guise of KMT troops, thinking that they might attempt in this way to link up with the Malayan communists, which would make things worse. When he met Mr. William J. Sebald, the US Ambassador in Yangon, on 18 December 1952, Ne Win informed him of the capture of a Chinese Communist officer, the defection of several hundred KMT troops to the Chinese Communists (Ne Win believed that they were actually communist agents), and their advance southward almost as far as Dawai. He also expressed grave concern over the danger that China might encourage Naw Sang (an army defector) and his troops, who were at the border ready to re-enter Myanmar to fight for the Myanmar Communists; this would open a new front, which would make Ne Win's fight against the Communist insurgents more difficult.[59]

Myanmar was also worried about being accused by China of harbouring its enemy, the KMT. The Myanmar government learned more about the intentions of the KMT forces from captured documents, which revealed plans to create problems between China and Myanmar.[60] Just a month after the Communists came to power in China, in November 1949, Premier Zhou Enlai warned that "any government which offered refuge to the KMT reactionary armed forces shall bear the responsibility for handling this matter and all its ensuing consequences".[61] In early 1950, the PRC warned that it would not tolerate Myanmar's accommodating KMT troops along her border.[62] Despite several incidents in which the PLA did cross the Myanmar border, offering technical excuses, China did not push Myanmar to the extent that the latter felt insecure and looked for assistance from the anti-communist bloc. Robert Taylor explained the Chinese position on this issue as follows:

The Chinese were certainly aware that a neutral Burma would be better protection to their southern border than a pro-Western, anti-communist Burma would be. If China had intended to rout the KMT, Burma might have either joined or been forced into the anti-communist bloc and the PRC's problems would have been more serious. Also, China was occupied at that time by the necessity of internal reconstruction following World War II and the revolution, and the war in Korea. Leaving the KMT problem to the Burmese made the most sense to the Chinese. To have themselves attacked the KMT in Burma would have been "playing the imperialist's game".[63]

Whatever the position of the PRC on the issue, Myanmar officials felt relieved by the PRC's understanding of the situation and the restraint of the Chinese government. Beijing had given an assurance to the Yangon government that the PLA would not enter Myanmar in pursuit of the KMT.[64] Nor did China use the BCP to pressure the Myanmar government. During his state visit to China in December 1954, Prime Minister U Nu publicly acknowledged his gratitude to the Chinese government on this matter. He said:

> If the PRC did not have goodwill toward our country, we would be in deep trouble… Taking pretext of the existence of the KMT troops in Myanmar, the PRC could turn Myanmar into a second Korea or second Indochina. However, with sympathy towards Myanmar, the PRC did not take any action against the KMT troops. Besides, China frequently expressed her understanding of us.[65]

The Chinese Communists were aware that the Myanmar government was trying her best to resolve the KMT issue both by diplomatic and military means.

At the same time, the Myanmar government tried to seek the good offices of India and the United States to persuade the Nationalist Chinese to evacuate the KMT. The Department of State in Washington failed to comply with Yangon's request, despite the recommendations of the US ambassadors in Myanmar at the time, David McKey and William J. Sebald, that Washington should assist in handling the KMT issue.[66] The Myanmar government was aware of US involvement in the KMT issue. In March 1953, Myanmar's Defence Minister U Ba Swe stated that his government had evidence of some American citizens training KMT troops, though he had no proof that they were US government agents.[67] The Myanmar intelligence community had knowledge of some American-owned companies supplying arms to the KMT, namely the Sea Supply Co., the Southeast Asia Corporation and the Bangkok

Commercial Corporation. In May 1953, Virginia Thompson reported Central Intelligence Agency (CIA) involvement with the KMT in the *Foreign Policy Bulletin* of the Council of Foreign Relations.[68] Ambassadors McKey and Sebald had not been informed of US involvement with the KMT forces. McKey eventually resigned as ambassador over the issue. Sebald first came to know about the CIA's activities from Ne Win.[69]

The US Embassy in Yangon had for some time been suggesting to Washington that provision of aid to the KMT troops in Myanmar would provoke strong anti-American feeling and the "Myanmar government, if not replaced by a pro-Communist one, would be forced to veer from neutrality to a more pro-Communist course".[70] The American ambassador in Yangon repeatedly asked the State Department to solve the KMT problem and to pressure Taiwan to evacuate KMT troops as soon as possible. His effort met with no success. With regard to the KMT issue, Robert Taylor has pointed out that the President, and perhaps the State Department, appears to have seen the KMT as a useful force to block Chinese Communist aggression into Southeast Asia. The CIA seems to have wanted to use the KMT primarily as a harassment force, to lure the Chinese government into invading Myanmar so as to force Yangon into the Western camp, within the framework of the United Nations.[71]

Finally, in March 1953, the Myanmar government brought the case to the UN General Assembly. This was partly due to the failure of other means to resolve the issue. Between 1950 and March 1953, the Myanmar government tried to resolve the KMT issue both by military means and also by negotiation with the Nationalist Chinese government in Taiwan through the good offices of the United States and India. The military operations, such as Operation Kengtung, Operation Frost, Operation Panglong, Operation Mogyo, and Operation Lakhum Bum, had been somewhat successful. However, the KMT became increasingly powerful as it continued to receive military aid from Taiwan and the United States. During the "Operation Naga Naing" (February 1953), the Tatmadaw began to realize that it would not be able to defeat the KMT militarily. This was perhaps a turning point in the process of resolving the KMT issue.

On 2 March 1953, in the Chamber of Deputies, Prime Minister U Nu explained that the government had been giving serious thought to the KMT issue and there were three courses of action, namely, (1) to take the matter up to the United Nations, (2) to negotiate with the Chinese Nationalist Government in Formosa through the good offices of those governments which had diplomatic relations with it, with a view to securing the withdrawal of its troops from the Union territory, and (3) to counter-attack the KMT aggressors using the armed forces of the Union. He further explained that taking the matter to the UN was not necessarily so simple since the Chinese Nationalist government could (1) flatly repudiate its own responsibility for the KMT troops operating in Myanmar by declaring that they had deserted from the Nationalist forces when the Chinese Nationalist Government evacuated to Formosa, and (2) come out with the more blatant assertion that the so-called KMT forces in Myanmar were in fact soldiers of the People's Republic of China wearing KMT uniforms. Besides, the Myanmar government was worried that Beijing might make the "present simple case of aggression a much more complicated issue" if steps were taken by the UN antagonize it. With these considerations in mind, the Myanmar government tried to resolve the issue by taking the second and third options. Yet the situation did not improve and the government eventually decided to take the issue to the UN. At the same time, Nu explained, "in order to dispel possible misunderstanding we have made arrangements by which our representatives can meet the representatives of the People's Republic of China to have full and frank discussion whenever occasion arises".[72] Meanwhile, the Myanmar government produced a book titled "Kuomintang Aggression against Burma" which documented the evidence concerning the KMT troops and foreign support for them. At the same time, Dr. Maung Maung, who later became a prominent political figure in Myanmar, authored a book entitled "Grim War against KMT".

The Myanmar government was disappointed with the resolution passed by the General Assembly, which referred to the KMT troops as unspecified "foreign forces", and recommended nothing more than negotiations. Meanwhile, the KMT issue had become more serious as the BCP, along with aboveground Communists, were engaging in propaganda warfare, accusing the Myanmar government of being an imperialist stooge. The Yangon government, thus pressed by the Myanmar Communists, became increasingly eager to solve the KMT issue as quickly as possible. Four-country talks, sponsored by the United States began in Bangkok on 22 May 1953. The Myanmar government sent a military delegation led by Colonel Aung Gyi, with the reservation that there be no face-to-face talks with the Nationalist Chinese, to whom Myanmar did not give recognition. The US and Thai delegations held talks with both the Myanmar and Taiwan delegations. The Taiwan delegation insisted on a general ceasefire whereas the Myanmar delegation guaranteed only safety zone. The Taiwan delegation was unwilling to cooperate in the evacuation of KMT troops.

As the talks dragged on, the leader of the US delegation warned the Taiwan delegation of the consequences of failing to cooperate in resolving the issue. He explained that the demand for a general ceasefire by all KMT forces throughout Myanmar was not practical and that it was senseless to say that Taiwan had no control over the KMT troops while the delegation was demanding a ceasefire.[73] The Taiwan delegation went back to Taiwan on 2 June for consultations. When it returned on 13 June, it put forward a new proposal, which was accepted with little modification, but was conditional upon transferring Mong-hsat and other important KMT camps to Myanmar. However, the agreement collapsed and the Taiwan delegation came up with other demands. Moreover, the Myanmar delegation was denied a visit to Mong-hsat with the US and Thai delegations, although this had been agreed upon earlier. At the request of the US delegation, the Myanmar delegation agreed to talk directly with the Taiwan delegation, provided that the latter had a mandate to act. Face-to-face talks took place between 14 and 23 June; however, the talks ended in disappointment for the Myanmar delegation, which withdrew its participation on 17 September 1953.[74]

The remaining three delegations continued discussions and reached a decision to evacuate 2,000 KMT troops, including their families, on 29 October. They asked the Yangon government for a guarantee of safe departure, which was accordingly granted. Despite agreement on the transfer of Mong-hsat, Mong-tung, Mong-yan, and Mong-yaung, the KMT failed to comply. The Tatmadaw then prepared to launch operations to capture all these towns. The talks in Bangkok continued and about 7,000 KMT soldiers were evacuated in 1954.[75] Nevertheless, about 4,000 KMT forces remained in the Myanmar border areas and the Tatmadaw finally launched operations to drive them out. The Myanmar government also intensified other ongoing military operations against the KMT. Major operations were carried out in 1954 and 1955, under the names of Operation Yuzana, Operation Bayint Naung, Operation Sinbyu Shin, and Operation Yang Gyi Aung. Between 1956 and 1961, the Tatmadaw carried out many localized operations to mop up the remaining KMT forces.

In the meantime, U Nu went to China in December 1954 on a goodwill visit. During his conversation with Mao Zedong, U Nu explained his position on the KMT:

> The attitude of China toward Burma [Myanmar] has been consistently correct. If the Chinese government had taken advantage of the presence of Kuomintang troops in Burma, that might face the Burmese government with many difficulties. But the Chinese government has never taken advantage of that and has instead shown sympathy with the difficulties of the Burmese government. On behalf of the government and people

of Burma, I wish to express our thanks to the Chairman for this correct and friendly attitude of the Chinese government.[76]

Mao Zedong certainly expressed his understanding of Myanmar's difficulties in resolving the KMT issue and guaranteed that China would never exploit the problem to undermine the peaceful relations between the two countries. He recognized that Myanmar did not intentionally allow the KMT to stay in the country. As long as Myanmar was taking adequate measures to resolve the issue, Beijing was happy to leave it to the Yangon government. China saw no reason to open a new Asian front in Myanmar, in addition to that in Korea, just to give Washington's containment policy a helping hand. After all, the Treaty of Friendship and Mutual Non-aggression signed in Beijing in January 1960 committed both China and Myanmar to refrain from supporting each other's enemies.

The KMT activities in Myanmar resurfaced in early 1960. This was partly due to Taiwan's decision to take advantage of China's difficulties during the Great Leap Forward period. The KMT who fled to Laos and Thailand from Myanmar's military operations in the late 1950s now began to return. According to the Myanmar government's estimate, at least 2,000 KMT troops were regrouped in three different locations: Keng-la, Mong Pa-liao and Mong Lin.[77] By early 1961, the KMT strength had increased to 6,000. At about that time, an agreement on coordinated military action against the KMT was reached between the Tatmadaw and the PLA. As a result, troops of both countries were allowed to cross the border up to ten miles in pursuit of the KMT. Exchange of combat intelligence and ration supplies was also agreed upon. "Operation Mekong" was conducted under this arrangement in December 1960.[78] The KMT troops were greatly pushed southward near the Thai-Myanmar border. In the later stages of this operation, the Tatmadaw captured many US-made weapons in crates with the US aid operations insignia stamped on them.[79] On 16 February 1961, the Myanmar air force also shot down a US Navy-type PB4Y long-distance patrol bomber which was dropping supplies to the KMT troops. The Tatmadaw suffered 18 men killed and 89 wounded.[80] A strong protest took place in front of the US embassy in Yangon. Finally the American government put pressure on Taiwan to remove KMT troops from the Myanmar border. In mid March 1961, the evacuation of about 4,000 KMT began. By August, the Myanmar government estimated that only about 700 KMT remained in Myanmar. In this way, the KMT issue, a possible excuse for Chinese intervention, was removed from Sino-Myanmar relations.

DEMARCATION OF THE SINO-MYANMAR BORDER

The Myanmar government had always displayed a great concern over the long-disputed frontier with China. The settlement of this undemarcated boundary had been a top priority for the Myanmar government of the time. Yangon confronted the border problem with China for the first time in 1948, when the Nationalist Chinese government refused to accept 1000 rupees as rent for the Namwan Assigned Tract, a perpetual lease negotiated during the colonial days. The coming of Chinese Communists to power did not resolve this frontier problem. Communist China published maps claiming areas north of Myitkyina as undemarcated Chinese territory. In this way, the PRC pursued a policy of what Holmes has called "cartographic aggression".[81] As early as December 1949, the Myanmar government attempted to discuss boundary demarcation with Beijing, but the PRC considered that the time was not appropriate for any substantial negotiations and expressed the desire to shelve the boundary question for the time being.[82]

There were three disputed border areas. These were: (1) Myanmar's northernmost boundary above High Conical Peak in Kachin State that included three Kachin villages; (2) the Namwan Assigned Tract; and (3) the Wa state boundary that included the Panghung-Panglao tribal area. In accordance with the two treaties on the Sino-Myanmar boundary line concluded between China and Britain in 1894 and 1897, the area north of Myitkyina was put aside to be delineated in the future. Both treaties left the Sino-Myanmar frontier north of 25' 35" N (High Conical Peak) open to different interpretations. The British claimed the watershed area of the Thanlwin river and the N'Maikha, a tributary of the Ayerwaddy, as the frontier of Myanmar. The Chinese never accepted this provisional boundary. Nevertheless, the British decided to maintain this watershed boundary at any cost. Between November 1897 and 1900, a joint Sino-British boundary commission demarcated the border from the High Conical Peak south to the Nanting River (23' 30" N) and from the Nam Hka (22' 10" N) to the Mekong, with the exception of the Wa state boundary, which was finally settled only in 1941. Another area of dispute in the territory north of High Conical Peak, a section of the Sino-Myanmar boundary line which had never been delineated in the past, was an area referred to as Hpimaw-Gawlum-Kangfang, names of the three local villages. In 1911, the British government sent its troops into this area. However, in a note dated 10 April 1911, it acknowledged that these three villages belonged to China, but were under British occupation. The Chinese government asserted that the Myanmar government might temporarily retain administrative jurisdiction over the three villages while final settlement was pending.

The second disputed and ill-defined area was the Meng-Mao triangular area, also known as the Namwan Assigned Tract, situated at the junction of the Namwan River and Shweli River. The fact that this area was Chinese territory had been formally and explicitly recognized by the British in the Convention of the Sino-Burmese Boundary Line of 1894. Nevertheless, without asking permission from the Chinese authorities, the British colonial authorities in Myanmar built a highway through this area to join Bhamo and Nankhan. By the time, Britain and China signed another convention on the Sino-Myanmar boundary line in 1897, Britain had secured recognition that this area was under "perpetual lease" and had asserted its jurisdiction. When Myanmar regained independence in 1948, this Namwan Assigned Tract became a perpetual lease to the Myanmar government. However, Beijing held the view that concrete steps should be taken to abrogate the perpetual lease of the Meng-Mao triangle area or Namwan Assigned Tract rather than continue the legacy of British humiliation of China. The third disputed area was an area in the Wa state, between the Nan Ting and Nan Kha rivers, that was ceded to Myanmar in 1941 in accordance with Iselin Line or 1941 Line. This area was known as "Panghung-Panglao" tribal area. On 18 June 1941, taking advantage of China's difficulty in its war with Japan, the British government secured some territory in the Sino-Myanmar frontier region in an exchange of notes with the KMT government. In fact, according to the "1941 Line", which revised the 1897 treaty on boundary demarcation, a large tract of land was ceded to the British in Wa state. The Communist Chinese government argued that the British imposed the "1941 Line" at a time when China had been distracted by Japanese aggression and civil war. For this reason, the agreement was void and the line must be reviewed, although both sides should maintain the *status quo* pending a final settlement. The PRC government refused to acknowledge the boundary treaties and conventions imposed by the British as it regarded them as "unequal treaties".

At the end of 1947, the Foreign Office of the Nationalist Chinese government in Nanjing issued a statement in which it declared that a mutually satisfactory solution to the boundary question could be sought through diplomatic channels in accordance with the treaty provisions and international laws. About the same time, Territorial Commissioner of the Chinese Ministry of the Interior voiced China's claim over disputed territory north of the High Conical Peak. Nanjing subsequently printed a map showing the area north of Myitkyina as belonging to China. The National Chinese government went further and legalized its claim in June 1948, when the Legislative Yuan held the first reading of a bill "to promote Sino-Burmese relations through the prompt settlement of a boundary dispute in which 250,000 square miles of territory are involved".[83] When the Chinese Communists came to power in October 1949, they applied the same tactics to claim the unsettled boundary. In December 1950, the PRC government published a map showing the area north of Bhamo as Chinese territory, although it was marked as undetermined. Subsequently, in March 1951, the same map was displayed among the PRC publications on show in the Chinese embassy pavilion in Yangon. This provoked a protest from the Myanmar government which instructed its ambassador in Beijing to seek explanation from the Chinese side. Yangon was assured that China had no territorial ambitions over Myanmar. With regard to the map, the Chinese authorities explained that they had merely reproduced it from old maps because a new map had not yet been drawn due to the unsettled status of the present boundary. U Nu assured his parliamentarians on 8 March that, "there are no problems between Asian countries like China, India and Burma, which cannot be solved through normal diplomatic channels… Sino-Burmese border has been shown as undemarcated boundary and we see no difficulty in sitting down together and demarcating boundary".[84]

In the early 1950s, several reports were made by the Tatmadaw commanders to the War Office about incursions of the PLA into Myanmar territory which was claimed by the Chinese. Moreover, Myanmar authorities were annoyed by Chinese activities on the border, which sought to foment secessionist sentiment among the various national minorities there. As early as 1953, the Chinese Communists tried to take a firmer grip on the territory claimed as Chinese. Between January 1953 and October 1955, China established five "autonomous areas" for national minorities in Yunnan near the Myanmar border.[85] Despite reports of PLA incursions, the Myanmar government remained restrained on the issue. On 25 March 1953, General Ne Win ordered Colonel Chit Myaing, Commander of No. 6 Brigade at Lashio, not to let Myanmar troops cross the Thanlwin River. The PRC claimed territory close to the Thanlwin River and the general wanted no clashes with the PLA.[86] However, Chit Myaing sent a 68-Day "Flag March" into the Wa sub-state on 17 January 1955. The purpose of this march was to show the people of the area that the Myanmar government had control over them. This had a positive result, and the Tatmadaw was able to nurture a good relationship with the peoples of Kokang, Mong Mao, Kaungti and Northern Wa sub-state.[87] About the same time, in October 1954, Yangon dispatched Colonel Saw Myint's mission to study the Sino-Myanmar border extending from the India-China-Myanmar trijunction in the west to the frontier with Laos in the east. One purpose of this mission, as already noted, was to determine how many PLA troops were on Myanmar's territory. The report of Colonel Saw Myint's mission, codenamed "Operation Yein Nwe

Par", subsequently became a point of reference for the Myanmar delegation in border negotiations.[88]

The issue of border demarcation was discussed during the visit of U Nu to China in December 1954. In a communiqué issued on 12 December, "the two premiers, in view of the incomplete delimitation of the boundary line between the two nations, agreed to settle the question in a friendly spirit at an appropriate time through normal diplomatic channels".[89] However, progress was very slow. Several rounds of negotiations and exchanges of letters followed. Meanwhile, evidence of increasing Chinese contacts with Kachins in the Hpimaw area came to light during the course of 1955. There was also a report that Chinese authorities had crossed the Myanmar border into Kachin state in September 1955, and taken a KMT suspect from a Kachin village.[90] Chinese identity cards were issued to some Kachin residents in the area. This led to the decision of the Myanmar government to hold a conference at Lweje, a border town in Kachin state, in February 1956, to foster loyalty among the Kachins and improve the prospects of a settlement with China.[91]

At the end of July 1956, the PRC proposed that the forces of the two countries maintain the status quo in the disputed areas pending a negotiated settlement. Premier U Ba Swe, who succeeded U Nu in June 1956, insisted that negotiations could not began until the Chinese troops withdrew from all territory claimed by Myanmar.[92] Myanmar's ambassador was recalled for consultations. The issue became the subject of increasing publicity in Myanmar. Finally, on 4 August 1956, Zhou Enlai wrote a letter to U Nu urging him to control the Myanmar press, which threatened the cordial relations between the two countries. Zhou tried to convince U Nu that Chinese forces were not crossing the Myanmar border. Four days later, U Nu declared that the border issue would be settled through peaceful negotiations and the press would be restrained.[93] Despite an exchange of letters between U Ba Swe and the Chinese government in late August and September, the two sides could not reach an agreement on the problems of recognizing the 1941 line, withdrawing Chinese forces from the disputed areas, or setting up a border commission.

Finally, U Nu was invited to China for discussions. In his capacity as the president of the AFPFL, U Nu accepted the invitation of the Chinese leaders to negotiate the border problem, and visited the PRC in October 1956. He was joined by some Kachin leaders whose territories were involved in the border negotiations. Reportedly, U Nu and the Chinese leaders worked out a "package deal" for the border problem. A press communiqué issued on 9 November, as U Nu left the PRC, stated:

In the talks, the Chinese side put forward the settlement of the Sino-Burmese boundary question a fair and reasonable proposal which takes into account the interests of both sides. The Burmese side promised to give consideration to this proposal.[94]

A month later, in December, Zhou Enlai paid a visit to Myanmar. His main purpose was to discuss the boundary issue further. Zhou consistently asserted that the boundary issue was a historical legacy and appealed for patience and mutual understanding. His speech on 11 December 1956 at the AFPFL gathering was intended to assure Myanmar that China would not display an attitude of "great-nation chauvinism" and was prepared to resolve the difference peacefully.[95] He and his counterpart, U Ba Swe, continued the discussions initiated by U Nu in China. No agreement was reached. China did not accept the Myanmar proposal on exchange of Hpimaw, Kangfang and Gawlum for the Namwan Assigned Tract.[96] However, the two prime ministers visited Meng-shih, a small town situated on the Sino-Myanmar border, on 16 December, to promote friendly relations between the two local communities. On 4 February 1957, U Ba Swe wrote to Zhou, offering to cede 56 square miles in the area of the three villages in return for the Chinese transfer of the Namwan Assigned Tract.[97] Nevertheless, there were disagreements over the size of the territory and other issues. In the meantime, U Nu reassumed the premiership in late February 1957. Soon afterward, in March, U Nu journeyed to Kunming to meet Zhou Enlai to continue the boundary negotiations. Zhou presented the new Chinese terms during his meeting with U Nu and said that U Ba Swe's proposal had failed to take China's basic requirements fully into consideration. Even so, he suggested, the Chinese government was inclined to exchange the Namwan Assigned Tract for the Panghung-Panglao tribal area on the Myanmar side of 1941 (Iselin) Line.

Meanwhile, on 9 July 1956, Zhou Enlai made a special report to the Fourth Session of the First National People's Congress (NPC), on the question of the Sino-Myanmar boundary demarcation. He indicated that settlement of this issue would be regarded as an important litmus test for Beijing's approach to its non-aligned neighbours. Of course it would also be seen as a test of China's commitment to the Five Principles of Peaceful Coexistence. Zhou pointed out that the Chinese government had not been able to deal comprehensively and systematically with the settlement of the Sino-Myanmar boundary problem in previous years. He also admitted that there had been an armed clash between Myanmar and China in November 1955. Zhou presented an outline of a tentative plan for dealing with the complicated boundary demarcation issue. In his report, Zhou acknowledged that the Chinese government's basic objectives were to protect Chinese national interests and to promote Sino-Myanmar friendship. At the technical level, Zhou confirmed that China claimed sovereignty over the Kachin villages (Hpimaw-Gawlum-Kangfang) and the Namwan Assigned Tract. Zhou's report and his proposals were approved by the National People's Congress on 15 July 1957. The NPC resolution explicitly suggested that the Chinese government should "secure the overall, fair and reasonable solution of the Sino-Burmese boundary question through concrete consultation".[98] In a letter to the Myanmar government, dated 26 July 1957, Zhou asked for 186 square miles in the area of the three villages and offered to exchange the Namwan Assigned Tract for approximately 86 square miles of Myanmar territory, west of the 1941 line, in the Panghung-Panglao area.

The Myanmar government then sent Justice U Myint Thein to Beijing to clarify the Myanmar position. Regarding the traditional line in the far north, the Myanmar government asked the Chinese government to accept the northern watershed of the upper Ayerwaddy, excluding the Taron Valley, as the boundary. If this proposal (which was implicit in a map appended to Zhou's letter of 26 July 1957) were accepted, a joint survey would be conducted to define the watershed. The Myanmar government stuck to the offer it had made in the Ba Swe letter of 4 February, which involved no exchange of the Namwan Assigned Tract for the Panghung-Panglao area.

In December 1957, Myanmar's Deputy Prime Minister U Ba Swe and U Kyaw Nyein paid a goodwill visit to China. They were informed of the Chinese position on the border issue by Zhou Enlai. The Chinese side raised a new point of reservation regarding the watershed principle. Myanmar asked Ambassador U Hla Maung to press the Chinese government to accept the watershed principle without any conditions, and to be satisfied with the Hpimaw-Gawlum-Kangfang area offered in U Ba Swe's letter of 4 February. On the exchange of the Namwan Assigned Tract for the Panghung-Panglao area, Hla Maung was instructed to suggest the existing lease agreement could be continued if China found it difficult to cede.[99] The Chinese reply on 30 July was, in essence, a reconfirmation of the position it had adopted in the talks with Myanmar's deputy prime ministers.

Meanwhile, in Yangon, the border issue was becoming a domestic political problem. Protests against the proposed transfer of the three Kachin villages broke out. Myanmar and Kachin leaders managed to convince the Kachin population to accept the transfer in the interests of the Union and the need for a secure boundary. At about the same time, in 1958, a split took place within the ruling AFPFL, and the political situation in Myanmar became tense. Finally, on 28 October 1958, U Nu transferred power to the Caretaker Government headed by General Ne Win. General Ne Win was aware of the problem and believed that his government, being above party politics, was best placed to tackle it. At the same time, the Sino-Myanmar border clashes in 1959 suggested the need for an urgent solution. General Ne Win settled the differences among politicians and national leaders and put forward a proposal on 4 June 1959:

(1) To continue to press the Chinese government to accept the principle that the boundary between Izurazi and Indian border should, with the exception of the Taron Valley, run along the watershed, this acceptance to be without any reservations.

(2) To adhere to U Ba Swe's offer in regard to Hpimaw, Gawlum and Kangfang to be returned to China; and that, apart from the adjustment which the acceptance of this offer would entail, the boundary between Izurazi and the High Conical Peak to run along the N'Maikha-Salween watershed.

(3) To agree in principle to exchange the Namwan Assigned Tract for the Panghung-Panglao tribal areas falling to the west of the 1941 line, and that apart from the adjustment which would be required as a result of the transfer of the Panghung-Panglao area to China, the 1941 line should be accepted by both sides.

(4) That China should surrender the right, under the 1941 Exchange of Notes, to participate in mining enterprises in the Lufang area.[100]

The Chinese reply of 24 September 1959 suggested that Myanmar proposal's of 4 June 1959 and the Chinese proposal of 30 July 1958 could constitute the basis for further negotiations. General Ne Win, believing that such negotiations would lead to several rounds of proposal and counter-proposal with no concrete results, sent a note to Zhou Enlai on 4 November 1959, in which he said that the proposal he had made was the best that was possible for a non-partisan Prime Minister and represented the maximum offer for a fair and equitable agreement between the two countries. His message clearly indicated that the border issue should be settled during his tenure as prime minister; otherwise it would drag on. As a result, Zhou Enlai extended an invitation to General Ne Win on 2 December 1959 and after some exchanges of notes and discussions, Ne Win finally went to China on 23 January 1960.

Five days later, Ne Win signed two agreements, one on the settlement in principle of the border problem and the other on the consolidation of peace and friendship between the two countries. The preliminary agreement on boundary demarcation was basically the same as the agreement reached previously on 12 November 1956 between U Nu and Zhou Enlai, with some minor differences. The most significant of these was that China agreed to cede the Namwan Assigned Tract to Myanmar in exchange for Panghung-Panglao and gave up its earlier claim to a much larger area. Myanmar was obliged to make only token concessions. What motivated the Chinese negotiators to come up with such conciliatory terms was not easy to judge. One possible explanation might be that China wished to refurbish its diplomatic image in the wake of Sino-Indian border conflict. Beijing, perhaps, wanted to assure its small neighbours that it did not harbour any desire for territorial gain and was willing to settle border issues peacefully. However this maybe, the boundary agreement and the treaty of friendship and mutual non-aggression were hailed in the Chinese press as diplomatic achievements and significant landmarks in Sino-Myanmar relations. Chinese propaganda clearly presented the successful and peaceful settlement of the Sino-Myanmar boundary issue as an example of peaceful coexistence between countries with different political systems. The joint statement issued on 29 January 1960 declared:

> The talks were marked by a spirit of utmost cordiality and full mutual understanding and paved the way for the conclusion by the two sides of the Treaty of Friendship and Mutual Non-Aggression between the People's Republic of China and the Union of Burma and the Agreement between the Government of the People's Republic of China and the Government of the Union of Burma on the question of the boundary between the two countries… The two Premiers viewed with satisfaction the remarkable advance made in recent years in friendly relations between China and Burma. This advance fully demonstrates the great vitality of the Five Principles of Peaceful Coexistence jointly initiated and firmly adhered to by the two countries. The two Premiers were convinced that the conclusion of the above-mentioned Treaty and Agreement will be a lasting monument to the growing friendship and mutual understanding between the New China and New Burma. The two Premiers pledged that the two Governments will ceaselessly strengthen friendly co-operation between the two countries, and continue to make joint contributions to the promotion of solidarity among Asian and African countries and the safeguarding of Asian and World Peace.

The tone of the joint statement reflected the mood of great satisfaction and achievement. General Ne Win was also apparently overjoyed by his successful deal with the Chinese government. While Zhou praised the "Pauk-Phaw" relations between the two countries, during the state banquet on 24 January 1960, Ne Win went a step further and said that the relationship was that of a "Nyi-Ako (brotherly)" friendship.[101]

While the technical matters were handled by border committees, the political aspect of the boundary agreement still needed certain adjustments. In Myanmar, after the general elections, U Nu became Prime Minister again in February 1960. One of his principal immediate tasks was to convince his parliament to accept the boundary agreement. On 28 April 1960, Nu gave a lengthy speech in the parliament. He emphatically stated:

> Considering the long and involved history of the Sino-Burmese boundary, and the fact our negotiations were in reality a continuation of the uncompleted negotiation between the British and Chinese, I believe that Burmese interests have been well served by the conclusion of this agreement. For the first time in history we shall soon have a well-defined, mutually agreed boundary between Burma and China. Thus a boundary which has defied solution for three quarters of a century has now been, to all intent and purposes, settled. The constant uncertainly which attended the absence of a mutually agreed boundary between China and Burma has been removed by this Agreement. It has thereby eliminated a major source of misunderstanding between our two countries and people.[102]

U Nu praised Zhou Enlai and Ne Win for their successful conclusion of the agreement. In his concluding statement, Nu said that the agreement would usher into a new era of even closer understanding and friendship between Myanmar and China. U Nu succeeded in securing parliament's acceptance for the agreement.

The two sides agreed to set up a joint Border Committee to work out solutions on specific questions regarding the Sino-Myanmar boundary enumerated in Article II of the agreement. The Joint Border Committee (JBC) met four times.[103] The first session, held between 28 June and 5 July 1960, laid the groundwork for a land survey, mapping, security measures and other logistical matters.[104] The survey was under the guidance of Brigadier General Aung Gyi, the Vice Chief-of-Staff, and Yao Zhongming, former Chinese Ambassador in Myanmar. On the Myanmar side, the task of border demarcation was undertaken as "Operation Burma Boundary (OBB)". Headquarters were established and the operation was directed by high ranking military personnel.[105] Operation Burma Boundary was carried out in three stages.[106] In fact, during the first session the Chinese team tried to direct Myanmar's attention to the size of territory to be transferred to China in the three-village area, the area under the jurisdiction of the Panghung tribes, and the matter of some villages intersected by the 1941 line, but the Myanmar team successfully deferred these issues to the second session in order to buy time for a better bargaining position. During the intervening period, under cover of overseeing the survey, the Myanmar team went to Hopan, the capital of Wa state, to talk to local chiefs. This gave Myanmar an advantage in dealing with the Chinese team. The Chinese accepted the area of the three villages as proposed in U Ba Swe's letter, with minor technical adjustments, fully aware that if Myanmar insisted on a plebiscite on Panghung, they had little chance of getting the area.[107] The third session of the committee was held in Yangon from 25 August to 4 September 1960. At this session, the Committee reviewed the draft treaty, detailed some survey work, and discussed the question of transfrontier land cultivation.[108] The fourth session of the Committee, held in Beijing from 20 to 28 September 1960, prepared the treaty for signing.[109] Within 298 days, a total of 402 boundary markers were erected.

Meanwhile, Zhou Enlai came to Myanmar on 15 April 1960 and stayed for four days during the Myanmar New Year. Needless to say, Zhou highlighted the successful conclusion of the boundary talks. He elaborated on the background of the Treaty of Friendship and Mutual Non-aggression. He said that U Nu had initiated the idea of the treaty during his trip to Kunming in March 1957, that the Chinese government had actively supported it and that General Ne Win had materialized it. In Zhou words, the treaty was a major step in further strengthening the existing Pauk-Phaw relations between the two countries.

After the boundary was physically demarcated, U Nu led a Myanmar delegation to China to sign the final document. General Ne Win was also a member of the delegation. The "Boundary Treaty between Union of Burma and People's Republic of China" was signed by U Nu and Zhou Enlai on 1 October 1960. On 13 October, "The Protocol between the Government of the People's Republic of China and the Government of the Union of Burma" was signed by Zhou Enlai and U Nu in Beijing. The protocol was an amplification of Article VII of the Boundary Treaty. The following adjustments were made:

(1) Myanmar ceded 59 square miles in the Hpimaw, Gawlum, and Kangfang area — 3 square miles more than U Ba Swe's offer

(2) Myanmar ceded 73 square miles in the Wa state — 11 square miles more than General Ne Win's offer;

(3) Myanmar gained 85 square miles comprising the Namwan Assigned Tract;

(4) Myanmar gained four villages and ceded two villages intersected by the 1941 line, which was now withdrawn;

(5) Myanmar gained about 5 square miles in the far north and ceded about 2 square miles in the eastern section, as a result of minor realignment of the boundary.[110]

The exchange of instruments of ratification of the Treaty took place in Yangon in January 1961. To attend the ratification ceremony as well as to commemorate the 13th anniversary of Myanmar's independence, a 400-member Chinese cultural delegation headed by Premier Zhou Enlai arrived in Yangon on 2 January 1961. The ceremony took place on 4 January 1961. Zhou Enlai and U Nu exchanged gifts. Myanmar gave 2,000 tons of rice and 1,000 tons of salt to the approximately one million Chinese living along the borders in China. In return, China presented 2.4 million metres of printed textiles and 600,000 porcelain plates to about one million Myanmar citizens residing along Myanmar's side of the border.[111] These gifts of cloth and plates are known in Myanmar as "Myitta Peik (loving kindness cloth)" and "Myitta Baganpyar (loving kindness plates)". Zhou Enlai praised the treaty as a "brilliant model for peaceful coexistence between the Asian peoples". While Zhou considered that the border demarcation negotiation had produced a "boundary of peace and friendship", some Myanmar leaders were more cautious, although occasionally optimistic. Dr. Maung Maung wrote, "the Treaty which has settled the boundary is not the end of all border problems, or other problems in Burma's relations with her big neighbour. It does, however, free the leaders of public life in Burma to devote their time and energies to work for national unity and strength, for consolidation and progress, without which the country must remain weak and exposed, the treaty notwithstanding".[112] Whatever the differences of opinion over these treaties, they marked a new era of peace and friendship between the two countries. During Zhou Enlai's visit to Myanmar in January 1961, China granted Myanmar credit of nearly US$84 million. Arrangements were also made to promote trade between the two countries and various development projects were set up in Myanmar with aid and technical assistance from Beijing. Thus, the initial period after the signing of the treaties can be considered as "Myanmar's honeymoon with China".

As noted above, in January 1960, along with the Agreement on Question of Boundary between the Two Countries, Myanmar and China signed the Treaty of Friendship and Mutual Non-Aggression. According to this treaty, Myanmar and China, with a view of strengthening good neighbourly relations and friendly cooperation, were to recognize and respect the independence, sovereign rights and territorial integrity of each other, to settle all disputes by means of peaceful negotiation, without resorting to force, not to carry out acts of aggression against each other, and not to take part in any military alliance directed against the other party. Moreover, the treaty also spelled out that both countries would develop and strengthen their economic and cultural ties in a spirit of friendship and cooperation, in accordance with the principles of equality and mutual benefit, and of mutual non-interference in each other's internal affairs. The treaty was a landmark in Sino-Myanmar relations. Although the signing of the mutual non-aggression pact, Article III of which stated that "each contracting party undertakes not to carry out acts of aggression against the other and not to take part in any military alliance directed against the other contracting party", may have formally limited Yangon's freedom of action in respect of its self-defense, for a neutralist country like Myanmar, this did not pose any foreign policy problem and, in fact, it even enhanced her security. The "package deal" was praised in the Chinese press as "a new example for friendship, cooperation and amicable relations among the Asian countries".[113] In December 1960, about the time the border demarcation named "Operation Burma Boundary" was being carried out, the Tatmadaw also launched a major military operation, "Operation Mekong", against the KMT remnants in the border area. It appeared to be a joint operation and that some 20,000 PLA troops were involved. By late 1961, all the outstanding issues between the two countries had been more or less resolved.

Various explanations can be offered for success in realizing the peaceful demarcation of the Sino-Myanmar boundary. One is that the Chinese had a strong desire for a secure frontier. The Sino-Soviet split and the armed clash with India might possibly have contributed to Chinese concerns about this matter. Another explanation might be that China wished to preserve her historical image as a great and benevolent Asian power in relations with her neighbours. A third explanation might be that China, by displaying flexibility and non-militancy in border settlements with less powerful neighbours, hoped to consolidate and develop her post-Revolutionary image as a champion of peaceful coexistence among nations in the spirit of the Bandung principles, somewhat tarnished by developments in Tibet. For Myanmar's leaders, particularly to the Tatmadaw, the sacrifice of a small portion of the national territory to remove a major cause of misunderstanding and a constant source of anxiety, was more than worthwhile. The Myanmar government subsequently tried to promote friendly relations with the PRC, as far as her foreign policy of neutralism permitted.

Notes

1. Sun Yat-sen once claimed: "We lost Korea, Formosa and Peng Fu to Japan after the Sino-Japanese war, Annam to France, Burma to Britain. In addition, the Ryukyu Islands, Siam, Borneo, Sarawak, Java, Ceylon, Nepal and Bhutan, were once tributary states to China". Mao Zedong shared a similar view. In his original version of "The Chinese Revolution and the Chinese Communist

Party", dated 15 December 1939, Mao Zedong wrote: "After defeating China in war, the imperialist powers seized many Chinese protectorates and parts of China's territory. Japan occupied Korea, Taiwan, the Ryukyu Islands, the Penghu Islands, and the port of Lushun, Britain seized Burma, Bhutan, Nepal and Hong Kong, and France occupied Vietnam. Even a miserable little county such as Portugal seized our Macao. In addition to annexing territory, they exacted huge indemnities. Thus heavy blows were struck at China's huge feudal empire". However, when it was reproduced years later in his *Selected Works*, the above paragraph was thoroughly censored and carefully rephrased to read as follows: "The imperialist powers have waged many wars of aggression against China, for instance, the Opium War launched by Britain in 1840, the war launched by the Anglo-French allied forces in 1857, the Sino-French War of 1884, the Sino-Japanese War of 1894, and the war launched by the allied forces of the eight powers in 1900. After defeating China in war, they not only occupied many neighbouring countries formerly under her protection, but seized or 'leased' parts of her territory. For instance, Japan occupied Taiwan and the Penghu Islands and 'leased' the port of Lushun, Britain seized Hong Kong and France 'leased' Guanzhouwan. In addition to annexing territory, they exacted huge indemnities. Thus heavy blows were struck at China's huge feudal empire".

2. Tibor Mende, *Southeast Asia between Two Worlds* (London: Turnstile Press, 1955), p. 154.

3. Ministry of Information, *From Peace to Stability* (Yangon: Ministry of Information, 1951), pp. 51–53.

4. Tin Maung Maung Than, "Myanmar and China: A Special Relationship? in *Southeast Asian Affairs* 2003 (Singapore: ISEAS, 2003), p. 191.

5. Ambassador U Thant. "Some Reflections on Burma's Foreign Policy", *The Guardian Monthly Magazine* (Vol. 8, No. 9; September 1961),

6. Dr. Maung Maung, *Burma in the Family of Nations* (Amsterdam: Djambatan, 1957), p. 147.

7. Richard Butwell, *U Nu of Burma* (Stanford, California: Stanford University Press, 1963), p. 172.

8. *People's China*, Vol. 1, No. 2 (16 January 1950), p. 3.

9. Doak Barnett, *Communist China and Asia: A Challenge to American Policy* (New York: Random House, 1960), p. 318.

10. Alexsandr Kaznacheev, *Inside a Soviet Embassy* (Philadelphia: J. P. Lippincott, 1962), pp. 189–191.

11. William C. Johnstone, *Burma's Foreign Policy: A Study of Neutralism* (Cambridge, Massachusetts: Harvard University Press, 1963), pp. 176–177.

12. Hugh Tinker, *The Union of Burma: A Study of the First Years of Independence* (London: Oxford University Press, 1967), fourth edition, p. 372.

13. Robert A. Holmes, *Chinese Foreign Policy Toward Burma and Cambodia: A Comparative Analysis*, unpublished PhD Dissertation, Columbia University, 1969, p. 21.

14. ကြည်ညွှန့်၊ *ချစ်ကြည်ရေး ချစ်ကြည်ရေးလို့ဆိုကာ* (ရန်ကုန်၊ အပေါင်းအသင်းစာပေ၊ ၁၉၆၈) [Kyi Nyunt, *In the Name of Friendship* (Yangon: Apaung-Athin, 1968)], pp. 78–80.

15. တပ်မတော်ထောက်လှမ်းရေး ညွှန်ကြားရေးမှူးရုံး၊ *အရှေ့မြောက်ဒေသ ဗကပ* (ပုံနှိပ်ခြင်းမရှိသောစာတမ်း၊ ၁၉၈၃) [Directorate of Defence Services Intelligence (DDSI), *The BCP in Northeast Myanmar* (unpublished, 1983)], p. 13.

16. တပ်မတော်ထောက်လှမ်းရေး ညွှန်ကြားရေးမှူးရုံး၊ *ပြည်တွင်းသောင်းကျန်းမှုသမိုင်း* (ပုံနှိပ်ခြင်းမရှိသော စာတမ်း၊ ရက်စွဲမပါ) [Directorate of Defence Services Intelligence (DDSI), *History of Insurgency* (unpublished, no date)], p. 1.

17. Ibid., p. 2.

18. J. H. Brimwell. *Communism in Southeast Asia: A Political Analysis* (London: Oxford University Press, 1959), pp. 312–313.

19. ရဲဘော်မြနှင့်အပေါင်းအပါများ၊ *သုံးပါတီရှိသည်မှာ* (ရန်ကုန်၊ မြယာပင်စာပေ၊ ၁၉၇၀) [Yebaw Mya and et al., *Three Parties Are* (Yangon: Myayarpin Sarpay, 1970)], pp. 4–9.

20. DDSI. *History of Insurgency*, p. 2.

21. ရဲဘော်သစ်မောင်၊ *ပြည်တွင်းသောင်းကျန်းမှုသမိုင်း* (ရန်ကုန်၊ သတင်းနှင့်စာနယ်ဇင်းလုပ်ငန်း၊ ၁၉၉၀) [Yebaw Thit Maung, *History of Insurgency* (Yangon: News and Periodical Enterprise, 1990)], Vol. 2, pp. 99–101.

22. တပ်မတော်ထောက်လှမ်းရေး ညွှန်ကြားရေးမှူးရုံး၊ *ပြည်တွင်းသောင်းကျန်းမှုသမိုင်း* [Directorate of Defence Services Intelligence, *History of Insurgency*], pp. 3–4.

23. Ibid., pp. 4–5.

24. ရဲဘော်မြနှင့်အပေါင်းအပါများ၊ *သခင်သန်းထွန်း၏နောက်ဆုံးနေ့များ* (ရန်ကုန်၊ မြယာပင်စာပေ၊ ၁၉၆၈) [Yebaw Mya and et al., *The Last Days of Thakin Than Tun* (Yangon: Myayarbin Sarpay, 1968)], Vol. 2, p. 657.

25. Ibid., p. 658.

26. Yang Meihong, *Yingsu Huahong: Wozai Mianggong 15 nian* [杨美红, 罂粟花红: 我在缅共十五年] — Red Poppies in Bloom: My 15 Years in the CPB — (Hong Kong: Tiandi Tushu Lit, 2001) quoted in Xiaolin Guo, *Towards Resolution: China in the Myanmar Issue* (Silk Road Paper, Johns Hopkins University-SAIS, March 2007), p. 38.

27. Central Intelligence Agency (CIA). *Peking and the Burmese Communists: The Perils and Profits of Insurgency* (Report prepared in 1971), pp. 11–12.

28. ရဲဘော်မြနှင့်အပေါင်းအပါများ၊ *သခင်သန်းထွန်း၏နောက်ဆုံးနေ့များ* [Yebaw Mya and et al., *The Last Days of Thakin Than Tun*], Vol. 2, pp. 660–661.

29. Ibid., pp. 677–681.

30. ကြည်ညွှန့်၊ *ချစ်ကြည်ရေး ချစ်ကြည်ရေးလို့ဆိုကာ* [Kyi Nyunt, *In the Name of Friendship*], p. 21.

31. Mao Zedong, *Mao Zedong on Diplomacy* (Beijing: Foreign Language Press, 1998), p. 138.

32. William C. Johnstone, *Burma's Foreign Policy: A Study of Neutralism*, pp. 163–164.

33. Ministry of Information, *From Peace to Stability*, pp. 98–101.

34. *The Nation* Newspaper (7 November 1950).

35. U Nu, *Premier Report to the People* (Rangoon: GUB, 1958), pp. 35–36.

36. Chinese People's Institute of Foreign Affairs, *A Victory for the Five Principles of Peaceful Coexistence* (Peking: Foreign Language Press, 1960), p. 2.

37. Ibid.

38. Mao Zedong, *Mao Zedong on Diplomacy*, pp. 137–138.

39. Ibid, p. 138.

40. Communiqué issued on 12 December 1954.

41. Kuo-kong Show, *Communist China's Foreign Policy toward the Non-aligned States*, unpublished PhD Dissertation, University of Pennsylvania, 1972, pp. 184–185.

42. *People's Daily* [人民日报] — *Rénmín Rìbào* (5 January 1956), p. 1.

43. *People's Daily* [人民日报] — *Rénmín Rìbào* (13 December 1956), p. 4.

44. Communiqué issued on 12 December 1954.

45. Ibid.

46. CD 28, *Report of Defence Services Goodwill Mission to China*, DSHMRI.

47. Soong Ching Ling, *Good Neighbours Meet* (Peking: Foreign Language Press, 1956), p. 43.

48. Ibid, pp. 298–299.

49. Francis Watson, *The Frontier of China* (London: Chatto and Windus, 1969), p. 89.

50. Press release on 9 November 1956.

51. Ministry of Information, *Kuomintang Aggression Against Burma* (Rangoon: Ministry of Information, 1955), p. 9.

52. Ibid., p. 3.

53. *New York Times* (29 January 1952).

54. Ministry of Information, *Kuomintang Aggression Against Burma*, p. 18.

55. CD 1017, *The Interrogation Report of Ex. KMT Major General Liu Shing Yie* (Date of surrender — 6 July 1956 and interrogated in August 1956, NBSD).

56. Royal Institute of International Affairs, *Collective Defence in Southeast Asia — The Manila Treaty and its Implications* (London: Oxford University Press, 1958), p. 59.

57. CD 1017, *The Interrogation Report of Ex. KMT Major General Liu Shing Yie*, p. 17.

58. Ministry of Information, *Kuomintang Aggression Against Burma*, pp. 10–11.

59. Department of State, *Foreign Relations of the United States, 1952–1954* (Vol. XII), pp. 41–42.

60. Ministry of Information, *Kuomintang Aggression Against Burma*, p. 159.

61. Evelyn Colbert, *Southeast Asia in International Politics* (Ithaca: Cornell University Press, 1977), p. 133.

62. William C. Johnstone, *A Chronology of Burma's International Relations 1945–1958* (Rangoon: Rangoon University Press, 1959), p. 19.

63. Robert H. Taylor, *Foreign and Domestic Consequences of the KMT Intervention in Burma* (Ithaca; Cornell University Southeast Asia Programme, 1973), pp. 30–31.

64. William C. Johnstone, *A Chronology of Burma's International Relations 1945–1958*, p. 24.
65. စာပေဗိမာန်၊ *ဂျနလရာ့မျတ်တမ်း* (ရန်ကုန်၊ စာပေဗိမာန်၊ ၁၉၅၅) [Burma Translation Society, *Record of China* (Yangon: Burma Translation Society, 1955)], p. 91.
66. Robert H. Taylor, *Foreign and Domestic Consequences of the KMT*, p. 23.
67. William C. Johnstone, *A Chronology of Burma's International Relations 1945–1958*, p. 32.
68. Virginia Thompson, "Burma and Two Chinas", in *Foreign Policy Bulletin*, Issue No. 23 (15 May 1953), pp. 1–2 & 8.
69. Warren Unna, "CIA: Who Watches the Watchman?" *Harper's Magazine*, No. 216 (April 1958), p. 49; David Wise and Thomas Ross, *The Invisible Government* (New York: Random House, 1964), pp. 130–131.
70. Department of State, *Foreign Relations of the United States, 1952–1954*, p. 18.
71. Robert H. Taylor, *Foreign and Domestic Consequences of the KMT*, p. 45.
72. Ministry of Information, *Kuomintang Aggression Against Burma*, p. 1.
73. CD 1493, *Report on the Bangkok Meeting*, DSHMRI, pp. 3–4.
74. Ibid., p. 12.
75. U Nu's Speech in the parliament (13 March 1962) — He gave a lengthy discussion on the KMT issue.
76. Mao Zedong, *Mao Zedong on Diplomacy*, p. 138.
77. စစ်သမိုင်းပြတိုက်နှင့် တပ်မတော်မော်ကွန်းတိုက်မှူးရုံး၊ *တပ်မတော်သမိုင်း* (ရန်ကုန်၊ စစ်သမိုင်းပြတိုက်နှင့် တပ်မတော်မော်ကွန်းတိုက်မှူးရုံး၊ ၂၀၀၃) [Defence Services Historical Museum and Research Institute (DSHMRI), *History of the Armed Forces* (Yangon: DSHMRI, 2003)], Vol. 4, p. 79.
78. Interview with Colonel Saw Myint (5 July 1996, Yangon).
79. DR 9398, *Report on the Operation Burma Boundary — Mekong Operation*, DSHMRI.
80. DR 9397, *Casualty Report on the Operation Burma Boundary — Mekong Operation*, DSHMRI.
81. Robert Holmes, *Chinese Foreign Policy toward Burma and Cambodia*, p. 32.
82. U Nu Speech in the Chamber of Deputies on 28 April 1960.
83. Dorothy Woodman, *The Making of Burma* (London: the Cresset Press, 1962), p. 522.
84. Ministry of Information, *From Peace to Stability*, p. 198.
85. They were (1) Xishuangbanna Thai Autonomous Area — January 1953, (2) Lancan Lahu Autonomous Unit — April 1953, (3) Thai-Shantou (Kachin) Autonomous Area — July 1953, (4) Nu-Jiang (Salween) Lisu Autonomous Area — August 1954, and (5) Gengma Tai Kawa Autonomous County — October 1955.
86. DR. 9453, *Interview with Colonel Chit Myaing*, pp. 285–286.
87. Ibid., p. 287.
88. CD 5, *Report on the Operation Yein Nwe Par*, Vol. 1+2+3, DSHMRI.

89. The Chinese People's Institute of Foreign Affairs (ed.), *A Victory for the Five Principles of Peaceful Coexistence* (Beijing: Foreign Language Press, 1960), p. 3.

90. Harold Hinton, *China's Relations with Burma and Vietnam* (New York: Institute of Pacific Relations, 1956), p. 41.

91. Ibid., p. 43.

92. Harold Hinton, *Communist China in World Politics* (London: McMillan, 1966), p. 314.

93. ဦးဇန်ထားဆင်၊ *ဒီမိုကရေစီပြောင်းပြန်* (ရန်ကုန်၊ အောင်စစ်သည်စာပေ၊ ၁၉၉၀) [U Zan Hta Sin, *Reversed Democracy* (Yangon: Aung Sithi Sarpay, 1990)], pp. 78–79.

94. The Chinese People's Institute of Foreign Affairs, *A Victory for the Five Principles of Peaceful Coexistence*, p. 6.

95. Speech on 11 December 1956.

96. Dorothy Woodman, *The Making of Burma*, pp. 530–531.

97. Ibid., pp. 531–532.

98. Kuo-kong Show, *Communist China's Foreign Policy toward the Non-aligned States*, pp. 198–199.

99. Ibid., pp. 533–535.

100. Ibid., p. 535.

101. ဝန်ကြီးချုပ်ချို့အင်လိုင်းကြိုဆိုရေးတရုတ်အမျိုးသားများကော်မတီ၊ *တရုတ်မြန်မာချစ်ကြည်ရေး မှတ်တမ်း* (ရန်ကုန်၊ ခေတ်မြန်မာပုံနှိပ်တိုက်၊ ၁၉၆၁) [Chinese Committee to Welcome Premier Zhao Enlai, *China-Myanmar Friendship Record — in Myanmar* (Yangon: Khit Myanmar Press, 1961), pp. 8–12.

102. Ministry of Information, *Burma* (Vol. IX, No. 4; October 1960), p. 4.

103. There were two more meetings after the signing of the Boundary Treaty.

104. CD 641, *Notes on the first session of the Chinese-Burmese Joint Committee*, DSHMRI.

105. CD 646, *Documents on the Operation Burma Boundary*, DSHMRI.

106. For detail, see Kay Khine, *Sino-Myanmar Relations: Operation Burma Boundary* (M.A Thesis, Department of International Relations, Yangon University, 1996)

107. CD 644, *Report of the Chinese-Burmese Joint Committee to the Permanent Secretary of Foreign Affairs*, DSHMRI.

108. CD 646, *Documents on the Operation Burma Boundary*, DSHMRI.

109. CD 648, *Boundary Treaty between the Union of Burma and People's Republic of China*, DSHMRI.

110. See Appendix (1) for detail.

111. Dr. Maung Maung, "Burma-China Boundary Settlement", *Guardian Magazine* (Vol. 8, No. 3; March 1961), p. 21.

112. Ibid., p. 23.

113. The Chinese People's Institute of Foreign Affairs, *A Victory for the Five Principles of Peaceful Coexistence*, editor's note.

3

SINO-MYANMAR RELATIONS
1962–1988
Into the Years of Living Dangerously

On 2 March 1962, the Tatmadaw, under the leadership of the then Commander-in-Chief, General Ne Win, carried out a military coup in the name of the Revolutionary Council and took over control of the State. The Revolutionary Council immediately issued a statement that it would not deviate from Myanmar's declared policy of "positive neutrality" in its conduct of foreign relations. A year later, the new government called Myanmar ambassadors back for consultations. On 2 September 1963, they were briefed on the council's approach to international affairs. General Ne Win said: "What is well-defined and clear-cut in our international relations, is our policy of strict neutrality of non-alignment. It is extremely important for our ambassadors to adhere to this policy in the discharge of their duties... Especially at this juncture when international politics is overshadowed by the split between the East and the West, the split doesn't stop with these two power blocs but at times has repercussions on us. Only if we can live up to our policy of neutrality, can we hope to meet the situation". Fearful of the spill-over effect of global Cold War in general and of the intensifying conflict in Indochina, in particular, the Myanmar government tried to avoid involvement in balance of power politics. Despite this undeniably realist worldview, the Revolutionary Council government had found isolation as the best course of foreign policy for the young nation.

Nearly two months after the military takeover, on 30 April, the Revolutionary Council proclaimed the "Burmese Way to Socialism". The Burmese Way to Socialism (BWS), heavily influenced by Marxist and Buddhist philosophies, subsequently became the political and socio-economic foundation upon which the Revolutionary Council based its policies. On 4 July, the Revolutionary Council formed the Burma Socialist Programme Party (BSPP) as a political organization to lead the socialist revolution in Myanmar. On 23 March 1964, the Revolutionary Council government issued a decree entitled "The Law Protecting National Unity". Under this law, all political parties except the BSPP were abolished and their assets appropriated. The Revolutionary Council now held a Marxist world view of class struggle between the forces of socialism and those of capitalism. Despite its strong support for anti-colonial struggles, at various international forums, and its apparent socialist orientation, however, the Revolutionary Council government did not prioritize Socialist solidarity and internationalism in its conduct of foreign policy. It was this failure to stress socialist solidarity in foreign policy that eventually triggered Chinese hostility towards Myanmar in the late 1960s.

Myanmar's China policy during the Revolutionary Council period was also framed in the context of the Five Principles of Peaceful Coexistence and strict adherence to so called "positive neutrality" and non-alignment. As the person who successfully negotiated the border demarcation treaty and the treaty of friendship and mutual non-aggression with China, Ne Win apparently held high hopes that his government would be well received by Beijing. This was in fact true. Two days after the coup, the Chinese government accorded the Revolutionary Council diplomatic recognition. Zhou Enlai cabled his greetings to General Ne Win and stated: "I am confident that the intimate relations of friendship and cooperation between China and Burma will be further strengthened and developed".[1] This was followed by exchanges of high level visits between the PRC and Myanmar. Liu Shaoqi, accompanied by Chen Yi, came to Myanmar for the first time in April 1963. The Chinese press praised Myanmar as being the first country to conclude a treaty of friendship and mutual non-aggression with China. Liu described Sino-Myanmar relations as "a brilliant example of amicable co-existence and friendly cooperation" for Asian and African countries. Myanmar also confirmed her support for China's admission to the UN.[2] The joint communiqué issued on 25 April stated that "constant consolidation and development of the friendly relations is a clear proof of the great vitality of the Five Principles of Peaceful Coexistence" and reaffirmed that "all nations should have the right to choose their own political and economic systems and their own way of life in keeping with their national requirements and aspirations and without any outside interference or pressure".[3]

Beneath the outwardly amicable relations between the two countries, however, there were certain signs of tension and irritation. These were the result of new developments on both the domestic and international fronts. In Myanmar, domestically, the government policy of nationalization, which included Chinese businesses, banks, schools, and newspapers, undermined China's political leverage. At the international level, the Revolutionary Council government maintained a strictly neutral and genuinely impartial foreign policy. It resisted all forms of political pressure, whether from the United States or the Soviet Union or China. In August 1963, a partial Nuclear Test Ban Treaty (NTBT) was concluded in Moscow. Myanmar considered this as a significant step toward the goal of banning nuclear tests in the atmosphere and underwater. It therefore signed and ratified the treaty. But China considered the treaty as a strategy by the established world nuclear powers to prevent the PRC from acquiring nuclear weapons. Myanmar's signing of the NTBT caused some discontent in China.

Between 1963 and 1966, China tried to gain Myanmar's support for the Chinese stand on various international issues, such as the Sino-Indian border dispute, the Afro-Asian Conference, Indonesia's *Konfrontasi* with Malaya and the Vietnam War. However, the Myanmar government refused to take a public stand on these issues. With regard to the Sino-Indian border dispute and, subsequently, war, as stated in the joint communiqué issued in April 1963 during the state visit of Liu Shaoqi, the Yangon government's position was that the issue should be resolved by the two parties entering into direct negotiations on the basis of the Colombo Conference proposals. This, Myanmar believed, might result in a settlement of the boundary question satisfactory to both sides.[4] However, the Myanmar government refused to endorse the PRC's call for convening an Afro-Asian Conference with a view to discussing the boundary issue.[5] Zhou Enlai and Chen Yi visited Myanmar again in February and July 1964. During the February visit, Zhou Enlai once more attempted to persuade Ne Win to support the Chinese position on the Sino-Indian border dispute and to generate enthusiasm for the idea of an Afro-Asian Conference. But Ne Win refused to take a position on the border dispute and told his counterpart that the proposed Afro-Asian Conference would have a divisive, rather than a unifying, effect on the non-aligned nations. Ne Win appeared to believe that Beijing might attempt to use the conference a forum to mobilize support for the Chinese stand in the border dispute. Although he finally agreed to consider taking part in the conference if one was held, he refused to give a public endorsement to the idea of holding the conference. According to some knowledgeable observers, after his meeting with Zhou, Ne Win was reported to have said that he "hated the Chinese more than ever".

The visit by Zhou Enlai and Chen Yi in July 1964 was seen by some Myanmar observers as a measure to offset any gain the Soviet Union may have made from First Deputy Prime Minister Anastas Mikoyan's visit less than a week earlier.[6] Nevertheless, Zhou tried to maneuver Ne Win into a pro-China position on the Vietnam War and Indonesia's *Konfrontasi*. Chinese leaders also attempted to persuade Ne Win not to allow Soviet over-flight rights in Myanmar airspace. But their efforts failed on all counts. The joint communiqué issued on 11 July 1964 expressed deep concern over the deteriorating situation in Southeast Asia, particularly in South Vietnam and Laos.[7] Yet the two sides took occasion to reaffirm their undertaking, contained in Article 3 of the Treaty signed in 1960, that both countries agreed neither to carry out acts of aggression nor to take part in any military alliance directed against each other. By 1964, China began to show some signs of disappointment with the Myanmar government. On 1 October 1964, on the 15th Anniversary of the founding of the PRC, Radio Peking broadcasted a congratulatory message sent by the BCP.[8] The BCP message accused the Revolutionary Council of having obstructed peace negotiations in 1963. The message declared: "The civil war in Burma has been going on for nearly 17 years now… the peace talks failed because of sabotage by imperialism, internal reaction and revisionism. The Communist Party of Burma will continue to uphold the three banners of national independence, democracy and peace in the country, and will strive for the establishment of a new Burma of real independence, politically and economically".[9] When the Myanmar government protested, through diplomatic channels, about the broadcast, the Chinese replied that they thought it was a good idea to publicize congratulatory messages, by whomever they were sent.[10] Nevertheless, the Chinese stopped airing any messages from the BCP until the outbreak of the anti-Chinese riots in Myanmar in June 1967. In this regard, the Myanmar government maintained a very strict press censorship policy even for foreign news. While it used AFP, Reuters and NCNA as the main sources of foreign news, it reported only factual and non-controversial issues, with no commentary. Any news items critical of China's domestic and foreign policies were never permitted to be published in state-owned media outlets. Despite this, Beijing protested over the use of the term "Red China" or the "Peking Government" in some private Myanmar newspapers and magazines.

Meanwhile, the war in Vietnam was escalating. The United States. sent combat troops to Vietnam in February 1965. In April, Zhou Enlai and Chen Yi made three stopovers in Myanmar. The first was on 3 April on their way back from Europe and Africa. The second was on 16 April on their way to the Tenth Anniversary celebration of the Bandung Conference in Jakarta. Then on 26 April, on their way back to China from Bandung Conference, Zhou Enlai and his party came to Myanmar and stayed for two days. During this visit to Yangon, Zhou Enlai was reported to have lectured Ne Win for three hours on the subject of the Vietnam War, urging him to display a spirit of socialist solidarity. A month later, on 21 May 1965, Peng Zhen (彭真), Vice Chairman of the Standing Committee of the National People's Congress, made a brief stopover in Yangon, on his way to Indonesia. Meanwhile, Myanmar's Foreign Minister, U Thi Han, cancelled his original plan to attend the second Afro-Asian Conference, to be held in Algiers, and returned home from the Federal Republic of Germany on 26 June 1965. This act was perhaps a sign of the Yangon government's displeasure over the conference, whose agenda, it suspected, was being excessively influenced by China.

On 24 July 1965, a Myanmar delegation led by General Ne Win went to China for a six-day visit at the invitation of Liu Shaoqi and Zhou Enlai. Mao Zedong received Ne Win on 26 July. During their meetings, Chinese leaders drew attention to developments in the Vietnam War, highlighting the "worldwide struggle against imperialism, colonialism, and neo-colonialism". Ne Win remained indifferent. At a state banquet, Liu clarified Beijing's policy toward the war in Vietnam:

> In order to really solve the Viet Nam question, the opinions of the Vietnamese people must be respected and the 'peace talk' hoax of the United States and its followers must be opposed, otherwise it will be detrimental to the Vietnamese people's cause of fighting against US aggression and for national salvation.[11]

In contrast, General Ne Win took a neutral stance and refrained from making any comments on the situation in Vietnam. So did the Myanmar press, which censored Liu Shaoqi's speech. General Ne Win carefully stated:

> Today a main source of international tension is a disregard of these elementary principles (five principles of peaceful coexistence) of international relations. Particularly dangerous to the newly independent, developing countries are flagrant outside interventions in their internal affairs on one pretext or another. Such interventions are bound to create great obstacle to the independent development of these countries whose primary task is to fulfil the hopes of their peoples who looking forward to a world in which they can live in peace and pursue their

political, economic, social and cultural advancement, free from outside interference.[12]

His statement was ambiguous. The joint communiqué issued on 1 August 1965 was also subtle on the subject of Vietnam.[13] Members of the Myanmar delegation must have carefully discussed and thoroughly gone through the draft with their Chinese counterparts to ensure that there were no elements in the communiqué that infringed Myanmar's declared policy of non-alignment. The communiqué stated that both countries were concerned with the "grave situation in Southeast Asia, particularly in Vietnam". It further stated: "They were of the view that a lasting settlement of the Vietnam question would be achieved only if the Vietnamese people were free to settle their own problems and determine their own future without any foreign interference. They considered that any ultimate settlement of the Vietnam question must respect the principles of independence, sovereignty, unity and territorial integrity of Vietnam embodied in the 1954 Geneva Agreement on Vietnam".[14] The carefully worded joint communiqué, it could be assumed, indicated that while Yangon would not publicly criticize Washington's position on Vietnam, it was not prepared to support the United States' agenda of creating an "independent" South Vietnam, separated from the North. Compared to strongly worded "China-Indonesia Joint Statement" issued on 28 January 1965, the communiqué was very weak. Nevertheless, the communiqué noted that the bilateral relations have been cordial and pledged further expansion of trade and economic relations. Myanmar also reaffirmed its support for China's right to the United Nations' seat.

When Liu Shaoqi paid his second visit to Myanmar in April 1966, he noted in a banquet speech that "Afro-Asian countries had waged unremitting struggle against imperialist subversion and interference and for the defence of national independence and sovereignty and they must heighten their vigilance, unite still more closely and preserve in struggle".[15] This was a subtle hint that Ne Win should show more anti-imperialist zeal. In connection with the Vietnam War, Liu tried to gain Myanmar's support. He stated:

> Both our countries are close neighbours of Vietnam. It is only natural that we are much concerned about the development of the situation in Vietnam and hope for an early restoration of peace there.... Two most essential points (in bringing peace in Vietnam) are: the immediate withdrawal of all US military forces in Vietnam and the recognition of the South Vietnam National Front for Liberation as the sole legal representative of the people in South Vietnam.[16]

General Ne Win showed nothing more than his deep concern over the escalation of the Vietnam War. When the joint communiqué was issued on 19 April, there was no mention of the Vietnam War. Apparently, once again, Liu Shaoqi had failed to gain Ne Win's support for the Chinese position on Vietnam. In the meantime, in China itself, the Cultural Revolution gained momentum and began to spill over in the area of foreign relations. Beijing's militancy was clearly apparent in the publication of the "Long Live the People's War" by Lin Biao in mid 1966. Beijing now advocated a policy of exporting revolution to other countries.

By late 1965 China had become increasingly dissatisfied with several aspects of Myanmar's foreign policy where Yangon's strictly neutral stance clashed with Beijing's own position. More than anything else, Myanmar's policy on the Vietnam War and her disinclination to take an anti-US position, coupled with her signing of the Nuclear Test Ban Treaty and her refusal to support a Chinese military training program for anti-Indian government Miso insurgents on Myanmar soil, among other things, made the PRC unhappy. Yet the PRC did not show her displeasure until anti-Chinese riots broke out in Myanmar in mid 1967. By October 1965, General Ne Win had openly admitted the failure of his government to achieve economic development as a result of the radical nationalization policy and recognized the need to look for outside assistance. He also acknowledged the consequences of "abandoning the self-defeating policy of virtual economic isolation that he had been adopted to please China, among others".[17] At the 1965 Party Seminar of the BSPP, General Ne Win eloquently stated his views on Myanmar's foreign policy:

> It is not possible for a nation to remain isolated. It must have relations with others. It must establish friendships and avoid generating ill-will. This is the principle. It is a good one and must be followed. But the practice is difficult.... . That is why in our relationships with other nations we will never attempt to reap advantage at the other's expense. Also, we will fraternize with others on a basis of equality. Of course, our relations will be closer with those countries which have programmes similar to ours. But even nations which have close relations with each other break out into quarrels arising out of misunderstandings. When lovers quarrel the ensuing hatred is more bitter. This is evident to our eyes. Therefore, we should be measured and moderate in our relations with others.[18]

By this time, Myanmar's neutralist foreign policy was becoming more expensive. General Ne Win began to experiment with a more diversified approach, travelling extensively to many countries, including India, Pakistan,

Sri Lanka, the Soviet Union, Czechoslovakia, Romania, the United States, Thailand and Japan. The Myanmar government sent hundreds of students to the Soviet Union and Eastern European countries for further studies. Moreover, as early as 1964, Yangon also sought economic policy advice from the Soviet Union.[19] In the United States, during his visit in September 1966, Ne Win was quiet on the Vietnam War and when the joint communiqué was issued, it simply mentioned that General Ne Win "had expressed Burma's desire for a political settlement of the Vietnam question on the basis of respect for her sovereignty, independence, unity and territorial integrity." A few months earlier, Ne Win also warmly received American Senator Mike Mansfield, the first high-ranking U.S. political figure to visit Myanmar since the 1962 coup. [Senator Mansfield's political view and anti-Vietnam War comments might have convinced Yangon that the senator was the most appropriate American political figure to visit Myanmar.] Besides, the Myanmar government procured various items of military hardware, such as aircraft and gunboats, from the United States. Between 1963 and 1967, the Tatmadaw bought six C-47D Dakotas, 23 Lockheed T-33 fighters, and 13 gunboats of various types from the United States. It also bought weapons factories from West Germany that could produce NATO-standard arms and ammunitions. All these measures, it might be assumed, might have annoyed the Chinese leadership. By the mid 1960s, it appeared that Beijing was increasingly dissatisfied and disappointed with Ne Win's strict neutralism. It therefore began to pursue a more assertive foreign policy toward Myanmar. The first manifestation of this was Beijing's decision to export the Cultural Revolution to Myanmar. This, in turn, led to Anti-Chinese riots, further deterioration of the Sino-Myanmar relationship, and, finally, open Chinese support for the BCP.

Until early 1967, there had been no clear signs of upcoming trouble in Sino-Myanmar relations at the official level. The "Myanmar Independence Day" reception on 4 January 1967 in Beijing was attended by Vice Premiers of the State Council, Chen Yi and Xie Fuzhi (谢富治), and Vice-Chairman of the National People's Congress Standing Committee Guo Moruo (郭沫若), along with other senior Chinese officials. On this occasion, the Myanmar ambassador remarked that the two countries had "continually strengthened and effectively developed perfect and broadening friendship and cooperation".[20] In a similar term, Chen Yi praised the Myanmar government as follows: "In the past few years, under the leadership of Chairman Ne Win, the Burmese Government and people have carried out unremitting struggles in the way of independence and development for safeguarding your national sovereignty and independence and developing your national economy and culture, and have achieved great successes. The friendship between the

Chinese and Burmese people is built on a deep and massive foundation. In the past few years, we have further developed the friendship and cooperative relations between our two countries. The Chinese government and people treasure Sino-Burmese friendship a great deal… The Chinese Government and people will, as they have done in the past, continue to support the Union of Burma in its struggle against imperialism for national independence and its pursuance of a policy of peace and neutrality, and will join hands with the Burmese Government and people to consolidate and develop the friendship and cooperative relations between our two countries".[21] With the benefit of hindsight, it can be seen that behind these diplomatic words, the CCP had been mobilizing anti-Myanmar government forces in China for a showdown.

THE 1967 ANTI-CHINESE RIOT

The anti-Chinese riot of 1967 in Myanmar was a turning point in the bilateral relationship. Paradoxically, the disturbances enabled the Myanmar government to finally gain control over the PRC's instruments of internal leverage. Since early 1964, China had speeded up its political and organizational activities among overseas Chinese in Myanmar. The Xinhwa correspondent, Yu Min-sheng, who arrived in Myanmar on 5 April 1964, was a key figure in infiltrating the Chinese community in Yangon. Despite its Communist ideological orientation, the Chinese government cultivated close relations with Overseas Chinese businessmen, although they were "class enemies", to promote its national interests. Some wealthy Chinese businessmen in Myanmar were working for the PRC cause. Beijing always treated such wealthy overseas Chinese businessmen as high profile figures. After the 1964 nationalization of industries and banks in Myanmar (including two Chinese banks and a number of Chinese businesses) the Beijing government must have realized that it had lost much of its ability to influence the overseas Chinese community in Myanmar. In term of mobilizing financial resources, according to an informed source, the Chinese Embassy in Yangon used three methods: (1) giving more margin of commission rate (from official two per cent to five per cent) for imports of Chinese goods into Myanmar; (2) collection of organizational funds out of profits from Chinese business; and (3) control of remittances by overseas Chinese.[22]

Aware of Beijing's influence over the Chinese community in Myanmar, the Revolutionary Council government monitored political activities of Chinese residents. This was partly because the government suspected that some Chinese were involved in making contacts with Communist insurgents.

The government was also aware of Communist Chinese activities in Chinese schools. Already in 1952, the then Myanmar government had required all Chinese schools in Myanmar to register with the government under the Private School Act. However, the level of compliance had never been satisfactory. When the Revolutionary Council came to power, realizing that some private schools, especially those operated by foreign communities in general and overseas Chinese in particular, were engaging in political and ideological education, it tried to bring them under tight control. In December 1962, there were 259 Chinese schools throughout the country attended by about 40,000 students. These schools were in reality subjected to little control by the Board of Education of the Myanmar government. They had their own curricula and language teaching programs. According to one study, out of 259 schools, only two claimed political neutrality. A total of 183 schools (70 per cent), with an enrolment of about 22,000 students (56 per cent) were clearly pro-PRC.[23] The position of the remaining 74 schools was less clear: they were under the supervision of one of two organizations, the 'right wing' Burma Overseas Cultural and Educational Advancement Association or the 'left wing' Burma Overseas Chinese Teachers' Union.[24] According to a former student, most of the schools were under the direction of the Chinese Embassy in Yangon. Usually, headmasters of the schools were pro-ROC whereas their deputies were pro-PRC. This was believed to be a common Chinese communist organizational tactic.[25]

In May 1963, the Myanmar government promulgated a new private school registration law which required all private schools with twenty or more students to register. No schools were allowed to offer courses unless they had a certificate of registration. A new socialist education system was introduced in 1964, and a uniform curriculum was prescribed for all schools. Notification No. 33, issued by the government on 26 March 1965, nationalized a total number of 883 private schools registered in Myanmar.[26] In March 1965 the government nationalized a further 129 schools. A year later, all the remaining 684 schools were absorbed into the state education system.[27] The result of this policy was the growth of private schools with less than 20 students, estimated at around 470 pro-PRC schools and 200 non- or anti-PRC schools. The curriculum of the pro-PRC schools was wholly based on Mao Zedong thought and the "History of the Chinese Communist Revolution and Literature". Moreover, there were also one-year special training classes designed to train communist cadres.[28] By 1967, the government realized that these schools had become the focal point of tension as the impact of the Cultural Revolution spilled over into Myanmar. These schools became arena to test the Myanmar government's ability to handle Chinese political pressure. Anti-Chinese riots erupted and Sino-Myanmar relations deteriorated. As China tried to export the Cultural Revolution to Chinese in Myanmar, Chinese diplomats as well as some militants created a number of incidents to dramatize their devotion to the Revolution. Confrontation between the two nations intensified and their relationship reached a nadir in their post-war history. As Holmes observed, Sino-Myanmar friendship became a casualty of the Chinese Cultural Revolution.[29]

Since 1966, the PRC had been openly calling for the allegiance of overseas Chinese to the motherland. The New Year Day's Message of the Head of the Overseas Affairs Commission in Beijing called on overseas Chinese to support the worldwide struggle against American imperialism. At the same time, steps were taken to encourage Chinese in Myanmar to support the Cultural Revolution. Well before the recall of Chinese diplomats from Myanmar, twelve Red Guards had been assigned to Yangon to mobilize Chinese support for the Cultural Revolution.[30] In January 1967, Ambassador Geng Biao (耿飚) and 21 members of the embassy staff in Yangon were recalled for so-called "consultation". In March, a group of fifteen people returned to Yangon, of whom at least four were Red Guards.[31] These Red Guards took charge of the Chinese Embassy in Yangon, while Xiao Ming remained as the titular *Charge d' Affaires*. Ambassador Geng Biao never returned to Yangon.

The Red Guards promoted the Cultural Revolution within the embassy premises and then extended it to the Chinese community in Yangon. They invited Chinese students to see Maoist plays and films on the Cultural Revolution, taught songs such as "Mao is the red sun in our hearts", and conducted cadre training classes in the embassy premises almost every morning.[32] Chinese teachers, senior students and junior students were organized, in Maoist fashion, as cadres, unit leaders and followers respectively. Their headquarters was the Chinese Teachers' Federation. This organization distributed Mao badges and armbands to students. The Myanmar government was puzzled by the discovery of a large quantity of Red Guard uniforms at the Xinhwa office.[33] The mastermind behind all these moves was Yu Min-sheng, a correspondent from the Xinhwa. He was very influential in the Chinese Embassy because of his party membership status. According to a Myanmar source, the Chinese government nominated Yu Min-sheng as a first secretary cum Xinhwa correspondent in early 1964, along with five other non-diplomatic personnel. Contrary to normal diplomatic practice, news of his nomination was passed on to some diplomatic missions in Yangon, before it had been accepted by the Myanmar government. Realizing that this was a move to take cover behind diplomatic immunity, the government rejected Yu Min-sheng's nomination, on the grounds that it was against diplomatic tradition.[34]

On 19 June 1967, the Ministry of Education issued a regulation which forbade the wearing of any political insignia except those approved by the ministry. The same evening, the Chinese Teachers' Federation held an emergency meeting to challenge the order and prepare a more aggressive defiance. Under instructions from their teachers, Chinese students ignored the regulation and formed groups in Red Guard fashion. The first demonstration of defiance against the government regulation by Chinese students took place on 22 June at two former Chinese schools in downtown Yangon. It was reported in Myanmar newspapers that Xinhwa correspondent Yu Min-sheng and three Red Guards from the Chinese Embassy came to the schools in a car from the embassy and distributed Mao badges and "Little Red Books" to students. When school authorities took action against those students who violated the regulation, the Chinese *Charge d' Affaires* in Yangon lodged a protest with the Myanmar Foreign Ministry on 23 June. The note argued that it was the legitimate right of the Overseas Chinese to wear Mao badges and that no one must deprive them of this right, and demanded the Myanmar government guarantee not to take action against those wearing the badge.[35] In their protest against the regulation of the Ministry of Education, Yu Min-sheng and the Red Guards were ubiquitous. On 26 June the Ministry of Education instructed school masters to remind students of the regulation and to appeal to parents to follow the rules. But the tension between school authorities and Chinese students escalated and anti-Chinese riots erupted. Chinese-owned businesses and residences, and even the Chinese Embassy, were targets of attack by the Myanmar public. On the next day, the government declared martial law and issued a dusk-to-dawn curfew in Yangon. The Ministry of Information urged restraint. A statement was issued on the same day and it said:

> People of the country:
> (1) The government of the Union of Myanmar is taking whatever action is necessary in connection with the prevailing situation at some schools.
> (2) It is necessary for the people and the Government to work together in order to prevent the present situation from worsening.
> (3) At the present time, the public is dissatisfied and holding demonstrations. While some are demonstrating in good faith, there could be also some trying to worsen the situation for various reasons.
> (4) The Government has the duty to protect the lives and property of foreign nationals residing as guests in the country, in the same way it is responsible to its own nationals. In particular, the Government has additional responsibility to protect the security of the members of Diplomatic Corps of various countries.

(5) The people should avoid acts which will harm the friendship between countries and create hatred between one people and another. Even when an unavoidable issue arises, the use of force and taking law into one's own hands should be avoided as much as possible. Instead, efforts should be exerted to settle it smoothly and amicably by adhering to the principle of 'let enmity be ephemeral and amity endure'.

(6) The Government shall stop, be it by citizen or by foreigner, the bullying of the minority by the majority, and the use of violence, in line with its responsibility.

(7) The Government will be able to concentrate on and attend to other matters as its responsibility to prevent public violence lessens. Thus, the people should now be satisfied, since they have already demonstrated their desire. The people as thus asked to stop their demonstrations in an orderly way, in accordance with the proper behaviour and attributes of citizens of a nation.

The official statement revealed that, despite a curfew, the government would allow the demonstrations against the Chinese in Myanmar and activities of the Chinese diplomats to continue, but in an orderly fashion. This was noteworthy since the Revolutionary Council rarely allowed such activities. The Revolutionary Council might have reasoned that the upheaval provided an opportunity to bring the Chinese community in Myanmar under its control. The government had thoroughly exploited Myanmar popular sentiment against Chinese who were practicing great Chinese chauvinism. The Chinese accused the Myanmar government of instigating and engineering the protest and Ne Win of carefully orchestrating xenophobia. Many Chinese in Myanmar were killed and their properties were destroyed. The government appealed to the public for tolerance "in the larger interest of friendly bilateral relations". The government evacuated a large number of Chinese families to Mingalardon cantonment. The official newspaper publicized an incident in which three Myanmar citizens were injured while protecting a Chinese neighbour. Other papers gave additional examples of Myanmar tolerance and forbearance. However, the demonstrations escalated out of control and angry crowds set fire to the Overseas Chinese Teachers' Federation building and attacked the Chinese Embassy. On 28 June, some demonstrators stormed the Chinese Embassy again, resulting in the death of a Chinese technician and the injuring of a diplomatic courier.

On 28 June, the Chinese Ministry of Foreign Affairs sent a protest note to the Myanmar Embassy in Beijing and demanded "that the Burmese government immediately take emergency measures to prevent further aggravation of the situation, guarantee the safety of the members of the Chinese

Embassy and the other Chinese agencies, of the personnel sent by China to undertake the Chinese loan projects in Burma and of the Overseas Chinese, as well as to protect their property and the property of the Chinese agencies, return the seized Chinese national emblem, and severely publish the culprits of these incidents".[36] In addition, the Chinese government reserved the right to demand compensation from the Myanmar government for all the losses and reminded Yangon that it must bear full responsibility for all the serious consequences arising out of the anti-Chinese demonstrations. On the same day, Chinese *Charge d' Affaires* in Yangon, Xiao Ming, put forward five demands on behalf of the Chinese government. It insisted that Yangon (1) Severely punish the culprits; (2) Give relief to the families of the victims; (3) Publicly offer apologies; (4) Guarantee the safety of the Chinese Embassy in Burma and the Chinese agencies and all their Chinese personnel; and (5) Immediately put an end to the fascist atrocities against Overseas Chinese.[37]

By then, the Chinese press began to brand the Revolutionary Council government as a reactionary government, a counter-revolutionary government, or a fascist government. Radio Peking broadcast anti-Myanmar government news and commentaries. The commentary on 29 June signalled the Chinese government's decision to overtly support the armed struggle of the Burma Communist Party. It said:

> Since its assumption of power, the Ne Win Government has all along pursued anti-communist and anti-people's policies. Its economic policy of harsh exploitation and plundering of the people has created extreme difficulties and chaos in the domestic economy. At present, class contradictions in the country have become acute, and the people's discontent with the government has been growing. The armed struggle waged persistently by the Burmese National Democratic United Front formed by the Burmese Communist Party and other revolutionary organizations has been steadily developing. In this situation, the Burmese Government is carrying out frantic anti-China and anti-Chinese activities, with the obvious aim of fanning up reactionary nationalist sentiments to cover up the class contradictions inside the country and to divert the strong resentment of the people against the reactionary government, which is caused by its economic policy of exploiting the people. It wants to use these actions to attack and weaken the forces and influence of the Burmese Communist Party and to stabilize its own rule. The Burmese government's attempt to use anti-China activities to achieve these aims can never be realized.[38]

Soon afterwards, an intense war of words between the two countries erupted. Some Myanmar newspapers serialized articles on Chinese interference in Myanmar internal affairs. *The Guardian* newspaper editorialized:

> There are in Burma many Chinese who have come to love and appreciate both the land and its people… There have been many instances of Chinese life and property being saved by Burmese neighbours, some of whom were actually hurt in doing this. The cause of the disturbance was the well-planned actions taken by a well-organized and carefully controlled group of Overseas Chinese, it is more than apparent. For some reason, they have taken the arrogant and Big Nation chauvinistic stand that they can live in a foreign country and refuse to comply with the laws of that country in force… It is this which the Revolutionary Government cannot possibly tolerate… and which caused the people to demonstrate against them. Unfortunately these demonstrations got carried away by mounting passion, and in the end the Government was having to protect the very people who challenged its authority.[39]

The Chinese government statements were increasingly belligerent. In the early stage, for example the statements issued on 28 and 29 June 1967, criticism was confined to Yangon's government's handling of the riots and its failure to defend Overseas Chinese interests. Later, Chinese statements began to portray the events as evidence of the Myanmar government's anti-China policies or anti-Chinese plots hatched in collaboration with "U.S. imperialism" and "Soviet revisionism".

Meanwhile, on 29 June, according to Chinese sources, about 200,000 Chinese nationals demonstrated in front of the Myanmar Embassy in Beijing. Another 400,000 joined the crowd on the next day. Despite the Myanmar government's appeal to the Chinese government to prevent such demonstrations, they continued. The Chinese official press also carried statements by the BCP. By early July 1967, it was apparent that the Chinese government openly endorsed the BCP's armed struggle and was prepared to lend its support. Mass rallies were organized in Beijing to denounce the Revolutionary Council government in Myanmar. China also filed a series of protests and demands through the Myanmar Embassy in Beijing and the Chinese Embassy in Yangon. The Myanmar government refused to comply with the Chinese demands, although it protected Chinese diplomats and their families. The public apology demanded by the Chinese government was never made. The Chinese government charged the Myanmar government with instigating the riots. General Ne Win was branded as "Chiang Kai-shek of Burma". Security measures taken by the Myanmar government to protect Chinese diplomats and their families were condemned as restrictions on their movements. Throughout the Myanmar government maintained an attitude of righteousness and indignation. As *The Guardian* insisted editorially: "Whatever the People's Republic of China may have chosen to say, the present trouble between this huge country and Burma is not of Burma's making… Shocked into a cruel disillusionment that her diligent scruples in nurturing neighboring friendship and in pursuing strict neutrality in international power-politics were not being respected as hoped, Burma, nevertheless, cannot be threatened into compromising sovereignty or her strictly neutral policy".[40] On 11 July 1967, the Myanmar Ministry of Foreign Affairs, through its embassy in Beijing, handed a note to the Chinese Foreign Ministry, explaining the situation in Myanmar. The note stated:

> The Government of the Union of Burma openly denies that charges that the recent riots had been instigated by the Government of the Union of Burma. The Government of the Union of Burma will carry out a full investigation in accordance with its legal duties and will take appropriate action in accordance with the laws of the Union. The Government of the Union of Burma is exerting every effort to protect the staff of the Chinese Embassy and Chinese experts, in accordance with international law, and is giving equal protection to both citizens and non-citizens alike. The Government of the Union of Burma is very sorry for the death of Mr. Liu Yi despite such protection. The family of the deceased should be comforted by the traditional friendship between the two countries and the strange circumstances of the incident. The correct security measures taken by the Government of the Union of Burma have prevented the recurrence of riots. Such security measures and other special measures taken for the safety of the staff of the Chinese Embassy should not be interpreted as restrictions on the movement of the Chinese Embassy staff.[41]

However, the Chinese government continued its protests. Meanwhile, on 14 July 1967, the Xinhwa correspondent in Yangon, Yu Min-sheng, was ordered to leave before noon on 17 July. He was accused of violating his agreement with the Ministry of Information — requiring him to work solely for the news agency — by interfering in the internal affairs of Myanmar by publishing in his *Xinhwa Bulletin* of 26 June 1967 the message of the outlawed BCP. This had led to the recall of Myanmar's ambassador from Beijing. The Chinese media's attacks on the Myanmar government persisted until early 1968, but with less frequency. Although some positive measures were taken by both sides after 1968, diplomatic relations were not restored until 1971. At one level, it could be argued that Beijing had been looking for an appropriate time and pretext to denounce the Myanmar government for the latter's failure to follow China's lead in international affairs and to publicly endorse the revitalization of the BCP. Who could have imagined that the bilateral relations would plunge into such a low point in early 1967? Until the outbreak of Chinese student demonstrations and the anti-Chinese riots, the state-to-state relations had appeared to be solidly based and there had been no indication that Beijing was prepared to thrown its weight behind the BCP's armed struggle.

The Myanmar government was chiefly concerned to avoid provoking China. However, Yangon was also culpable for allowing the situation to deteriorate so badly. The Myanmar government's propaganda had proved to be a massive stimulant to renewed nationalist sentiment. Yangon sought to make the most out of the riots and the deterioration of the bilateral relationship, exploiting the situation to gain public support for some of its domestic policies, such as anti-BCP campaign. According to an official source in Myanmar, no fewer than 1.1 million people participated in the demonstrations in 288 different areas. Forward, a bi-weekly magazine of the BSPP, editorialized that there was a "patriotic spirit behind demonstrations" and "a popular retort to offensive tirades against Burma uttered from a foreign country".[42] It appeared that the government's firmness and uncompromising stand in the face of Chinese political blandishments had earned a renewed legitimacy for the Revolutionary Council in the eyes of general public. In addition, the Myanmar government was given an opportunity to crack down on pro-Beijing leftist leaders and illegal propaganda outlets. In the wake of the events, a longtime pro-Communist newspaper, *Ludu*, was shut down. With the support from the Myanmar public, and many Chinese as well, the Myanmar government managed to bring the Chinese community firmly under its control. In the post riot period, Communist China no longer had much leverage over the Chinese community in Myanmar. With regard to this event, Melvin Gurtov remarked:

> "The phasing and timing of Peking's responses suggest that the Maoist leadership finally supported the CPB [BCP] not because of any new finding of strength in the Burmese Communist movement, but because the situation in Burma had developed to the point where Peking had to choose between backing down or supporting its officials and overseas Chinese, some of whom had lost their lives. And Peking's choice seems in turn to have been compelled by the actions of those ultraleftists in the CPR Embassy and other agencies who considered themselves duty-bound not merely to fulfill the static function of representing Chinese interest abroad, but also to be active publicists of the thoughts and works of Mao Tse-tung. These zealots, when challenged in this latter role by the GUB, probably to their and Peking's surprise, responded as had their compeers on the mainland —by taking up the challenge and rejecting either retreat or compromise — and thus set in motion a chain reaction of increasingly intransigent statements and actions in

Rangoon and Peking. Peking's choice of second alternative may have been further influenced by the extremist tide that, by late June, had once more engulfed the Cultural Revolution. Conceivably, the return of extremism further influenced Mao and the more radical members of the Central Committee not to let the crisis subside without backing China's warnings of "consequences" with deeds.[43]

Despite strong political pressure from China, the Revolutionary Council government continued to maintain strict neutralism in its foreign policy. In the midst of the riots and demonstrations, the Myanmar government confirmed its foreign policy stance in the *Mirror* newspaper published on 3 July 1967. The newspaper stated: "After the recent anti-Chinese disorders, it has been asked whether Burma would submit and yield or would choose to depend on other countries. If the 700 million Chinese are armed with the thought of Mao Tse-tung, the 25 million Burmese are armed with sincerity and love. Burma will not renounce her neutrality".[44] The Myanmar government apparently held a view that as long as it preserved neutralism in its foreign policy, it could maneuver to restore friendly relations between the two countries. Neither balancing against nor bandwangoning with China was the policy of choice for the Myanmar government. Yangon repeatedly confirmed its strictly neutralist foreign policy and declared that it would "never discard the said policy in favour of bowing to foreign influence and command".[45]

In the aftermath of the demonstrations, the Myanmar government terminated the Chinese development assistance program. In accordance with the Treaty of Economic and Technical Cooperation between the two countries, signed on 9 January 1961, the Chinese government had provided an interest free loan of K400 million (US$84 million) to build two suspension bridges and seven factories in Myanmar. The two bridges were Kunlon Bridge and Tarkaw Bridge. The seven factories were two hydro-electric plants, a tyre factory, a textile factory, a plywood factory, a sugar mill, and a paper mill. The construction of Kunlon Bridge, which began on 19 February 1964, had been completed on 22 December 1965. The construction of Tarkaw Bridge began in June 1966, but it was suspended a year later in the wake of anti-Chinese riots in Myanmar and return of Chinese technicians. Construction was resumed only in early 1970s. The bridge was completed on 25 February 1974 and officially opened on 23 March. As far as the factories were concerned, at the time of the suspension of Chinese aid, only the sugar mill in Bilin had been completed. It was officially opened on 15 November 1966. The hydroelectric plants to be constructed in Kengtung and Kunlon and the tyre factory in Insein were merely at the stage of preliminary survey works. The paper mill in Sitaung had been about 80 per cent completed. The plywood factory in Swa, construction of which had begun on 20 January 1966, had been nearly completed and was officially opened on 17 October 1969. Likewise, the textile factory in Meikhtila had been almost completed. The test run began in July 1967 and the factory was opened in January 1968. Therefore, out of the K400 million loan negotiated in 1961, only K153.4 million had been utilized for development projects by the time of the suspension of the aid programme in mid 1967. On 6 October 1967, the Myanmar government demanded the withdrawal of all Chinese technicians from PRC funded projects in Myanmar. Subsequently, in November, a total of 412 Chinese technicians left Myanmar in three groups. Some Overseas Chinese also went back to China. According to an official Myanmar source, about 1500 Chinese left Myanmar during the first five months of 1968.[46]

By 1968, Beijing's attacks on the Myanmar government had become less frequent and more subdued. Some sings of rapprochement could be observed but no concrete steps were taken. The Chinese Red Cross donated Yuan 10,000 to the Myanmar Red Cross for the relief of hurricane victims in May. The Chinese *Charge d' Affaires* in Yangon laid a wreath at the Martyr's Mausoleum on 19 July. Myanmar military officials attended the PLA Day hosted by the Chinese Military *Attaché* in Yangon on 1 August 1968. Ne Win sent a National Day greeting to Zhou Enlai in October 1970. A new Myanmar ambassador to China was appointed in November 1970. However, the Chinese government, by this time, was determined to openly support the BCP's armed struggle.

CHINESE OVERT SUPPORT FOR THE BCP

Successive governments in Myanmar firmly believed that during the 1950s and 1960s the Chinese government or the Chinese Communist Party maintained clandestine contacts with the BCP Headquarters in Central Myanmar, either through certain overseas Chinese or the BCP branch office in Beijing. Yet the Chinese did not go beyond that low-level support. Meanwhile, the Revolutionary Council issued an amnesty order on 1 April 1963. During his April 1963 state visit, according to some observers, Liu Shaoqi discussed the matter of negotiations with the BCP with General Ne Win. Because of this, some Myanmar observers speculated that the Yangon government's call for peace talks with all insurgent groups, including the BCP, in June 1963 was a result of Liu Shaoqi's advice. Nevertheless, the Chinese influence over the BCP in the peace negotiations with the Myanmar government was later revealed by both Myanmar and Chinese media.

According to one interpretation, the Chinese wanted to save the BCP from extinction as the party had suffered many serious political and military setbacks since the late 1950s. When the Revolutionary Council issued its amnesty order in 1963, at a time when most aboveground left wing political organizations supported the BWS, a number of prominent Communists had accepted the amnesty. The Chinese advice of "peace talks" had in this way averted a grave danger of a BCP collapse. According to articles which appeared in the Chinese press during the Cultural Revolution, Liu Shaoqi had advised the BCP to consider the amnesty offer of Ne Win's government, hide their weapons, reorganize their army into national defence units, and return to legal political activities. Another view was that Liu had simply advised the BCP to pursue a peaceful transition to power.[47] In any case, the Chinese intention seems to have been to save the BCP from a total collapse. The Chinese Communists may also have feared a mass surrender of BCP rank and file, which would have meant the loss of another Chinese mechanism of leverage in Myanmar. Alternatively, the Chinese might have considered the Revolutionary Council to be a progressive force and rationalized the BWS as a national democratic phase of social revolution. In this scenario, the BCP would have been advised to pursue a united front strategy. Certainly, the Myanmar government was friendly toward the Chinese government. While many points remain unclear, there is a good reason to believe that the Chinese government used its influence with the Yangon government and the BCP to promote a ceasefire and peace negotiations. The Chinese appear to have wanted a positive outcome from the peace talks. They urged the BCP to abandon the policy of armed struggle in favour of an aboveground united front, in which the Communists would eventually have predominant influence. It can be suspected that Beijing viewed this strategy as a short cut to power for the Myanmar Communists as well as a means to maintain or increase Chinese influence over the government in Yangon.

The 1963 peace talks offered a perfect opportunity for the CCP to re-establish firmer control over the BCP HQ in central Myanmar. When the Myanmar government called for the peace talks, Chinese Communists organized an emergency meeting of the BCP (Overseas), at which a resolution was passed, authorizing Aung Gyi and Tin Shein to lead a delegation immediately to Yangon to negotiate with the government.[48] Beijing appeared to be confident that some form of peace settlement could be reached between the Myanmar government and the BCP. On 10 July 1963, the Central Committee of the CCP gave instructions to the BCP delegation on its negotiation strategy. The CCP urged the Myanmar Communists to be prepared to take advantage of the Revolutionary Council government.[49] The advance party of the Overseas BCP delegation left Beijing for Yangon on 11 July. There were seven members altogether.[50] After their arrival, the delegation first contacted the Chinese Embassy in Yangon, which briefed them on the political, economic and military situation in Myanmar. According to one Myanmar source, Beijing told the delegates that they should first talk with the Leftist parties in Yangon and meet Thakin Kodaw Hmaing's "Internal Peace Group". If the situation appeared to be favourable, they should be prepared to openly advertise the existence of the BCP.[51] A second eleven-member group, headed by Bo Zeya, arrived in Yangon on 23 July.[52] The two groups then proceeded to the BCP HQ in Bago Yoma on 11 August, after a dinner at the Chinese Embassy in Yangon. A third group of eleven delegates led by Ba Thein Tin arrived in Yangon on 3 September.[53] Whatever the outcome of the negotiations, the entire affair provided a golden opportunity for the Beijing-trained Communists to return to Myanmar where they could play a major role in shaping the future policy of the BCP. When the peace talks collapsed on 14 November 1963, only Thakin Ba Thein Tin and Yebaw Thein Htike returned to China. The remaining 27 delegates joined their HQ in Bago Yoma.

It is difficult to apportion blame for the breakdown of the peace talks. What was clear, however, was that the BCP delegates spent a great deal of time in Yangon organizing mass rallies in support of the BCP and making contacts with various leftist political forces to pressure the government. Moreover, the BCP's efforts to improve its military position during the talks annoyed the government. The talks did not go beyond the stage of ceasefire negotiation. There is no information about the extent to which the Chinese may have advised the BCP delegation during the peace talks after the initial phase. It appears that the Chinese basically left the negotiation tactics in the BCP's hands but that the Myanmar Communists had misjudged the situation and took a number of initiatives that proved detrimental to the peace talks. Certainly both the Chinese and Myanmar Communists wanted the talks to go on as long as possible. The breakdown of the talks must have been a disappointment to the Chinese.

After the collapse of the peace negotiations, the BCP held a Central Committee meeting on 25 December 1963. The BCP eagerly sought Chinese advise about the future course of its armed struggle since it was now bankrupt politically, organizationally and militarily. In February 1964, the Chinese sent a top secret message to the BCP HQ and instructed the party to continue the armed struggle. Two months later, the CCP sent a political, organizational and military program by wireless to the BCP. This was popularly known as "the 1964 Line". The Chinese were fully aware that the BCP in central and lower Myanmar had been suffering from severe military setbacks and was not capable of mounting an offensive. It was against this background that the Chinese decided to play a more active role in the internal affairs of the BCP. By late 1964, the CCP was firmly in control of BCP affairs; the CCP, in fact, now dominated the BCP through its trained cadres who had joined the HQ after the collapse of the peace talks. The Chinese ever managed to keep the extremely shaky and discredited Than Tun as Chairman of the BCP with the help of these Beijing-trained cadres.[54]

Strongly supported by these cadres, Than Tun introduced Maoist-style campaigns and the Cultural Revolution into the BCP. The anti-revisionist campaign led to the execution of several prominent BCP cadres including some Central Committee members. In spite of the Chinese attempt to revitalize the BCP's armed struggle in central and lower Myanmar, the party continued to suffer political, organizational and military setbacks, both because the government's counter insurgency programme proved effective and because of its own mistakes. When Sino-Myanmar relations reached their nadir in 1967, the Chinese decided to openly support the BCP's armed struggle. There were several reasons for this decision. First, as the BCP's zone of operations in the central Myanmar began to wane, under the impact of the government's counterinsurgency campaign, the CCP apparently decided to open up a second front to relieve the military pressure on the HQ area of Bago Yoma. Second, having realized that the Revolutionary Council was not likely to bow to Chinese pressure, the CCP decided to apply the leverage of Communist insurgency. Third, viewing itself as the champion of the Third World, the CCP decided to export revolution on a global scale.

In 1964, the CCP reactivated training programmes for the BCP members residing in China. Apart from senior members and cadres of the BCP in Beijing, there were two prominent groups within the BCP (Northeast) area. One group was known as Guizhou group and the other was Sichuan Group.

The Guizhou group was mostly comprised of Kachin nationals led by Naw Seng, an army deserter who had captured many important towns during the early days of Myanmar's civil war. In October 1950, the group fled into China and took refuge there. CCP cadres lectured them on Communism and finally sent them to a mercury factory in Guizhou province. Hpalang Gam Di and Khan Man were other prominent leaders of the group. While in China, they were treated as Chinese citizens. During his visit to Yangon in 1954, Premier Zhou Enlai admitted to his Myanmar counterpart that the Chinese government had offered asylum to the Naw Seng group. However, there were reports that individuals and families who wanted to go back and resettle in Myanmar, taking opportunity of the government's amnesty, had been prevented from doing so. After nearly 15 years of residence in China, the group was finally mobilized by Beijing for political purposes.

In early 1964, Lin Htin (alias Soe Thein) and Htoo Shin from the BCP (Overseas) visited the mercury factory and held discussions with the group. The two BCP cadres gave them a month long series of lectures on Marxism-Leninism and the history of the BCP. The BCP cadres came again in July 1967, together with cadres from the CCP, and asked the group to cooperate in the revolutionary cause of the BCP. Since the group's members had a strong desire to go back to Myanmar, they agreed. Nearly 450 members subsequently received military training from PLA instructors. After a month of training, they were sent to Kunming and then to Htan San, a military camp on the Sino-Myanmar border.

The Sichuan group was primarily formed from among the BCP members who had come to China in the early 1950s. From January 1954 to July 1956, the BCP members took various political and military courses provided by the CCP. Subsequently, from August 1956 to July 1960, the group received further political training at Sichuan University. After the training programme, the group undertook fieldwork at a steel factory in Nei Jiang, Sichuan, until March 1964. In this way, the Sichuan group had first-hand experience of the socialist construction of China. Some of the members of the group later went to the Soviet Union for further studies. During the peace talks with the Revolutionary Council in late 1963, some members came back to Myanmar and, after the breakdown of the negotiations, joined the BCP Headquarters in Bago Yoma. After completing their fieldwork, the Sichuan group underwent an intensive political refresher course from March 1964 to August 1965. The group was then subdivided into two: one section received training in Chongqing and the other in Chengdu. Then, for a year from April 1966, the two subgroups, known as Chongqing company and Chengdu company, toured the PRC separately to study the Chinese Revolution. About the same time, in June 1966, a group of forty BCP members led by Bo Sein Maung joined the BCP (Overseas). Somewhat after this, another group of 100 BCP members led by Bo Hla Thaung and U Tun arrived at Mangshi on the Sino-Myanmar border. The Chongqing and Chengdu companies of the Sichuan group met in Beijing in June 1967 where they were welcomed by Zhou Enlai and other senior members of the CCP. The entire group then went back to Chongqing to hold a meeting, attended by Thakin Ba Thein Tin. The main topic was the launching of a new military front in the border area. In July the Sichuan group went to Chengdu from where they were airlifted to Kunming. Their final destination was Htan San where they met the Guizhou group.

These two groups formed the core of the BCP troops, supported by Chinese volunteers trained by the PLA.[55]

Since mid-1967, the CCP had trained overseas Myanmar Communists in China for a military offensive to open a new front in the Northeast Border region of Myanmar. In fact, in the mid 1960s, acting on the advice of the CCP, the BCP (Overseas) had instructed Thakin Tin Tun to establish a base in the Indaw-Kyaukku area and to study the feasibility of penetrating Myanmar. Subsequently, in 1966, Tin Tun drew up the "Moe Lone Hein" plan, which proposed the penetration and occupation of Myanmar with Chinese military assistance.[56] The BCP (Overseas) assigned Bo Thuya and Yebaw San Thu to special duty in the Shan State for the same purpose.[57] The CCP now tried to activate the opening of a military front in the Shan State. The Guizhou and Sichuan groups formed the core of the BCP (Northeast) troops, receiving training from No. 57 PLA brigade. In late December 1967, the BCP troops, joined by Chinese volunteers and some troops from No. 7688 PLA unit, marched into Myanmar. On 1 January 1968, a BCP military unit launched a major offensive against an outpost manned by the Tatmadaw and this opened the new military front in the North-east border region of Myanmar. Within a few years, the BCP had successfully established a 20,000 square km "liberated zone", known as the Northeast Military Region, located along Sino-Myanmar border, adjacent to Yunnan province, with Ba Thein Tin and Khin Maung Gyi as political commissars and Naw Seng as military commander.[58]

The CCP subsequently provided various kinds of assistance to the BCP. One form of assistance was the "Military Advisory Teams". In fact the term "military advisory team" did not exist in official Myanmar Communist documents. It was usually referred to as "Mae-Myan-Yae-Aphwe" in Myanmar and "Wei-Wen-Tuan (慰問團)" in Chinese, meaning a team sent to convey greetings and appreciations. However the PLA advisors were very visible on battle fronts. The Chinese wanted to make sure that the BCP made a good start in the Northeast. In order to assist the striking forces, in early 1968, a Chinese advisory team of about twenty PLA personnel, known as No. 808 team, was attached to the BCP's No. 303 Regiment. The team played a major role in the famous 40-day battle at Kunlon in October 1971. It was finally recalled to China only in July 1972.[59] Another team of military advisers, most of whom were from the Baoshan military region, was attached to the BCP's No. 404 Regiment until October 1971. The Tatmadaw estimated that there were about 200 Chinese military advisors with the BCP (Northeast) in the late 1960s. Moreover, several Chinese artillery officers were attached to BCP troops.[60] Among the various forms of Chinese assistance, both tangible and intangible, the exchange of combat intelligence was especially vital for the

BCP in military operations. The BCP relied heavily on intercepted messages passed on by the PLA.

Chinese assistance in training was strengthened after the formal establishment of the Northeast Military Region on the Myanmar side of the border in 1968. Before that, BCP members had to undergo training in various places. After 1968 the CCP offered courses in Mangshi in Yunnan; indeed, Mangshi could be regarded as a BCP cantonment. It was commonly referred as No. 30357 Military Training Camp. [The number appeared to be a combination of No. 303 BCP Regiment and No. 57 PLA Brigade.] The CCP offered various political and military courses. Important courses were the Junior Officer Course and Senior Commander Course, which usually lasted for about nine months. According to a Myanmar intelligence source, some 140 BCP trainees underwent a Senior Commander Course in September 1974. Prominent among the trainees were Pheung Kya-shin, Pheng Kya-phu and San Maung, all of whom later emerged as top commanders. The CCP encouraged local Chinese people on the border to join the BCP forces. Many volunteers, including doctors, joined the BCP between 1968 and 1975.[61] Some of them remained with the BCP until the collapse of the party in 1989.

Between December 1967 and December 1973, China supplied enough arms and ammunition to equip three PLA brigades or 10,000 soldiers. According to one estimate, between 1968 and 1978, Chinese assistance to the BCP in arms and ammunition amounted to more than 40 million Yuan.[62] China also granted the BCP 2 million Yuan per year for general military expenditure.[63] It was believed that China supplied about 30,000 rifles, millions of rounds of ammunition, a few hundred pieces of heavy artillery, more than 60 trucks and six anti-aircraft guns.[64] During the same period, whenever the BCP launched major military operations, the CCP supplied the required ammunition. For example, during the Konlone Battle of 1971, cases of bullets were transported to the front line by trucks and during the retreat about a million rounds were abandoned.[65] China also supplied various types of mines, hand grenades, wireless sets, mine detectors, compasses, binoculars, military maps, and explosives. About 20 to 50 trucks were used for every shipment of material and equipment. It was only in October 1978 that the CCP began to scale down its assistance to the BCP.[66]

The CCP helped the BCP to construct roads on the China-Myanmar border as well as within the so-called liberated areas of the BCP (Northeast). China also provided the BCP with telecommunications facilities. Telephone exchanges were installed. Another substantial contribution was radio facilities. In the period between 1967 and 1971, the CCP allowed the BCP to use Radio Peking for propaganda. Subsequently, in 1971, a team was organized at the Kunming Broadcasting Station to operate the "Voice of the Burmese People (VOBP)". The transmission was originally in four languages — Bamar, Chinese, Jeingpaw, and Shan. Later, the Wa and Kayin languages were included. The VOBP began broadcasting on 28 March 1971. China also provided medical facilities for the BCP. The CCP helped the BCP open hospitals for the local populations in the "liberated areas".[67] Moreover, No. 71 PLA Hospital in Teng Chong, No. 108 PLA Hospital in Zhe Fang, No. 145 PLA Hospital in Mong Htwe, No. 66 PLA Hospital in Gengma, and No. 61 PLA Hospital in Lancan were resolved exclusively for the BCP. The BCP Central Committee members and brigade level cadres could go to the No. 43 PLA Hospital in Kunming. [68]

TOWARDS RAPPROCHEMENT AND NORMALIZATION

Massive Chinese support to the BCP created a new front of communist insurgency in the northeast border region of Myanmar, the severity of which was revealed in the Myanmar media for the first time in November 1969. In his opening address to the fourth Party Congress of the BSPP on 6 November 1969, General Ne Win stated:

> In regard to the clashes which have happened on the border, I wish to appeal to the members present here, and to the people in the country, to restrain themselves and not give vent to anger or passion. The force, which are up against us openly declare that they are bolstered by external aid, but we do not wish to bear any grudge or bitterness against anyone. One question may be asked: do you have the strength to retaliate if you wish? And I must honestly answer, no. Be that as it may, our way of life is that we shall be true, even if others act otherwise. Therefore, I appeal to the people of the country to remain calm not to be provoked into anger and harsh words or drastic action, by the clashes on the border.[69]

His concern for the relationship with the PRC was apparent in his speech:

> Here I wish to reiterate that we wish to maintain friendly relations with all our neighbours, with all the members of the family of nations in fact. With our neighbours, we wish to keep up good relations... Now specifically to mention China with which our present problem is connected, we should like to restore the cordial and friendly relations which formerly prevailed between our two countries. We shall strive towards that end, but it takes two to make a friendship... Even in the midst of the clashes on the border, and the present situation, we shall

do what we can on our part to restore the old friendship. We keep on trying to hold the situation from getting worse. The ugly incident of 1967 must be attributed to turns in bad fortune, and we try to forgive and forget.[70]

Indeed, Ne Win was very angry with China although he tried all possible means to restore normal diplomatic relations. At an educational fair in December 1970, while reviewing with his entourage a booth organized by the Burma Research Society, Ne Win had reportedly said that the real threat for Myanmar was China. He had put his finger on a map featuring China and pressed so hard that he punched a hole in the paper. Nevertheless, Ne Win refrained from accusing China for promoting insurgent activity but said vaguely: "The people who are against us have openly declared they are getting external aid". Nor he made any public statement about Chinese policy toward Myanmar. Ne Win ordered the Tatmadaw to be defensive in its military operations in the Northeast border region, particularly to avoid provoking any direct Chinese military intervention. He insisted that it was not to launch any offensive near the Sino-Myanmar border. The Myanmar government realized that the best way to handle the new BCP military front was to promote friendly diplomatic relations with China.

Meanwhile, during its own version of Cultural Revolution, the BCP lost many of its most capable leaders and commanders. Among the Central Committee members, Yebaw Goshal and Yebaw Htay were killed on 18 June 1967 and Bo Yan Aung on 26 December 1967. Than Tun was assassinated by one of his soldiers on 24 September 1968. The government intensified its military operations against the Communists in central and lower Myanmar while it maintained a totally defensive position in the northeast; in fact, the government practically lost control over the area east of the Thanlwin (Salween) river to the BCP (Northeast). The most able Beijing trained BCP commanders were either captured or killed during these operations. The BCP in central and lower Myanmar was forced to retreat. By mid 1975, the party had ceased to exist in these parts of Myanmar. The BCP's armed struggle was solely to the northeast border region, where it enjoyed the support of the Chinese.

Parallel with these efforts, the Myanmar government tried every possible way to restore normal diplomatic relations with China. It was even reported that General Ne Win went to Pakistan to talk with Chinese officials.[71] Despite various difficulties (military, political and economic), the Myanmar government showed no signs of changing its foreign policy in favour of either the United States or the Soviet Union. Myanmar remained non-committal on

Moscow's proposal for an Asian Collective Security System. Any conspicuous move towards the Soviet Union or the United States might have provoked serious Chinese intervention in Myanmar affairs. There were still tensions along the Sino-Myanmar border. In the early 1970s, according to a Myanmar intelligence source, the PRC deployed a large number of PLA troops along the Myanmar border; in December 1970 about 9,000 PLA troops were stationed there; in February 1972, despite some reduction in number, it was estimated that about 2,000 PLA soldiers, 700 military police, 450 regular police and 1,300 militia were still deployed near the Myanmar border.[72]

The first major step to restore normal diplomatic relations between the two countries came in August 1970 with the appearance of high-ranking Myanmar military officers at a reception given by the Chinese military *attaché* in Yangon to celebrate the 43rd anniversary of the PLA. Two months later, on 1 October 1970, General Ne Win, for the first time since 1966, sent a letter of felicitation to Zhou Enlai, on the 21st anniversary of the foundation of the PRC. A Myanmar ambassador was posted back to Beijing in November 1970 and a Chinese ambassador returned to Yangon in March 1971. A major breakthrough in the normalization of diplomatic relations came with the visit of Ne Win to China at the invitation of Zhou Enlai in August 1971. An internal document of the Myanmar government observed:

> Between 1969 and 1971, China had repositioned itself in the ever changing international situation and decided to pursue a more liberal approach in its foreign policy. China also tried to improve her relations with the United States. China was deeply concerned with growing Soviet influence within the Non-Aligned Movement. Therefore, China tried to improve her diplomatic image by promoting cooperation and building confidence with regional neighbors. After the 1971 War of Liberation in Bangladesh, confidence building with the Myanmar government had become increasingly important. Therefore, China distinguished the party-to-party relationship from that of the state-to-state relationship and it tried to restore normal diplomatic relations with Myanmar and invited U Ne Win for a state visit. It was just a few days away from the fall [death] of Marshal Lin Biao. It was also a time that the Maoists in the ILD of the CCP had been praising so much about the BCP. Nevertheless, Premier Zhao Enlai had expressed his friendship towards Myanmar people and his sincere appreciation for Prime Minister U Ne Win's effort to restore bilateral relations.[73]

While in China Ne Win met Mao Zedong and other Chinese leaders. Outside Beijing he was accompanied by Zhou Enlai himself, as a gesture of close friendship. Ne Win reportedly discussed the question of the overseas Chinese in Myanmar and compensation for the death of a Chinese technician during the riots. Zhou made it clear that he opposed dual citizenship for overseas Chinese. Ne Win subsequently promised to grant citizenship to those Chinese who applied for it. Ne Win met Zhou Enlai altogether five times to discuss bilateral relations, and both expressed deep regret about what had happened between the two countries in 1967. On one occasion, Zhou Enlai mentioned the fact, in a seemingly casual manner, that Ne Win had visited the United States in the mid 1960s. Perhaps he meant to suggest that Ne Win's U.S. visit had been disturbing for Chinese leaders. Zhou also offered to restore the Chinese development aid program suspended in 1967. At state dinners, both sides recalled their amicable Pauk-Phaw relations.[74] Ne Win apparently kept quiet on the question of Chinese assistance to the BCP. The visit was a major step in restoring the bilateral relationship, although full normalization of Sino-Myanmar relations was still some years away. On 24 September 1971, at the second interim meeting of the Central Committee of the BSPP, General Ne Win reported on his visit to China and gave credit to Zhou Enlai for his part in the restoration of friendly relations between the two countries.[75]

After the normalization of relations between the two countries in 1971, Myanmar learned to live with China's "two-pronged" policy; this is, maintaining official diplomatic relations with the Yangon government on the one hand and actively supporting the BCP insurgency on the other. In November 1975, following a visit by his Foreign Minister in August, U Ne Win again journeyed to Beijing, this time at the invitation of Chairman Zhu De of the Standing Committee of National People's Congress. He was welcomed in Beijing by Vice Premiers Deng Xiaoping (邓小平) and Zhang Chunqiao (张春桥), a member of the notorious "Gang of Four". No official explanation for this visit was offered, but there was speculation that Ne Win might have discussed Chinese policy towards the BCP. The visit also confirmed Myanmar's policy toward PRC under a new government, elected in early 1974. This was the first time Ne Win visited China as the President of Myanmar. He was received by Mao Zedong and Zhu De. By this time, Zhou Enlai was gravely ill. This gave rise to the question of who was going to be the host for Ne Win in Beijing. On 5 November, Deng Xiaoping sent a memo to Mao asking whether he or Zhang Chunqiao should host the Ne Win visit. Mao responded that Deng would be the host and, at the same time, he crossed out the Foreign Ministry's proposal for Jiang Qing, wife of Mao Zedong and a member of the Gang of Four, to meet Ne Win.[76] Ne Win held discussions with Deng Xiaoping for three days. The two countries pledged not to join any military alliance targeting the other, reaffirmed their adherence to the Five Principles of Peaceful Coexistence, agreed to refrain from hostile acts against each other and to settle difference through peaceful means. At the state dinner given by Deng Xiaoping, the Vice Premier drew attention to the danger of [Soviet] hegemonist expansion in Southeast Asia. Ne Win avoided the issue, merely stating in general terms that Myanmar would not accept any foreign military bases which might pose a threat to other countries, especially neighbours. Yet the joint communiqué issued at the end of the visit declared that: "the two sides reaffirmed that the people of each country have the right freely to choose their own political, economic and social system according to their national needs and aspirations free from outside interference [and] opposed any design of hegemonist expansion in any part of the world by any nation or a group of nations".[77] In his speech at the state dinner Ne Win emphasized the importance of friendly bilateral relations: "It is of vital importance that our two sides should make every effort to consolidate and maintain the friendly relations. The friendship should be nurtured and maintained not by us only but also by our coming generations. Differences may, of course, arise at times in the relations between our two countries. Even in a family, differences do occasionally arise. If, as is natural, such differences arise between our two countries, we should resolve them with patience, mutual understanding and accommodation, always determined that our friendship must prevail".[78]

Meanwhile, when the BCP (Northeast) realized that the BCP HQ in central Myanmar was about to collapse, it organized a Special Bureau of the Central Committee. An extended Central Committee meeting was held not long after the fall of the BCP HQ and the deaths of Chairman Thakin Zin and Secretary Thakin Chit in Bago Yoma on 15 March 1975. Ba Thein Tin assumed Chairmanship of the BCP, Pe Tint became the First Vice-Chairman and Khin Maung Gyi the Second Vice-Chairman. A new Central Committee was formed on 31 March 1975. The newly reorganized BCP Central Committee began to consider moving the HQ from Mangshi (China) into Myanmar since there was no longer a BCP HQ in central Myanmar. In 1975, the CCP and the BCP signed an agreement of mutual cooperation for a ten year period. As a result, China delivered arms and ammunition to the BCP on a regular basis until 1978. However, in April 1977, the CCP built a factory to produce M-21, M-22, and M-23 rifles and ammunition in Pangsan. This was codenamed the "774 Central Weapons Factory". The factory could produce up to 10,000 rounds per day, but due to shortages of raw materials and manpower, it actually produced about 2,000 rounds per day. In March 1976, a 40 horsepower hydropower generator station was constructed at Mongko under the supervision of Chinese technicians. It became operational in October 1976.[79] Almost two years later, in May 1978, an 80-KV power station was built in Pangsan under the Chinese aid programme.[80] When the BCP HQ was moved into Pangsan in 1979, the CCP delivered twenty 120mm guns and sixty anti-aircraft guns, and twenty million kyat in Chinese currency to the BCP. By 1980, China had already supplied about 60,000 rifles. The supply of arms and ammunition continued during the early 1980s.[81]

Despite the positive developments in Sino-Myanmar relations outlined above, China thus continued to support the BCP and there was heavy fighting between the Tatmadaw and the BCP throughout the 1970s. However, after the death of Mao Zedong in September 1976 and the coming to power of Deng Xiaoping in 1978, China substantially reduced its moral and material support to the BCP. This was partly due to fatal mistakes committed by the BCP and partly due to the changing policy in China. There was a major power struggle in China from late 1975 to early 1978. The BCP's chief mentor, Keng Sheng (康生), passed away in Beijing on 16 December 1975. Less than a month later, on 8 January 1976, Zhou Enlai died of cancer. President Ne Win sent a message of condolence to the Chinese government. The Chinese media printed the BCP's message of condolence as well.[82] In the message, the BCP, while praising Zhou Enlai, attacked the "revisionism and anti-party schemes of Liu Shaoqi and Lin Biao".[83] The attack on Liu Shaoqi was significant at that point of time since Deng Xiaoping was linked to Liu. At that time, Mao was gravely ill and not able to make any policy decision. Hardliners within the CCP launched a vicious campaign and manoeuvred to oust Deng Xiaoping and other moderates. They temporarily succeeded and, by April 1976, had managed to reassert their positions within the CCP hierarchy. Deng Xiaoping was accused as being a Capitalist-roader, revisionist, or Right deviationist, and was dismissed from all posts both inside and outside the Party on 7 April 1976. But the BCP made a grave mistake in the wording of its message to the CCP on the 55th Anniversary of the founding of the Party on 1 July 1976. Unlike other Communist parties in Asia, the BCP, while openly supporting the hardliners, attacked "the revisionist clique headed by Liu Shaoqi". The message also stated: "the movement to repulse the Right deviationist attempt at reversing correct verdicts, and the decision of the Central Committee of the CPC on the measures taken against the Rightist chieftain Deng Xiaoping are in full accord with Marxism-Leninism-Mao Zedong Thought".[84] Zhu De died on 6 July 1976. The Chinese press also printed the BCP's message on this occasion.[85] A little over two months later, Mao Zedong passed away on 9 September 1976. In its message of condolence, the BCP again attacked Deng Xiaoping.[86] The message also attacked the Myanmar government and said: "We will apply ourselves to the study of Marxism-Leninism-Mao Zedong Thought and make efforts to integrate it more correctly with the practice of the Burmese revolution. We will unite all the revolutionary classes, strata and the people of all nationalities of Burma and work to the best of our ability to overthrow the reactionary rule representing imperialism, feudalism and bureaucratic-capitalism and build a new Burma".[87] In the message, the BCP portrayed China as "the reliable bulwark of the world proletarian revolution".[88] When Hua Guofeng (华国锋) was appointed the Chairman of the CCP Central Committee as well as the Central Military Commission, the BCP sent a congratulatory message on 22 October 1976 and tried to secure continuous assistance from the Chinese. The BCP sought further strengthening of "deep and militant unity" between the CCP and the BCP, which is "based on Marxism-Leninism-Mao Zedong Thought and proletarian internationalism and formed in the struggle against the common enemies, imperialism, particularly social-imperialism, revisionism, and the reactionaries".[89] The widely publicized reception and banquet given by Hua Guofeng to Ba Thein Tin and Pe Tint, Chairman and Vice Chairman of the BCP, on 18 November, seemed to be a confirmation that the CCP would continue to support its "comrade-in-arms" and to foster "the continuous growth of the revolutionary friendship and militant unity" between the two parties.[90] Yet this commitment did not prove to be enduring. Deng Xiaoping reassumed power at a Central Committee meeting in Beijing in July 1977 and the Chinese government began to abandon support for the communist revolutions across Asia. The Chinese official press stopped reporting on BCP activities. Deng had become the *de facto* leader of China; Hua Guofeng was denounced and replaced by Zhao Ziyang (赵紫阳) as Premier in 1980 and by Hu Yaobang (胡耀邦) as Party Chairman in 1981. Now the BCP found itself obliged to reevaluate China as the reliable "bulwark of the world proletariat revolution".

When Deng Xiaoping became Chairman of the Central Military Commission of the PRC in 1978, the BCP leaders decided to move their HQ to Pangsan. The BCP leadership sensed that there would be a change of policy on the part of the Chinese government. The Chinese asked the BCP to move its radio station from China into Myanmar. In January 1978, a group of Chinese technicians came to Pangsan and chose a new site for the radio station. The VOPB broadcast from Pangsan began in 1979. Faced with this new situation, the BCP Central Committee met for a marathon meeting that lasted from November 1978 to June 1979. The Party's 40th anniversary on 15 August 1979 was subdued. In his lengthy speech, Ba Thein Tin emphasized that the Party must be "self-reliant" and, without being specific, said that the BCP "had made many mistakes" during its 40-year long history. Moreover, "non-interference" was declared as a major aspect of the BCP's relations with "fraternal communist parties". In 1979, China stopped supplying combat intelligence and withdrew Chinese military advisors.[91]

In 1980, the CCP arranged an excursion trip for a high-level BCP delegation to visit historic sites in China. From Simao, a border town in Yunnan, the delegation travelled in PLA vehicles to Kunming, the provincial capital, where they boarded an aircraft to Xi'an, the capital of Shaanxi, some 1,200 kilometres to the north. The delegation visited Yan'an and Nanniwan, the legendary base area of the Long March where Mao Zedong and the CCP had survived during the Civil War and the Japanese Invasion. The BCP delegation then journeyed to Jiangxi province in southeast China to visit Jinggangshan where the Long March had begun. The entire purpose of this political pilgrimage to the sacred sites of the Chinese revolution was to highlight the importance of self-reliance. The delegation was finally brought into Beijing to meet Qiao Shi (乔石), Deputy Director of the International Liaison Department of the CCP, who conveyed the message that the CCP had decided to stop its support for the BCP's armed struggle and that the BCP would from now on have to be self-reliant. However, Qiao Shi assured the BCP delegation that China would continue to provide aid for a five-year period of transition so that the BCP could adjust to the new situation.[92] Low level non-military aid continued until around 1985. In 1985, when China cut off electricity to the radio station, the VOPB went off the air. However, China delivered a mobile transmitter to the BCP in 1986 and transmission was resumed in February 1986. The mobile transmission was carried out in Khunma village until it was occupied by Wa troops in April 1989.[93] By 1983, the CCP had closed down various medical facilities inside China for the BCP. The PLA hospitals were no longer exclusively for the BCP rank and file; but a special ward was retained in each hospital for battalion level cadres and above. In 1986, these special wards were also closed and free medical care ceased to be given to BCP members, apart from a special arrangement for Central Committee members.[94]

In the post-Mao era, government-to-government relations between Myanmar and China gradually improved. The visit in February 1977 of Madame Deng Yingchao (邓颖超), widow of the late Chinese Premier Zhou Enlai, in her capacity as Vice Chairperson of the Standing Committee of the People's Congress, was reciprocated by U Ne Win in April the same year. Five months later, in September, Ne Win went to China again accompanied by his Foreign Minister. During this trip, the Myanmar Foreign Minister held exploratory talks with officials from Chinese Foreign Ministry about the possibility of a visit by Deng Xiaoping. Ne Win also created an environment conducive to further strengthening of government-to-government relations.

In late November 1977, Ne Win became the first and only Head of State of a non-Communist country to visit Kampuchea at a time when the PRC-backed Khmer Rouge was still in power. This can be seen as an attempt to bring Kampuchea out of its diplomatic isolation. Although it is difficult to know whether Ne Win's visit was a calculated move, it must have impressed the Chinese leadership.

In overall assessment of the Sino-Myanmar relationship between 1967 and 1977, an internal document prepared by the research unit of the Myanmar Commander-in-Chief's Office observed:

> Even in the post Cultural Revolution era, until the fall of the Gang of Four in 1976, as the Gang of Four in general and Yeo Wenyuan (姚文元) in particular was in control of the International Liaison Department (ILD) of the CCP, the Sino-Myanmar relationship had failed to improve significantly. In fact, Yeo Wenyuan was the person behind the CCP's statement issued in September 1967, which mentioned that the BCP's revolution had made great progress as the Party upheld the Mao Zedong Thought. In the post-Lin Biao era, although Zhou Enlai and Deng Xiaoping had attempted to improve China's diplomatic relations, in accordance with the changing international situation, they could not do so. They also failed to improve the Sino-Myanmar relations due to the fact that the Gang of Four had dominated the ILD. Until the end of 1975, Zhang Chunqiao and Yeo Wenyuan frequently met BCP leaders and showed support. Three months after the visit of Myanmar Foreign Minister, on 11 November 1975, U Ne Win, President and Chairman of the State Council, visited China. By this time the health of both Mao Zedong and Zhou Enlai had deteriorated. The administration was in the hands of Vice Premier Deng Xiaoping. However, both the "Gang of Four" and the "Wang Dongxing (汪东兴) Group" attacked Zhou Enlai and Deng Xiaoping. During President Ne Win's call on Zhu De, Chairman of the NPC, representatives from three groups were also present... Zhang Chunqiao from the "Gang of Four", Wu De (吴德) from the "Wang Dongxing group", and Tan Zhenlin (谭震林) from the "Zhou Enlai group". These groups dominated the party, the army and the administration respectively... However, during the visit, notwithstanding the difficulties, Deng Xiaoping had expressed a genuine desire to maintain good relations with Myanmar by stating that "the social system of a country must be chosen and decided only by its own people and must not be imposed by any other country". During his trip to China, President Ne Win held discussions with Vice Premier Deng Xiaoping for three times within three days. He also called on Chairman Mao Zedong and had cordial conversation. Both Deng Xiaoping and

Zhang Chunqiao were present on the occasion. Zhang Chunqiao was the person who met Thakin Ba Thein Tin of the Burma Communist Party on 25 January 1975 in Beijing and held discussion in family spirit.[95]

Nevertheless, Sino-Myanmar relations markedly improved after the state visit of Deng Xiaoping in January 1978, as part of his Southeast Asian tour. At various receptions he and his host waxed lyrical about the strong ties of Pauk-Phaw friendship between the two countries. At the same time, hinting that Myanmar should take a pro-China and anti-Vietnamese position in the Kampuchea-Vietnam border war, Deng said: "As for the disputes among Asian countries, we have always stood for seeking resolution through friendly consultations on the basis of the principles of peaceful co-existence. We are sure that as long as the people of Asian countries strengthen their unity and persist in the struggle, they certainly will be able to frustrate any plot of imperialism and hegemonism and win greater victories in their struggle to safeguard their national independence and State sovereignty". However, Ne Win made no comment on the subject; Myanmar was not prepared to commit itself to China's attempt to forge a united front with all non-Communist countries in Southeast Asia against alleged Vietnamese and Soviet hegemonist expansion. In his speech, Ne Win said: "Whenever there is rift between us, we must attach the utmost importance to friendship, and show tolerance, patience and determination, so that there will be no problems that cannot be resolved". Deng pledged his host that China would provide more economic assistance to Myanmar.[96] While in Singapore, Deng learnt that Southeast Asians were more afraid of the Chinese dragon than the Russian bear. Admittedly, in Malaysia, Deng said that government-to-government relations were different from party-to-party relations, a hint that the CCP would continue to support the revolutions of the regional Communist parties, including the BCP. In June 1978, a high-level Myanmar military delegation led by the Chief-of-Staff, General Thura Kyaw Htin, went to China. This was the first such delegation since 1956. No details of the talks were reported in the press. In September, the new Myanmar Foreign Minister, U Myint Maung, went to China to further consolidate the improving bilateral relations. Subsequently, in November 1978, Deng Xiaoping made a brief stopover in Yangon and held discussions with U Ne Win. As promised, a Sino-Myanmar economic and technical cooperation agreement was signed during the visit of Prime Minister Maung Maung Kha to China in July 1979. Myanmar's withdrawal from the Non-Aligned Movement (NAM) in September 1979, on the grounds that the movement was deviating from its original aims, no doubt brought much pleasure to the Chinese government. China had viewed the movement as a tool of Soviet hegemonist expansion. Two months after Myanmar's withdrawal from the NAM, the Chinese Foreign Minister Huang Hua (黄华) visited Myanmar. All these exchanges, and Myanmar's change of policy toward the NAM, resulted in improved government-to-government relations and a downplaying of party-to-party relations with the BCP.

By late 1979, signs of changes in Chinese foreign policy towards Myanmar became more apparent. This was partly due to the evolving security environment in Southeast Asia. The Vietnamese invasion of Kampuchea and the Sino-Vietnamese war had impacted upon the Chinese security calculus. The Chinese now provided full scale support to the Khmer Rouge in Kampuchea. The Myanmar government, although it continued the diplomatic recognition to the Khmer Rouge, was particularly quiet about the Sino-Vietnamese war. Meanwhile, on 28 May 1980, in commemoration of the successful conclusion of the Sangha of All Orders for Purification, Perpetuation and Propagation of the Sasana, the BSPP government issued a general amnesty order. Insurgents who returned to the fold within 90 days of the date of issue of this order were to be pardoned for any crime they might have committed, except for murder, rape, grievous hurt or loss of property reported by private citizens. Many prominent politicians living in exile or involved in armed struggle, including former Prime Minister U Nu, took up the offer. Prisoners were granted remission of sentences; 23,935 prisoners gained their freedom, including 1,957 politicians. A total of 2,257 insurgents returned home, including 456 members of the BCP.[97] However, the BCP ignored the amnesty order and responded with an attack on Mong Yawng. Nevertheless, the Party proposed talks in September, after the amnesty had expired. The official overture for peace talks came from the BCP on 23 September 1980. Thakin Ba Thein Tin proposed (a) negotiations for cessation of fighting within the country and for building internal peace, (b) a ceasefire between the two sides, (c) discussions between delegations from both sides, and (d) that the discussions be kept secret. U Ne Win replied that a ceasefire was impossible; that he was willing to hold discussions if the BCP wished to send a delegation secretly under existing conditions; that the security of this delegation was guaranteed, and that a government delegation had been formed.[98]

U Ne Win paid a visit to China in October 1980. During his stay in Beijing he conferred with important Chinese leaders such as Hua Guofeng, Deng Xiaoping, Li Xiannian (李先念) and Zhao Ziyang. Yet, despite tacit understanding on many questions, the issue of Chinese support to the BCP could not be resolved. The Chinese leaders "advised and encouraged" Ne Win to open up negotiations with the BCP. Deng Xiaoping arranged a meeting between Ne Win and Thakin Ba Thein Tin. This meeting ended, disappointingly without success. However, Ne Win promised Deng that he would open a venue for further negotiations. As a result, peace talks were held in Lashio between a BCP delegation and a BSPP delegation. As promised, on 16 October, the BSPP informed the BCP that a team led by a senior Central Executive Committee member would negotiate with them. The BCP responded, three months later, that its Vice Chairman would lead the BCP team. The negotiations took place in May 1981, over four sessions. The BCP delegation made three demands: (a) permission for continued existence of the Burma Communist Party; (b) permission for continued existence of their armed forces which came into being together with the Burma Communist Party; and (c) permission for existence of the border area where they maintained their bases. Since both sides could not agree on the terms, the BSPP delegation called off the talks on 9 May.

Ne Win was disappointed with what he believed as continued Chinese interference in Myanmar's internal affairs. He was determined not to visit China again until the issue of China's support for the BCP could be resolved. He explained his encounter with the Chinese leaders and the BCP chairman to his colleagues in melancholy tones.[99] Relations between the two countries cooled. In fact, Ne Win was angry. Since his return from China in October 1980, Ne Win had been reading books on Myanmar's history and literature, and asked his party Foreign Affairs Committee to prepare a paper on Sino-Myanmar relations. On 29 December 1980, Ne Win made a surprise appearance at a paper reading session organized by the Burma Research Society, held at the Institute of Economics. After listening to a paper, he gave a speech in which he asked Professor Daw Than Swe from the Myanmar Language Department why there was no epic on Myanmar's victory over Qing China in 1769 while there were epics on the victories over Assam and Siam. He said that Myanmar should have an epic entitled "Victory over China" and showed the audience books dealing with the mid-18th century Myanmar's struggle against Imperial China to illustrate his point.[100] In January 1981, shortly after a visit to Myanmar by the Vietnamese Prime Minister Phạm Văn Đồng, Premier Zhao Ziyang came to Yangon, possibly to confirm Myanmar's position vis-à-vis the Soviet Union and Vietnam. At a state dinner, Zhao, referring indirectly to Vietnam and the Soviet Union, declared that "tension in Southeast Asia has been created by the small and big hegemonists". Myanmar's leaders, as always, avoided the issue. Foreign Minister U Chit Hlaing's China visit in July 1982, it may be assumed, was simply to introduce himself as the new Foreign Minister, since he assumed the duty only in November 1981.

A number of senior members of the BSPP and the cabinet tried to resolve this unhappy state of affairs and maintain normal and stable diplomatic relations with China. An opportunity came in November 1983, when the State Councilor and Vice Premier cum Minister of Foreign Economic Relations and Trade Madame Chen Muhua (陈慕华) visited Yangon. During her visit, she invited Myanmar's Deputy Prime Minister Thura U Tun Tin to visit China. The Deputy Prime Minister told his counterpart, obliquely, that his visit should help resolve an existing issue between the two countries. Soon afterwards, in February 1984, Chinese Foreign Minister Wu Xueqian (吴学谦) came to Myanmar. A few months later, the Chinese government extended an official invitation to the Myanmar Deputy Prime Minister. As a result, with the approval of the Cabinet, a Myanmar delegation led by Thura Tun Tin went to China in June 1984. Tun Tin was received by Deng Xiaoping, President Li Xiannian, and Vice Premier Wan Li (万里) [on behalf of Premier Zhao Ziyang]. Li Xiannian confirmed to Tun Tin that China would not interfere in Myanmar's internal affairs and it would follow the Five Principles of Peaceful Coexistence. Likewise, during his meeting with the Myanmar Deputy Minister, Deng Xiaoping noted that there was a minor issue between Myanmar and China and that he was determined to resolve it fairly soon. Tun Tin immediately cabled Deng's message back to Yangon. He also conveyed Ne Win's best regards to Madame Deng Yingchao (邓颖超) [Mrs. Zhou Enlai], Madame Wang Guangmei (王光美) [Mrs. Liu Shaoqi], and Madame Zhang Qian (张茜) [Mrs. Chen Yi].[101]

During the tour, Tun Tin held informal discussions with Chinese Foreign Minister Wu Xueqian, Ambassador Huang Mingda, and Councillor Chen Baoliu on the possibility of inviting Myanmar's President U San Yu to China, so that U San Yu could invite Chinese President Li Xiannian to Myanmar in return, which would then give an opportunity for Li Xiannian to invite Ne Win to China to meet Deng Xiaoping. If the meeting between Deng Xiaoping and Ne Win were to take place, then both parties could discuss the issue. When he came back, Tun Tin immediately submitted a report on his China visit to the BSPP leaders. Soon afterwards, the Chinese Ambassador Huang Mingda asked Tun Tin about the progress on the question of mutual visits by the two presidents, as he was about to go back to China. In the meantime, after hearing Tun Tin's report, Ne Win immediately authorized President San Yu to go on a trip to China. Tun Tin passed on this news to the Chinese Ambassador. As a result, San Yu's China visit was materialized soon after the Pyithu Hluttaw meeting. Thus, leading a high level delegation, U San Yu went to China in October 1984. The Myanmar President was received by Deng Xiaoping, Li Xiannian, and Hu Yaobang. The visit resulted in fruitful and frank discussions on the issue of the BCP. Deng told San Yu that he was determined to resolve the issue eventually. However, he asked for Myanmar's understanding on the issue of supplying food and provision to the BCP while arms supplies were being discontinued. As planned, San Yu invited Li Xiannian to visit Myanmar in the near future.[102]

Official relations between the two countries were further consolidated by the visit of Chinese President Li Xiannian in March 1985. During his visit, Li Xiannian declared that China would never practice Hegemonism and that it would oppose the practice of the great suppressing the small and the strong bullying the weak. At a state dinner, he portrayed the relationship between the two countries as follows:

> Over the years, there has been a steady development of Sino-Burmese relations despite international vicissitudes. This is attributed, first and foremost, to the vision shown by the leaders of our two countries for bilateral relations. Sino-Myanmar relations were once affected by the internal problems in China. yet our Burmese friends adopted a forward-looking attitude, which deeply touched us. In recent years, the friendly relations and cooperation between our two countries, in the political, economic, cultural and other fields have developed further. The successful visit to China by President U San Yu last October gave a fresh impetus of the Chinese Government to steadily enhance the friendship and develop amicable cooperation between the two countries. We are convinced that, through joint efforts, the friendly relations and cooperation between China and Myanmar will yield brilliant and rich results.[103]

The following day, the editorial in *The Guardian* [Myanmar] newspaper characterized the nature of Myanmar's foreign policy as follows:

> Pursuing an independent foreign policy in international affairs, Myanmar has safeguarded its state independence and national dignity. It does not attach itself to any big power of group or group of powers, nor does it yield to outside pressure. In handling relations with other countries, Myanmar has adopted a positive approach of "promoting friendship and removing suspicion and hatred", and enhanced its amicable relations with other countries, neighbouring countries in particular, thus winning admiration and appreciation from the international community.[104]

Exactly two months after Li Xiannian's visit to Myanmar, at the invitation of Deng Xiaoping, Ne Win went to China as the Chairman of the BSPP, on a party-to-party basis. Deng Xiaoping praised Ne Win as a "far-sighted and outstanding statesman of Burma" and "one of the most intimate, close and respected old friends of China".[105] Ne Win held talks with Hu Yaobang, the General Secretary of the CCP, at which the Chinese policy towards the BCP was reportedly discussed. Ne Win stressed that "it is of vital importance that these fine traditions of warm, friendly and close relations which have prevailed between our two countries in the past, right up to the present, be maintained in the future also". He further stated that:

> Unavoidable difficulties could, of course, have arisen between us due to extraneous factors beyond our control. However, on such occasions, all that was needed was for the leaders of both sides to meet and hold discussions, to substantially contribute towards achieving a peaceful solution.

However, Chinese leaders placed more emphasis on the need for economic development in Third World countries, including Myanmar. Deng Xiaoping stated: "The development of these countries, being a force in itself for maintaining and preserving international peace, could provide more assurance to the cause of international peace. These assurances are in harmony with the basic interests of the people of the world."[106] A very similar message on the need for an open door economic policy and economic restructuring was passed on to Myanmar leaders by Zhao Ziyang in April 1986, during the state visit to China of Prime Minister Maung Maung Kha, and by Vice-Premier Qiao Shi in May 1987 during his visit to Yangon. In essence, government-to-government relations between the two countries improved substantially in the late 1980s at the expense of party-to-party relations between the CCP and the BCP.

In 1985, Hu Yaobang, the General Secretary of the CCP, met Ba Thein Tin in Beijing. This was the last meeting between two party officials of equal status. At this meeting, Hu Yaobang mentioned that the CCP and the Chinese government were in fact the same; the Chinese government was prepared to base its foreign relations on the principles of peaceful coexistence, and revolution would no longer be exported. The CCP had decided to correct the mistakes it had made during the years since 1968. The agreement on mutual cooperation with the BCP was due to expire. As final assistance to the BCP, Hu promised to deliver three million Yuan, twenty million Kyat and five million rounds of ammunition. This was duly delivered. The CCP also asked the BCP to close down its liaison office and communications center in Beijing. When the Myanmar government demonetised its currency notes in 1987, the BCP lost twenty million Kyat. Ba Thein Tin met an official from the International Liaison Department of the CCP in Kunming and discussed relations between the two parties. However, the Chinese side confirmed China's position as stated by Hu Yaobang. For the loss of Kyat twenty millions, the Chinese government promised to compensate one million Yuan.[107] In 1987, during the Sisiwan-Tarpan battle, the Chinese permitted the Tatmadaw's shelling and the movement of its infantry columns into their territory. Some witnesses said that the Chinese military officers even waved their hands to greet the Tatmadaw officers. This was confirmed by memoirs published by commanders involved in the operation.

As the bilateral relationship normalized, Beijing resumed development aid to Yangon. During his visit to China in July 1979, Prime Minister U Maung Maung Kha signed with Chinese Premier Hua Guofeng an agreement on economic and technical cooperation which provided US$64 million for development projects. In 1984, Beijing extended another US$15 million in aid. During the visit of Lu Xuejian, Vice Minister of Foreign Economic Relations and Trade, to Yangon, China provided an interest free loan of 80 million Yuan for the construction of the Yangon-Thanlyin Bridge. Bilateral trade also grew steadily after 1974, although the amount was small. More importantly, illegal border trade flourished. Lashio and Bhamo were major points of entry for Chinese commodities. The prevalence of Communist insurgency in the Northeast border area of Myanmar since 1968 had seriously discouraged official overland border trade between the two countries. The official trade existed only through normal overseas trade with the main entry port at Yangon. According to official trade statistics published by the Myanmar government, the total value of Sino-Myanmar bilateral trade between 1974 and 1988 was K2,987.2 million (approximately US$495 million). China enjoyed a trade surplus of K1,035.4 million (approximately US$172 million). This figure did not, of course, reflect the reality of the bilateral trade relations between the two countries. In another set of data provided in the publication "Burma: Century of Statistics", between 1974 and 1988, the total value of Sino-Myanmar trade was US$381.72 million, with US$186.1 million trade surplus for China. In reality, since the early 1970s Chinese consumer goods, along with Thai products, had flooded the Myanmar market through illegal trade. Every household in Myanmar relied on cheap Chinese products, such as toiletries, cloth, medicines, electronics and so on. Muse-Lashio and Bhamo were the two major gateways for these Chinese products. The volume and impact of the illegal Chinese trade with Myanmar was difficult to assess. Yet it was China and Thailand that practically helped fill the gap created by the badly performing centrally-planned socialist economy in Myanmar.

After an eight-day visit by Myanmar Foreign Minister U Ye Goung, which began on 4 May 1988, the Chinese government invited U Tun Tin again in the same month to introduce the new leaders in the Chinese government. During

TABLE 1
Myanmar's Trade with China (1974–1988)
(Million)

Year Apr–Mar	Export Kyat	Import Kyat	Value Kyat	Balance Kyat	Year	Export US$	Import US$	Value US$	Balance US$
1974–75	212.8	127.5	340.3	+85.3	1974	3.60	19.16	22.76	-15.56
1975–76	102.9	111.9	214.8	-9.0	1975	16.35	20.51	36.86	-4.16
1976–77	3.2	68.1	71.3	-64.9	1976	0.06	9.32	9.38	-9.26
1977–78	6.8	135.3	142.1	-128.5	1977	0.18	18.68	18.86	-18.50
1978–79	3.4	125.0	128.4	-121.6	1978	0.98	18.14	19.12	-17.16
1979–80	78.6	120.6	199.2	-42.0	1979	1.79	17.60	19.39	-15.81
1980–81	40.2	209.1	249.3	-168.9	1980	4.89	29.30	34.19	-24.41
1981–82	29.2	180.5	209.7	-151.3	1981	5.47	25.99	31.46	-20.52
1982–83	8.4	250.5	258.9	-242.1	1982	13.81	34.51	48.32	-20.70
1983–84	30.5	237.1	267.6	-206.6	1983	14.38	34.82	49.20	-20.44
1984–85	4.9	149.7	154.6	-144.8	1984	13.23	33.52	46.75	-20.29
1985–86	165.3	176.7	342.0	-11.4	1985	3.71	8.92	12.63	-5.21
1986–87	137.0	94.9	231.9	+42.1	1986	3.52	9.61	13.13	-6.09
1987–88	152.7	24.4	177.1	+128.3	1987	2.68	8.48	11.16	-5.80
					1988	1.81	7.70	9.51	-5.89

Source: Statistical Yearbook; Century of Statistics.

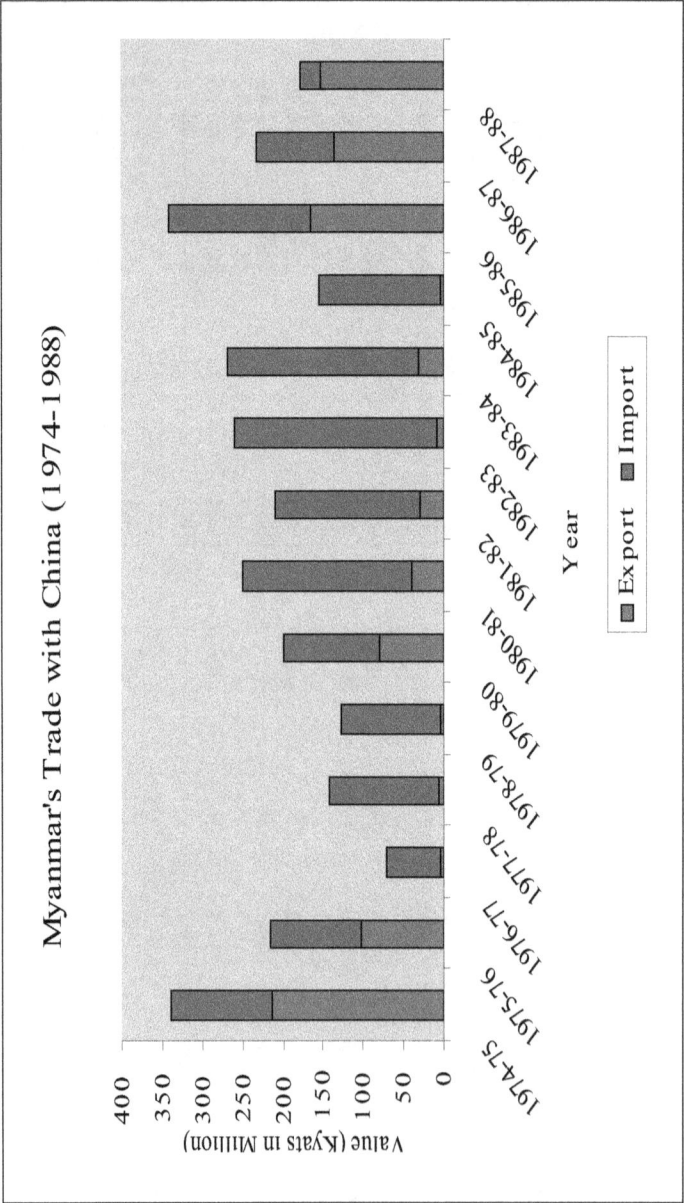

Myanmar's Trade with China (1974-1988)

his nine-day visit from 25 May, apart from meeting with old acquaintances, such as Madame Chen Mu Hua and Vice Premier Wu Xueqian, Tun Tin was introduced to President Yang Shangkun (杨尚昆), Vice President Wang Zhen (王震), and Premier Li Peng (李鹏). By the time the BSPP government fell from power in September 1988, Sino-Myanmar relations were back on track. The good relationship forged during these years, after much difficulty, was carried over into a new era of mutual cooperation.

Notes

1. *New China News Agency* (7 March 1962)
2. *Peking Review*, Vol. VI, No. 17; 26 April 1963, pp. 7–8.
3. *Peking Review*, Vol. VI, No. 18; 3 May 1963, pp. 10–11.
4. *Peking Review*, 3 May 1963, p. 11
5. Ralph Pettman, *China in Burma's Foreign Policy* (Canberra: Australian National University, 1973), p. 26; Robert A. Holmes. "Burma's Foreign Policy toward China Since 1962", *Pacific Affairs* (45:2; Summer 1972), p. 244.
6. Chi-shad Liang. *Burma's Foreign Relations: Neutralism in Theory and Practice* (New York: Praeger Publisher, 1990), p. 85.
7. *Peking Review*, Vol. VII, No. 29, 17 July 1964, p. 6.
8. *Xinhwa* News Bulletin (2 October 1964)
9. Ibid.
10. သိန်းဖေမြင့်၊ *မော်စီတုံးတရုပ်ပြည်နှင့် မြန်မာ့အချုပ်အချာအာဏာ* (ရန်ကုန်၊ နန္ဒာတိုက်၊ ၁၉၆၇)
    Then Pe Myint, *Mao Zedong's China and Myanmar's Sovereignty* (Yangon: Nanthar Press, 1967), p. 57.
11. *Peking Review*, Vol. VIII, No. 31, 30 July 1965, p. 7.
12. *Working People's Daily*, 25 July 1965.
13. *Peking Review*, Vol. VIII, No. 32, 6 August 1965, p. 30.
14. *Peking Review*, Vol. VIII, No. 32, 6 August 1965, p. 30.
15. *Working People's Daily*, 18 April 1966.
16. *Working People's Daily*, 17 April 1966; *Peking Review* (Vol. 9, No. 17; 22 April 1966), p. 6.
17. Myo Myint, *China Factor in Burma's Foreign Policy* (unpublished paper), p. 9.
18. Burma Socialist Programme Party, *1965 Party Seminar* (Yangon: BSPP Press, 1966), p. 16.
19. The government invited a Soviet Central Committee member, Uranovsky, to Myanmar for discussions on economic policy. It also sent at least one study team to the Soviet Union for the same purpose. (*Living Color*, June 2007. Interview with Thakin Tin Mya).
20. *New China News Agency* (4 January 1967).
21. Ibid.
22. *Min Bao Newspaper* (Hong Kong) — 24 August 1967.

23. Holmes. *Chinese Foreign Policy toward Burma and Cambodia*, p. 166.
24. Ibid.
25. Interview with Daw Htwe Kyi (2 November 1996, Yangon).
26. *Guardian* (2 April 1965).
27. Holmes, *Chinese Foreign Policy toward Burma and Cambodia*, p. 168.
28. Frank N. Trager, "Sino-Burmese Relations: the End of the Pauk Phaw Era", *ORBIS* (Winter 1968; Vol. XI, No. 4), pp. 1039–1040; ကြည်ညွန့်၊ ချစ်ကြည်ရေး ချစ်ကြည်ရေးလှုံ့ဆော်ကာ [Kyi Nyunt. *In the Name of Friendship*], Vol. 1, pp. 68–71.
29. Holmes, *Chinese Foreign Policy toward Burma and Cambodia*, p. 182.
30. ကြည်ညွန့်၊ ချစ်ကြည်ရေး ချစ်ကြည်ရေးလှုံ့ဆော်ကာ [Kyi Nyunt. *In the Name of Friendship*], Vol. 1, p. 55.
31. Ibid., p. 52.
32. Ibid., p. 53.
33. ကြည်ညွန့်၊ ချစ်ကြည်ရေး ချစ်ကြည်ရေးလှုံ့ဆော်ကာ [Kyi Nyunt. *In the Name of Friendship*], Vol. II, pp. 9–10.
34. ကြည်ညွန့်၊ ချစ်ကြည်ရေး ချစ်ကြည်ရေးလှုံ့ဆော်ကာ [Kyi Nyunt. *In the Name of Friendship*], Vol. I, pp. 61–62.
35. Diplomatic Protest note delivered by the Chinese Embassy in Yangon.
36. Chinese Protest Note (dated 28 June 1967).
37. *Peking Review* (7 July 1967).
38. Peking Radio Broadcast (29 June 1967, 04:30 GMT).
39. *Guardian*, 2 July 1967.
40. *Guardian*, 10 July 1967.
41. Diplomatic Note Dated 11 July 1867.
42. *Forward* (Vol. V, No. 24; 1 August 1967), p. 1.
43. Melvin Gurtov, *China and Southeast Asia — The Politics of Survival* (London: Heath Lexington Books, 1971), p. 118.
44. The Mirror (3 July 1967).
45. Brigadier San Yu's speech on 22 April 1968 at the passing out parade of 10th Intake of DSA.
46. *WPD* (23 May 1968).
47. Jay Taylor, *China and Southeast Asia: Peking's Relations with Revolutionary Movements* (New York: Praeger Publishers, Second Edition, 1976), pp. 199–200.
48. Central Intelligence Agency, *Peking and the Burmese Communist* (CIA secret report), p. 13; ရဲဘော်မြနှင့်အပေါင်းအပါများ၊ သခင်သန်းထွန်း၏နောက်ဆုံးနေ့များ [Yebaw Mya and et al., *The Last Days of Thakin Than Tun*], Vol. 1, p. 7.
49. ရဲဘော်မြနှင့်အပေါင်းအပါများ၊ သခင်သန်းထွန်း၏နောက်ဆုံးနေ့များ [Yebaw Mya and et al., *The Last Days of Thakin Than Tun*], Vol. 1, p. 7.
50. These were Yebaw Aung Gyi, Thakin Pu, Yebaw Khin Gyi, Yebaw Aung Nyein, Yebaw Chit Maung, Yebaw Nyo, and Yebaw Tin Shein. (DDSI, *History of Insurgency*, p. 5).
51. Than Tun, vol. 1, p. 9.

52. These were Bo Zeya, Yebaw Thet Tun, Bo Ba Nyunt, Bo Ba Phyu, Bo San Pe, Bo Shein, Yebaw Min Aung, Yebaw Soe Win, Yebaw Zaw Lay, Yebaw Aung Khin, and Yebaw Tun Nyein.

53. They were Thakin Ba Thein Tin, Yebaw Myo Tint, Yebaw Tun Shein, Ko Tun, Yebaw Pe Thaung, Yebaw Thein Htike, Yebaw Taik Aung, Ma Khin Khin Kyi (alias) Ma Myo Thant, Ma Tin Wai, Yebaw Nyan Kyaw, and Yebaw Maung Ko.

54. At the Central Committee meeting held in June 1962, Than Tun's leadership was seriously challenged by Goshal, chief ideologue of the BCP. Goshal blamed Than Tun for the enormous losses suffered by the Party in the period between 1958 and 1962. Goshal and some of Than Tun's opponents moved to replace Than Tun as Chairman. When the voting took place, four were in favour of the motion and three were against with five abstentions. Since the vote of the majority of those present at the meeting was required, i.e., seven, to elect a new Chairman, Than Tun barely survived. However, it was clear that Than Tun did not have the support of the majority.

55. For detail, Maung Aung Myoe, *Counterinsurgency in Myanmar: The Government's Response to the Burma Communist Party*, unpublished PhD Thesis (Canberra: Australian National University, 1999).

56. ကကကြည်း (သုတေသန)၊ အရှေ့မြောက်တိုင်းစစ်ဌာနချုပ်နယ်မြေအတွင်းရှိ သောင်းကျန်းမှုသမိုင်း (ပုံနှိပ်ခြင်းမရှိသောစာတမ်း) [Army (research), *History of Insurgency in the Northeast Command* (unpublished paper)], p. 47.

57. ရဲဘော်ဘခက်၊ "ငြိမ်းချမ်းပန်းကမ်းခဲ့ပေမယ့်" *ပြည်သူတို့နှင့်အတူ* (ရန်ကုန်၊ မြရာပင်စာပေ၊ ၁၉၇၀) [Yebaw Ba Khet. "Although the Peace was Offered" *Together with the People* (Yangon: Myayarpin Press, 1970)], p. 41.

58. ကကကြည်း (သုတေသန)၊ အရှေ့မြောက်တိုင်းစစ်ဌာနချုပ်နယ်မြေအတွင်းရှိ သောင်းကျန်းမှုသမိုင်း [Army (research), *History of Insurgency in the Northeast Command*], p. 48.

59. ကကကြည်း (သုတေသန)၊ တရုတ်-မြန်မာဆက်ဆံရေးအကျဉ်းချုပ် ၁၉၄၉-၁၉၈၄ (ပုံနှိပ်ခြင်းမရှိ သောစာတမ်း) [Army (Research). *Sino-Myanmar Relations in Brief, 1949–1984* (unpublished paper)], p. 47.

60. ကကကြည်း (သုတေသန)၊ ဗကပအရှေ့မြောက်စစ်ဒေသ သမိုင်းအကျဉ်းနှင့် အလားအလာသုံးသပ်ချက် (ပုံနှိပ်ခြင်းမရှိသောစာတမ်း) [Army (Research). *Brief History of the BCP Northeast Region and Assessment on its Future* (unpublished paper)], p. 5.

61. တပ်မတော်ထောက်လှမ်းရေး ညွှန်ကြားရေးမှူးရုံး၊ အရှေ့မြောက်ဒေသ ဗကပ [Directorate of Defence Services Intelligence (DDSI), *The BCP in Northeast Myanmar*], pp. 140–141.

62. Ibid., p. 158.

63. တောခိုကျောင်းသားဟောင်းများ၊ *ထို့ကြောင့် ... ၍*ဆို့ (ရန်ကုန်၊ ဦးတင်မောင်ဝင်း၊၁၉၉၁) [Former Underground Students. *Therefore — It is* (Yangon: U Tin Maung Win, 1991)], p. 222.

64. တပ်မတော်ထောက်လှမ်းရေး ညွှန်ကြားရေးမှူးရုံး၊ အရှေ့မြောက်ဒေသ ဗကပ [Directorate of Defence Services Intelligence (DDSI), *The BCP in Northeast Myanmar*], pp. 160–161; FUS. *Therefore — It is.* pp. 223–225.

65. တော်ခိုကျောင်းသားဟောင်းများ၊ *ထို့ကြောင့် ... ၎င်းသို့* [Former Underground Students. *Therefore — It is*], p. 224.

66. ကကကြည်း (သုတေသန)၊ *တရုတ်-မြန်မာဆက်ဆံရေးအကျဉ်းချုပ် ၁၉၄၉-၁၉၈၄* [Army (Research*). Sino-Myanmar Relations in Brief, 1949–1984*], p. 48.

67. တပ်မတော်ထောက်လှမ်းရေး ညွှန်ကြားရေးမှူးရုံး၊ *အ‌ရှေ့မြောက်ဒေသ ဗကပ* [Directorate of Defence Services Intelligence (DDSI), *The BCP in Northeast Myanmar*], p. 171.

68. တော်ခိုကျောင်းသားဟောင်းများ၊ *ထို့ကြောင့် ... ၎င်းသို့* [Former Underground Students. *Therefore — It is*], p. 49.

69. General Ne Win's Speech at 4th Party Seminar (6 November 1969).

70. Ibid.

71. *Far Eastern Economic Review* (20 February 1969).

72. DSHMRI, File 163/7/U-1.

73. တော်ခိုကျောင်းသားဟောင်းများ၊ *ထို့ကြောင့် ... ၎င်းသို့* [Former Underground Students. *Therefore — It is*], pp. 34–35.

74. ချစ်ကြည်ရေးကြည်ညွှန့် *ခေတ်လေးခေတ်တရွတ်မြန်မာဆက်ဆံရေး* (ရန်ကုန်၊ မိုးနတ်စာ‌ပေ၊ ၁၉၇၆) [Chitkyiye Kyi Nyunt, *Sino-Myanmar Relations under Four Periods* (Yangon: Moe Nat Press, 1976)], pp. 165–168.

75. BSPP Central Committee (24 September 1971).

76. Frederick C. Teiwes and Warren Sun. *The End of the Maoist Era: Chinese Politics During the Twilight of the Cultural Revolution, 1972–1976* (New York: M.E. Sharpe, 2007), p. 404.

77. ချစ်ကြည်ရေးကြည်ညွှန့်၊ *ခေတ်လေးခေတ်တရွတ်မြန်မာဆက်ဆံရေး* [Chitkyiye Kyi Nyunt, *Sino-Myanmar Relations under Four Periods*], pp. 190–221; *Peking Review* (Vol. 18, No. 47; 21 November 1975), p. 9.

78. *Peking Review* (Vol. 18, No. 47; 21 November 1975), p. 8.

79. တပ်မတော်ထောက်လှမ်းရေး ညွှန်ကြားရေးမှူးရုံး၊ *အ‌ရှေ့မြောက်ဒေသ ဗကပ* [Directorate of Defence Services Intelligence (DDSI), *The BCP in Northeast Myanmar*], p. 171.

80. တော်ခိုကျောင်းသားဟောင်းများ *ထို့ကြောင့် ... ၎င်းသို့* [Former Underground Students. *Therefore — It is*], p. 50.

81. DDSI, Statement given by U Sai Aung Win (29 June 1990).

82. *Peking Review* (Vol. 19, No. 3; 16 January 1976), p. 25.

83. *Peking Review* (Vol. 19, No. 3; 16 January 1976), p. 25.

84. *Peking Review* (Vol. 19, No. 31; 30 July 1976), p. 31.

85. *Peking Review* (Vol. 19, No. 29; 16 July 1976), p. 29.

86. *Peking Review* (Vol. 19, No. 40; 30 September 1976), p. 59.

87. *Peking Review* (Vol. 19, No. 40; 30 September 1976), p. 60.

88. *Peking Review* (Vol. 19, No. 40; 30 September 1976), p. 59.

89. *Peking Review* (Vol. 19, No. 46; 12 November 1976), p. 14.

90. *Peking Review* (Vol. 19, No. 48; 26 November 1976), p. 3.

91. တော်ခိုကျောင်းသားဟောင်းများ၊ *ထို့ကြောင့် ... ၎င်းသို့* [Former Underground Students. *Therefore — It is*], p. 173.

92. Xiaoling Guo, *Towards Resolution: China in the Myanmar Issue*, March 2007,

pp. 44–45 (quoted from Yang Meihong. *Yingsu Huahong: Wozai Miangong 15 nian*, 2001, p. 263.

93. တောခိုကျောင်းသားဟောင်းများ။ *ထို့ကြောင့် ... ကြွသို့* [Former Underground Students. *Therefore — It is*], p. 194.

94. Ibid., pp. 640–641.

95. ကကကြည်း (သုတေသန)၊ *တရုတ်-မြန်မာဆက်ဆံရေးအကျဉ်းချုပ် ၁၉၄၉-၁၉၈၄* [Army (Research). *Sino-Myanmar Relations in Brief, 1949–1984*], pp. 33–39.

96. Cheng Ruisheng, *1978: Deng Xiaoping's First Foreign Visit after being reinstated* www.cppcc.gov.cn/rmzxb/cqzk/200408190038.htm (accessed 12 August 2007).

97. Min Maung Maung, *The Tatmadaw and Its Leadership Role in National Politics* (Yangon: News and Periodical Enterprise, 1993), pp. 227–228.

98. *16th CC Meeting of the BSPP* (14 May 1981), DSHMRI.

99. Interview with Former Prime Minister Thura U Tun Tin (9 August 2007).

100. On this very occasion, Ne Win declared the dissolution of the Burma Research Society.

101. Interview with Former Prime Minister Thura U Tun Tin (9 August 2007).

102. Ibid.

103. *Working People's Daily* (6 March 1985).

104. *The Guardian* Newspaper (6 March 1985).

105. *South China Morning Post* (13 May 1985).

106. *Working People's Daily* Newspaper (8 May 1985).

107. Testimony given by Sai Aung Win (29 June 1990).

4

SINO-MYANMAR RELATIONS 1988–2010
Towards Closer Cooperation

Myanmar's China policy since 1988 has been essentially directed toward securing and consolidating Chinese political support for the government in international and regional forums. To this end, the Myanmar government makes full use of its geopolitical realities, geostrategic position and economic resources to keep China committed to Myanmar's cause. Although Myanmar has cultivated a very close Pauk-Phaw relationship with China and although China has practically become Myanmar's security guarantor, Yangon has always tried to find alternatives to counter China's growing influence in the country. This is by no means intended as a balance against China since Beijing does not currently pose a threat to Myanmar. To the government in Yangon (or Naypyitaw), Myanmar occupies a strategic position that deserves attention from Beijing. In September 1991, in the state-owned newspaper, a senior Tatmadaw officer stated: "The two nations have resolutely resolved that whoever governs them and whatever systems they practise, they will continue to uphold the traditional friendship for ever and ever because these two nations, according to geopolitics, are interdependent".[1] Again, a decade later, in the words of an official spokesman of the SLORC/SDPC government, Myanmar is "the weak link in the regional China containment policy", although he did not elaborate further.[2] It is fairly clear, however, that the Myanmar leadership believes that China has always regarded their country as an important factor in her security calculus.

When the International Crisis Group (ICG) published a timely report entitled "China's Myanmar Dilemma" on 14 September 2009, detailing China's frustration over what was described as the "erratic and isolationist behaviour of the military leadership" in Naypyitaw, the report, citing interviews with Chinese diplomats, stated that "while China holds a prominent place in Myanmar's foreign policy, the reverse is hardly true and Myanmar is currently a low priority for Beijing". It further noted that "this loss of priority has been noted by Myanmar, which has become increasingly suspicious of China's strategic intentions [and] many in Myanmar fear that China might use it as a bargaining chip in its relations with the U.S.".[3] Just four days later, state-owned newspapers in Myanmar [in both Myanmar and English languages] published an article titled "To serve as a land bridge", which basically highlighted the geopolitical and geo-economic significance of Myanmar in Asia. The article claimed that "being situated between Southeast Asia and South Asia as well as between China and India, Myanmar occupies a strategic position in terms of geopolitics". The article further observed that "China's energy security will not be guaranteed so long as it relies on the Malacca Strait for the shipment of oil. If it lays an oil pipeline from Kyaukphyu deep water seaport to Yunnan, it will enjoy energy security and the benefit of less cost due to shorter distance".[4] The article reveals Naypyitaw's perceptions of China's grand strategy, of its strategic interests in the Indian Ocean, and its growing concern for energy security. It presents the view that Myanmar is a vital factor in China's security calculations. By adhering to Beijing's rhetoric about Washington's attempts to contain China and about the Chinese desire to expand its strategic presence into the Indian Ocean, and by reinforcing China's fear that the Malacca Straits might possibly be blockaded by unfriendly powers, the Myanmar government feels that it can expand its space for diplomatic maneuver. Moreover, in the light of the new global distribution of power and the geopolitical realities of the post-Cold War period, Beijing has been following the "policy of good neighborliness" since the early 1990s. The hallmarks of this policy are accommodation and restraint in China's relations with her neighbors as well as the application of political-diplomatic support, military-security ties, and economic cooperation in the forms of trade, aid and foreign investment as foreign policy strategies towards neighbouring countries.

When the Tatmadaw organized a military *coup d'etat* and took over the state in the name of the State Law and Order Restoration Council (SLORC) on 18 September 1988, after the heavy-handed crackdown on the anti-government demonstrations that aimed to overthrow the BSPP and institute a regime change, and the Chinese government adopted a position of neutrality, the military authorities were convinced that Sino-Myanmar relations were on the right track. Initial Chinese policy towards Myanmar at the time of the 1988 political upheavals was one of wait-and-see. On 8 September 1988, about ten days before the military takeover of the state, at a weekly press conference held by the Chinese Ministry of Foreign Affairs, the official spokesman stated that Myanmar was a "neighboring country with a long tradition of friendship with China and the Chinese government was concerned with recent developments in Myanmar, and it hoped that the situation would be resolved by the best means available and as early as possible so that peace and stability would be maintained throughout Myanmar that would lead to economic prosperity and development in socio-economic life of people".[5]

The Chinese government was, however, alarmed by the brief, yet potentially threatening, presence of a US naval flotilla comprised of the aircraft carrier *Coral Sea* and four other warships in Myanmar's territorial waters on 12 September 1988.[6] The PLA had immediately deployed troops along the Sino-Myanmar border and put them on high alert. Although there was no evidence of Chinese involvement in the "conspiracy of the BCP to take over the state power" (Beijing was either unaware of such a conspiracy or unwilling to take risks,) the PLA appeared to be making preparation to take over the area east of the Thanlwin River with the assistance of BCP troops if a US invasion were to take place. Some informed sources indicated that Tatmadaw representatives met Chinese authorities to clarify the situation and ensure that the matter would be resolved as quickly as possible before any further complications took place.[7]

Subsequently, at the weekly press conference held on 22 September 1988, four days after the coming of the SLORC to power, the official spokesman from the Chinese Foreign Ministry stated that the Chinese government was extremely concerned with the recent developments in Myanmar and that China had firmly believed in and followed the five principles of peaceful coexistence; China would not interfere in the internal affairs of Myanmar and hoped that the Myanmar government would resolve internal problems on its own in a sound way, avoid bloodshed, and restore normalcy as early as possible. On 13 November 1988, during his stop-over in Bangkok, Premier Li Peng explained China's policy towards Myanmar in the following terms:

> China has consistently adhered to a policy of non-interference in the internal affairs of other countries, and Myanmar is no exception. Myanmar is a neighboring country of China. We hope that the situation there can be stabilized. There exist trade relations between China and Myanmar, which have not been suspended.[8]

By early 1989, the Chinese government had indicated a clear stand of support for the military regime in Myanmar. The Tiananmen Square incident of June 1989 further strengthened Beijing's position on Myanmar. In the wake of its severe suppression of pro-democracy movements in Beijing, the Chinese government came to face the same kind of Western criticism and sanctions as were being experienced by its Myanmar neighbor. Sino-Myanmar relations were further cemented by the exchange of bilateral visits as well as military and security co-operation, and trade, aid and investment. Moreover, the relationship received further impetus from the participation of both countries in regional organizations.

In the years since 1988 Sino-Myanmar relations became increasingly intimate, with multi-sectoral linkages extending beyond the traditional sphere of political-diplomatic ties to military-security and deeper economic cooperation. Several factors enabled the two countries to forge a closer relationship. The most important one was Chinese decision to refrain from interfering in Myanmar affairs. Beijing had by now learned, from long experience, that state-to-state relations would serve Chinese interests better. China took advantage of the West's condemnation and isolation of the Myanmar military regime and emerged as the country's major security guarantor. As noted above, the Tiananmen Square "incident" of May 1989 further strengthened the bilateral relations.

In the post Cold War security environment, some scholars and policy makers tend to see a rising China as a major challenger to the U.S. hegemonic position. The Chinese government has also appeared to hold a view that the United States follows a "containment policy" against China, and that the emergence of United States as the sole superpower [or hyperpower] in a unipolar world, at least in political and strategic terms, has not been in Chinese interests. China desires to secure a stable and peaceful regional security environment and to assure its neighbors that it does not constitute a threat. This is to some extent because she does not want to see unfriendly powers establishing foothold in her neighborhood. It is in this context that Myanmar has come to assume an important place in China's security calculus in terms of both geopolitics and geostrategy. China has consistently assured Myanmar that it did not pose any security threat. China has also helped the Myanmar government resolve its internal security issues by encouraging insurgents and the various armed groups operating along the Sino-Myanmar border area to conclude ceasefire agreements, while at the same time helping to strengthen the military capability of the Myanmar armed forces. The Myanmar government was grateful for these services and, therefore, China was considered a friend.

One of the most important factors that facilitated the development of SLORC's cordial relations with China was the latter's decision to withheld her support for the BCP and ethnic insurgencies along the Sino-Myanmar border. Just two months before the fall of the BCP, in February 1989, Ba Thein Tin and Myo Myint again met officials from the ILD in Kunming and explained their activities and achievements during the 1988 uprising in Myanmar. This was the last meeting between the two parties. The officials reconfirmed the Chinese government's policy towards Myanmar and said there would be no change of policy on the issue of resuming aid to the BCP.[9] The CCP also closed down its ILD offices for the BCP in Beijing and Kunming. However, it maintained liaison offices in Mong-Ah, Mong-Gu, Wan-Tain, and Shweli. Subsequently, these offices were closed down and a new office was set up in Teng Chong after the Wa rebellion in April 1989. The Teng Chong office was finally closed down in May 1990.[10]

At the time of Kokang mutiny on 12 March 1989, Ba Thein Tin was in hospital in Lanchan (China). He immediately called Politburo and CC meetings and declared the mutiny counter-revolutionary. The BCP leaders tried to suppress the mutiny by using Wa troops but with no success. The Wa group joined the mutiny on 17 April by capturing Pangsan. No. 815 Military region followed suit on 19 April. Several BCP leaders fled into China, while some were detained by the Wa. The Wa leader Chao Ngi Lai asked the ailing Ba Thein Tin to choose either to remain with him or to follow the other BCP leaders across the Chinese border. As Ba Thein Tin chose the second option, Chao Ngi Lai sent him to China.[11] As a result of the mutinies, BCP leaders first moved into Meng Lian, a Chinese border town, where another CC meeting was held on 7 May 1989. It was decided to send a delegation to persuade Wa to continue the armed struggle. The attempt proved futile. The BCP leaders then briefly moved back into Myanmar before they resettled in Teng Chong. The ILD representative warned the BCP leaders that they could not engage in political activities while in Chinese territory. If they want to carry on their revolution, they should leave China and do so in Myanmar. The CCP also asked the BCP to submit, by December 1989, a list of Chinese volunteers who wanted to resettle in China. The CCP promised to grant pensions to the members of the 1975 CC, who abandoned politics and desired to remain in China.[12] In November 1989, Khin Maung Gyi went to Beijing, looking for assistance from other communist countries. He was denied assistance by Chinese officials in contacting the embassies. Chinese authorities said that they could give him nothing more than phone numbers. Khin Maung Gyi contacted the embassies of Mongolia, Laos, North Korea, East Germany, Rumania, Albania, Cuba, USSR, and Bulgaria. Only the North Korean and

Albanian embassies received him and told him that they would help when opportunities arose.[13] In February 1990, in Teng Chong, when the BCP published a propaganda leaflet known as "Pyithu Ahnar", Chinese police raided the residence of Yebaw Tun and seized machines and documents used for propaganda. The Chinese reminded that the BCP leaders could settle in China only if they did not engage in political activities. By then, the Chinese had completely abandoned the BCP. The Chinese government also actively encouraged ethnic insurgents to enter ceasefire agreements with the SLORC government, as it wanted to maintain regional peace and stability necessary for smooth and better trade flow between Yunnan Province and Myanmar.

SINO-MYANMAR POLITICAL RELATIONS

Politically, Sino-Myanmar relations have witnessed the development of ever closer bilateral links. The Chinese government provides the political-diplomatic support that the Myanmar government badly needs. The PRC has confirmed its commitment to the Five Principles of Peaceful Coexistence with Myanmar and has emphasized the importance of the principle of non-interference in the internal affairs of one country by another. The Chinese government rarely makes public comments criticizing Myanmar's internal affairs. The exchange of state visits between the two leaderships attests the close relations between the two countries. In 2004, General Khin Nyunt, the then Prime Minister, even described the current state of Sino-Myanmar relations as "Nyi-Ako" [sibling] relations, a step higher than the usual "Pauk-Phaw" [kinsfolk] relations. It is now clear that both sides cherish the "Pauk-Phaw" relationship. In his message to the Myanmar Head of the State on 4 January 2007, Hu Jintao stated: "China and Myanmar are good-neighboring countries linked by common mountains and rivers while the two peoples enjoy profound Pauk-Phaw (胞波) friendship". Similarly, Premier Wen Jiabao sent a message to his Myanmar counterpart and said: "The further development of the Sino-Myanmar friendly relations with the deepening of exchanges and cooperation in all fields has brought substantive benefits to both peoples. The Chinese Government treasures the Pauk-Phaw friendship between China and Myanmar, and is willing to make joint efforts with the Myanmar side for the consolidation of the traditional friendship, the enhancement of mutually beneficial cooperation, and the continuous promotion of the relations between China and Myanmar".

Frequent exchanges of state visits between the two countries testify the importance of bilateral cooperation. Visits of Myanmar leaders have been intended to consolidate the existing friendly bilateral relations and to secure

Chinese support for their country in various international and regional forums. The first state visit by a Chinese dignitary to Myanmar since 1988 was by Secretary General of the State Council Luo Gan in January 1991 to officially hand over the National Theatre, a gift of President Li Xiannian in 1985, to the Myanmar government.[14] About eight months later, Senior General Saw Maung, Chairman of the SLORC, paid his first state visit to China. On 20 August 1991, claiming that the objective of the visit was to strengthen and promote the existing friendly relations between the two countries which were established by previous leaders, Saw Maung, leading a 53-member delegation, went to China. He held discussions with President Yang Shangkun, Party General Secretary Jiang Zemin, and Premier Li Peng. The Chinese Premier confirmed his government's foreign policy towards Myanmar in the following term:

> Our country and Myanmar are the ones which initiated and have adhered to the Five Principles of Peaceful Coexistence. Our policy is to prevent interference in internal affairs of other countries. Every country has to tackle its own internal affairs within the country.[15]

Striking a similar note Saw Maung said: "It has been over forty years that China and Myanmar have maintained Pauk-Phaw relationship as established under the guidance of the leaders of the two nations. The fact that there exists no major or minor problem that cannot be solved between the two nations is witness to the correctness of the relations laid down by leaders of the two nations. During this period, our two countries have enjoyed better understanding and greater cooperation with sympathy towards each other." During the visit, despite some speculation about so-called secret agreements that enabled Chinese military advisers to develop naval bases in Myanmar by renting military facilities along the Myanmar coastline, the Chinese and Myanmar governments signed nothing but the "Agreement for Construction of Television Station" and China provided RMB50 million loan.[16]

About eight months after his return from China, in April 1992, Saw Maung was replaced as SLORC Chairman by General Than Shwe. To meet the new Chairman, Chinese State Councillor and Minister for Foreign Affairs Qian Qichen came to Myanmar on 1 February 1993 for a three-day visit. He held discussions with General Than Shwe and Lieutenant General Khin Nyunt, Secretary-1 of SLORC. It was reported that, during the visit, both sides exchanged views on bilateral relations, regional and other internal issues of common interest and expressed hope that the good-neighbourly relations between two countries would be further strengthened and developed. Qian Qichen's visit appears to have been a show of support for the SLORC new leadership. In July 1993, the Vice Chairman of the Standing Committee of the National People's Congress, Buhe (布赫), came to Myanmar to commemorate the Yangon-Thanlyin Bridge, a much publicized landmark of Sino-Myanmar friendship. The bilateral relationship went smoothly and more exchanges of high level visits followed. Secretary-1 Lieutenant General Khin Nyunt journeyed to China in September 1994. His visit was reciprocated by Premier Li Peng, leading a 100-member delegation in December. Li Peng's visit was to commemorate the 40th Anniversary of the Five Principles of Peaceful Coexistence. Li Peng declared that his visit would expand relations "both in scope and depth between China and Myanmar". He remarked: "History over the past four decades and more proves that friendship between China and Myanmar is in keeping with the fundamental interests and the shared aspirations of our two peoples, and is conducive to peace and stability in the region".[17] Li Peng and Khin Nyunt reportedly exchanged views on political, economic and social development in both countries, discussed promoting friendship and cooperation in the regional context, and pledged to strengthen bilateral trade and exchange of technical know-how for the development of agricultural sector. A year later, in December 1995, Li Ruihuan (李瑞环), Chairman of the China People's Political Consultative Conference and Member of the Politburo Standing Committee, came to Myanmar.

Soon afterwards, in January 1996, Senior General Than Shwe made his first visit to China in his capacity as Head of State and Head of Government. He was received by President Jiang Zemin and senior Chinese leaders. It appears that Myanmar informed China of its intention to join the ASEAN. In his conversation with Jiang Zemin, Than Shwe stressed the need to work for regional cooperation to secure regional stability and progress and noted that Myanmar had been working closely with ASEAN. In the joint communiqué issued at the end of the visit, on 13 January 1996, both countries declared their intention to "constantly consolidate and promote the Sino-Myanmar friendship and cooperation and the traditional Pauk-Phaw friendship between the two peoples". Myanmar reiterated that it would firmly follow the "One China" policy and recognize Taiwan as an inalienable part of China. A year after Than Shwe's visit, in March 1997, State Councillor and Secretary-General of the State Council Luo Gan came to Myanmar again and signed three agreements on bilateral cooperation. Then in October, Vice Premier Wu Bangguo visited (吴邦国) Yangon to sign a Framework Agreement on a Preferential Loan with Interest Subsidized by the Chinese Government.

Meanwhile, on 15 November 1997, the SLORC was rejuvenated as the State Peace and Development Council (SPDC). The four top leaders of the SLORC were retained while new members were recruited. During his state visit to China in June 1999, Lieutenant General Khin Nyunt, now Secretary-1 of SPDC, attended the signing of the Agreement on Economic and Technical Cooperation between Myanmar and China. Khin Nyunt held discussions with Premier Zhu Rongji, Chairman of the Chinese People's Political Consultative Conference (CPPCC) with Li Ruihuan, with State Councillor Luo Gan, and with Defence Minister Chi Haotian. After the State Councilor Ismail Amat's visit to Yangon from 31 May to 4 June 2000 to celebrate the 50th anniversary of the establishment of diplomatic relations between the two countries, General Maung Aye, as Vice Chairman of the SPDC, went to China on 5 June 2000, at the invitation of Vice President Hu Jintao. During his seven-day stay in China, Maung Aye witnessed the signing of the Framework of Future Bilateral Relations and Cooperation. A month later, Vice President Hu Jintao reciprocated the visit. During Hu's three-day visit to Yangon, from 16 to 18 July 2000, Myanmar and China signed three agreements for further bilateral cooperation.

The state visit of President Jiang Zemin to Myanmar in December 2001 represented a high point in the development of Sino-Myanmar relations since 1988. There had been a sixteen-year interval between Jiang Zemin's visit and the previous one by President Li Xiannian in 1985. The Chinese government declared that the visit was "of significance for pushing forward the overall development of bilateral good-neighborly friendship and cooperation in the new century".[18] On his arrival in Yangon, Jiang Zemin declared that China and Myanmar were good neighbours bound by "a profound Pauk-Phaw friendship fostered in the long-term and in close contacts between the two peoples". During his meeting with Than Shwe, the Chinese president stressed that the bilateral friendship was in conformity with the common aspirations and fundamental interests of the two peoples, that the development of China-Myanmar good-neighbourly relations was an important component of China's foreign policy, and that this established principle would not change. He also promised that China would make concerted efforts with Myanmar to comprehensively implement the joint statement on bilateral cooperation so as to enable the two peoples to be good neighbours and partners forever and carry on their friendship from generation to generation.[19] In reply, Than Shwe was quoted as saying: "Myanmar attaches importance to the comprehensive development of friendly cooperation with China" and thanked the Chinese leader for Beijing's "generous support and assistance over the years".

Jiang Zemin's visit was interpreted by some observers as an attempt to please the Yangon leadership. Myanmar leaders had been somewhat unhappy with Premier Zhu Rongji's five-nation trip in May 2001, which had included

Pakistan, Nepal, the Maldives, Sri Lanka and Thailand; Zhu had left Myanmar out in his schedule. Zhu Rongji became Prime Minister in March 1998. Zhu did not seem to have a good impression of Myanmar's leaders and never paid a visit to the country during his entire tenure as premier. In fact, to this day, he has never been to Myanmar at all. About the same time, there were unconfirmed reports that Zhu had rejected a number of Myanmar's proposals for development assistance primarily for economic reasons, while Li Peng had been inclined to support them on political grounds. In addition, it was also around this time that Myanmar had begun to cultivate closer relations with India and Russia. Thus, Jiang Zemin's visit could well be viewed as a move to maintain China strategic gains and influential position in Myanmar.

To reciprocate Jiang's visit, Senior General Than Shwe paid his second visit to China, as the chairman of SLORC/SPDC, in January 2003. During the trip, on 7 January 2003, Jiang Zemin once again confirmed "China's set policy to maintain good-neighborly friendly relations of cooperation with Myanmar and to always remain a good neighbor, a good friend and a good partner of Myanmar".[20] He reiterated that China supported the efforts made by the Myanmar government to safeguard the country's independence and sovereignty and to pursue a path to development that was in harmony with its national situation. However, Jiang also advised Myanmar to improve its investment environment so as to facilitate Chinese investment and cooperation. As a way of showing his appreciation, Than Shwe thanked his counterpart for the "selfless and sincere help from China," which had played an important part in Myanmar's economic development, and characterized China as "the most sincere friend of Myanmar".[21] Somewhat overestimating his capacity to influence regional affairs, Than Shwe said that "Myanmar, as a member of ASEAN, is ready to strengthen coordination and cooperation with China in the international and regional affairs and to help China strengthen its relations with ASEAN".[22] Vice President Hu Jintao, during his meeting with Than Shwe on 8 January, noted that during the course of more than fifty years of diplomatic ties, China-Myanmar relations, based on the Five Principles of Peaceful Coexistence, had withstood the test of many international and domestic changes, made steady progress and displayed great strength and resilience under the guidance of leaders from both countries. While Hu Jintao told Than Shwe that China would always consider Myanmar a good neighbor, friend and partner, and make joint efforts to deepen reciprocal cooperation in various fields and to create an even more attractive future, the latter replied that Myanmar regarded China as its most reliable friend and would educate younger generations to pass the torch of bilateral Pauk-Phaw friendship from generation to generation.[23]

Meanwhile, new political developments were unfolding in Myanmar. On 30 May 2003, the government and the Union Solidarity and Development Association (USDA) which it sponsored cracked down the opposition movement led by Aung San Suu Kyi in Depeyin, Sagaing Division. The Depeyin incident saw a few dozen of Aung San Suu Kyi's supporters killed and several others arrested. Among those arrested were Aung San Suu Kyi herself and her lieutenant, Tin Oo. The international community was totally outraged, and strongly condemned this heavy handed crackdown. ASEAN was seriously concerned and took the unusual diplomatic initiative to pressure the Myanmar government to resolve the internal political deadlock and move towards political transition. The United States government tightened its sanctions against Myanmar. This incident triggered a series of chain reactions which eventually led to the hearing of the Myanmar case at the United Nations Security Council (UNSC). Realizing that China was a major stakeholder in Myanmar's affairs, foreign governments and international organizations requested Beijing to exercise its influence in Yangon to help bring about political change. As a responsible member of the international community, China began to pressure Myanmar's leaders to fulfill their promises and international obligations. ASEAN began to show interest in Thailand's proposed "Bangkok Process" to bring about political change in Myanmar.[24] Against this background, the Myanmar government introduced a number of measures to ward off international criticism and to prevent further interference in the country's internal affairs. General Khin Nyunt was appointed as Prime Minister on 25 August 2003. Five days later, Khin Nyunt came up with a "seven-point roadmap" for political transition in Myanmar, which included the resumption of the National Convention suspended since 1996. Khin Nyunt also went on a diplomatic charm offensive designed to convince the international community and regional neighbors that Myanmar was on the right track. Khin Nyunt also attempted to project his image as a reformer.

From late 2003, the Chinese government began to adopt a more assertive policy towards Myanmar, encouraging Yangon to introduce political change, while continuing to defend the country in international and regional forums and providing more development assistance. It appeared that the Chinese government had thrown its support behind Khin Nyunt, possibly seeing him as the next leader in Myanmar. A possible indication of this was that Khin Nyunt's tenure as Prime Minister witnessed an increase in Chinese development assistance. In March 2004, Vice Premier Wu Yi (吴仪) came to Myanmar as part of her Asian tour. During her stay, which extended from 23 to 27 March, Wu Yi held discussions with Khin Nyunt on bilateral relations and economic cooperation. This was followed by the signing of 21 agreements, memorandums of understanding, or agreed notes between the two countries. Madam Wu Yi's visit resulted in a further strengthening of economic and trade ties with Beijing agreeing to provide a new preferential loan and extra funding for infrastructure and agricultural projects. Madam Wu was accompanied by a 40-member business delegation. A senior member of Madam Wu's delegation said that the visit would pave the way for a more extensive and practical bilateral relationship. Madam Gao Yan, the Vice Chair of the China Council for the Promotion of International Trade, a member of the delegation, predicted that Chinese investment in Myanmar would grow rapidly as China was interested in building infrastructure and industrial parks in the country.[25]

During her meeting with Than Shwe on 25 March in Yangon, Wu recalled that, on the basis of the traditional "Pauk-Phaw" friendship, which now extended back for half a century, Sino-Myanmar amicable and neighborly ties had continuously developed. She noted: "We are not only the joint advocators of the Five Principles of Peaceful Coexistence, but have also become the pattern to abide by these principles in development of ties between nations". Moreover, subtly exercising Chinese political influence, Wu was quoted as saying, "China hopes that Myanmar will have a stable political situation, national conciliation and economic development". At the same time, she reiterated Beijing's view that Myanmar's internal affairs should be coordinated and resolved by the government and people themselves. Wu reportedly said that, while respecting Myanmar's sovereignty, the international community should, in a positive and constructive manner, extend assistance to Yangon. In addition, she expressed the hope that the Myanmar government could push the developing situation in a more positive direction. At the meeting, Than Shwe also observed that the peoples of Myanmar and China enjoyed a deep traditional friendship and that the intimate exchanges between successive leaders of the two countries had played an important role in fostering the development of bilateral ties. Than Shwe was quoted as saying that "China's selfless and long-term aid and support extended to Myanmar has also played an active role in promoting Myanmar's economic development and the improvement of its people's living standard, which Myanmar people would never forget". He stressed that Myanmar regarded China as a true friend, and hoped the two sides would strengthen friendly collaboration in the sectors of trade, economic cooperation and so on. Than Shwe also emphasized that Myanmar, as always, held that Taiwan had been an inalienable part of China since ancient times and no matter how the situation changed, Myanmar would unshakably adopt a "One-China" policy.[26] While the government press in Myanmar completely censored the content of this meeting and related discussions, *Xinhua* reported them in considerable detail. The semi-official weekly paper, *The Myanmar Times*, however, was allowed to publish a somewhat censored report.[27]

Four months later, in July 2004, Khin Nyunt journeyed to Beijing. During this visit to China, he held discussions with President Hu Jintao, Premier Wen Jiabao and the Chairman of National People's Congress, Wu Bangguo. Hu Jintao pledged to further expand and deepen the mutually beneficial cooperation with Myanmar. This was followed by the signing of 12 agreements, contracts and memorandums. Khin Nyunt met Wen Jiabao on 12 July. During their discussions, Wen Jiabao reminisced: "China and Myanmar are friendly neighbors of each other, and the two peoples have been living in peace and amity since ancient times and established Pauk-Phaw friendship. In recent years, relations between the two countries have maintained good momentum, with cooperation in politics, economy, culture and some other areas constantly expanding. To cement the traditional friendship and deepen the mutually beneficial cooperation is not only the common aspiration of people of the two countries but also the shared goal of the two governments".[28] Stressing the importance of building good-neighborly relationships and partnerships with neighboring countries, Wen promised that China stood ready to consolidate the Pauk-Phaw friendship with Myanmar and deepen cooperation with it in all areas so as to promote the comprehensive development of bilateral relations. China, he said, would continue to provide economic assistance to Yangon within its available resources with the ultimate goal of improving Myanmar's capability for self-development. Having made these pleasant diplomatic remarks, Wen stated, significantly:

> China hopes Myanmar will maintain its political stability, economic development and national amity, with its people living and working in peace and contentment. What happened in Myanmar is its internal affairs and should be addressed by the government and people of Myanmar themselves through consultations. The international community may provide constructive help to Myanmar on the precondition of showing respect for its sovereignty. *As a neighbor and friend of Myanmar, China hopes that Myanmar will address the existing problems in a timely and appropriate manner so as to accelerate the process of political reconciliation and democratization in a real sense and embark on the road to unity, stability, peace and development at an early date.* (Italic are mine)[29]

In his reply, Khin Nyunt thanked "China for its selfless assistance in an effort to help with Myanmar's national construction and economic development" and expressed the hope that the two sides would enhance their pragmatic cooperation in various sectors. "Myanmar is grateful for and takes seriously the recommendations of the Chinese friends, and will actively commit itself to maintaining national unity and political stability, continue the democratization process it has mapped out and develop good-neighborly and friendly relations with its neighboring countries, including China", he pursued.[30] During Khin Nyunt's visit Hu Jintao also confirmed China's continued support for Myanmar, observing that:

> People of China and Myanmar have enjoyed long-standing friendship. Five decades ago, China and Myanmar, together with India, jointly advocated the Five Principles of Peaceful Coexistence and made them basic guiding principles for development of relations between countries. In recent years, leaders of the two countries have maintained frequent exchanges of visits, the mutual political trust has been enhanced, achievements in their economic and trade cooperation are remarkable, and the two sides have maintained coordination in international as well as regional affairs. China appreciates and is thankful for the long-term adherence by Myanmar to the one-China policy and its understanding and support for China's lofty cause of reunification, and *China supports Myanmar in its efforts to maintain social stability, promote national reconciliation and expand foreign exchanges...* China follows a policy of bringing harmony, security and prosperity to neighbors. On the basis of the Five Principles of Peaceful Coexistence, China stands ready to develop long-term, stable, good-neighborly and friendly relations of cooperation with Myanmar, further expand and deepen the mutually beneficial cooperation, actively promote regional as well as sub-regional cooperation and jointly push relations between the two countries and relations between China and ASEAN for further development.[31]

The official press in Yangon, however, briefly reported that China had declared that it would never interfere in Myanmar's internal affairs and that, the Chinese President expressed his pleasure at the development of the Sino-Myanmar relationship based on the Five Principles of Peaceful Coexistence and had promised to strengthen understanding and cooperation between the two countries.[32] In his response, to President Hu Jintao's remarks, according to official Chinese press release, Khin Nyunt was quoted as saying,

> Over a long period of time, the two sides have borne mutual respect and trust and offered mutual support for each other. The people of Myanmar will never forget the precious support provided by China. Myanmar will, as always, continue to follow the one-China policy and stand by China

firmly and forever on the Taiwan issue… Myanmar will continue to
press ahead with the process of its domestic political reconciliation and
democratization and establish a democratic system suited to the national
context of Myanmar.[33]

On 13 July, during his visit to Beijing, General Khin Nyunt also called on the
Chairman of the National People's Congress of China Wu Bangguo. While the
official media in Myanmar reported the meeting very briefly, noting merely
that "they discussed matters relating to strengthening friendship, cooperation
and mutual respects between the two countries", the Chinese press and
official statements provided a somewhat more detailed account.[34] According
to Chinese press, Wu noted that China was committed to developing good-
neighborly, friendly and cooperative relations with Myanmar and that there
were no outstanding issues between the two countries. He further said: "To
consolidate the traditional friendship and deepen the mutually beneficial
cooperation conforms not only to the interests of the two peoples but also to
the regional peace and stability. China will as always continue to follow the
friendly policies towards Myanmar and constantly promote relations between
the two countries towards deepened development".[35]

During the visit, when asked at a press conference held by the Chinese
Foreign Ministry in Beijing on 13 July about the implications of international
criticism concerning Sino-Myanmar relations, the Chinese official
spokesperson, while reiterating China's policy of good neighborliness and
non-interference in Myanmar's internal affairs, stated: "As a friendly and close
neighbor, we hope that Myanmar can maintain political stability and economic
growth and its people can live in happiness. As to its internal question, China
always handles it according to the principle of non-interference in other's
internal affairs. The democratic process of Myanmar is a gradual process
and needs a stable and favorable external environment. The international
community should create a benign environment for the democratic process
of Myanmar on the basis of respecting its sovereignty without interfering in
its internal affairs".[36]

Early in 2004, to facilitate bilateral cooperation between the two
countries, Khin Nyunt formed the "Leading Committee for Implementation
of Myanmar-China Economic Agreements". The first public meeting of
the committee was held on 21 February 2004.[37] After his return from
China, Khin Nyunt immediately organized two meetings. The first was
the Coordination Meeting on the Implementation of Agreements between
the Union of Myanmar and the People's Republic of China on Border
Areas Management and Cooperation held on 23 July 2004. Khin Nyunt

discussed promoting cooperation to ensure the maintenance of law and order in border areas between the two nations. Also taken up were the issues of border areas development and the fight against drugs.[38] Three days later, on 26 July, Khin Nyunt chaired another meeting of the Leading Committee for Implementation of Myanmar-China Economic Agreements to coordinate the speedy implementation of agreements and memorandums of understanding on energy, hydroelectric power, mining, industrial development, transport, communications and agriculture. At the meeting, he was reported as saying that "Myanmar was in a strategic position which can link South Asia and Southeast Asia regions and promotion of cooperation among those countries will be very useful to both Myanmar and neighbouring and regional countries".[39] He grouped bilateral cooperation issues into 29 sectors. About two months later, on 1 October, Khin Nyunt called another meeting of the Leading Committee for Implementation of Myanmar-China Economic Agreements. At this third meeting, he called on all the ministries to accelerate implementation of the agreements between the two nations.[40]

On 18 October 2004, Khin Nyunt was removed from the premiership and placed under house arrest. He was eventually given a deferred sentence for a long prison term. There were a number of reasons for this dramatic development, including irreconcilable institutional tensions and rivalries between the intelligence corps and the infantry, Khin Nyunt's increasing departure from the norms of collective leadership and collective responsibility, and his failure to share credit for more progressive government policies. As a result of these events, Khin Nyunt's military intelligence establishment was dismantled and all of his subordinates and staff were either imprisoned or forced to retire.[41] Rumors that the Chinese leadership had tried to cultivate deeper and stronger personal ties with General Khin Nyunt, a situation that the regime's top leaders were unlikely to tolerate, since as they believed that the latter held a pro-China policy and attached less significance to relations with other major powers, and that he would become future Head of the State, could not be substantiated. In any case this could not have been a cause for Khin Nyunt's downfall. Contrary to widely circulated speculation, Khin Nyunt's departure from Myanmar's political scene did not precipitate any shift in the overall foreign policy direction of the government. All this confirmed that it was really Senior General Than Shwe who had the final say in major policy decisions. To maintain some sort of balance in Myanmar's relations with major regional powers, whenever possible, had long been one of his objectives. Another objective had been not to rely exclusively on the efficacy of just one Veto at the UNSC. It was for this reason that Than Shwe had always tried to ensure that he himself and senior members of the SPDC paid important and well publicized visits to India and Russia, as well as to China. However this may be, Myanmar's China policy remained unchanged, despite Khin Nyunt's political demise.

Lieutenant General Soe Win became Prime Minister. After less than a month in office, Soe Win travelled to China to attend the China-ASEAN Business and Investment Summit held in Nanning. He met with Vice Premier Madam Wu Yi (吴仪) and discussed promotion of bilateral economic cooperation. Madame Wu Yi declared that Myanmar's internal problems could only be solved by the government and people of Myanmar themselves, and that outside pressures would be unhelpful.[42] About the same time, in late July 2005, Chinese Foreign Minister Li Zhaoxing (李肇星) arrived in Yangon to show support for Yangon's decision to relinquish the ASEAN Chairmanship for 2006, by not attending the ASEAN Regional Forum. In fact China had stood solidly with the Myanmar government on the ASEAN chair issue from the very beginning. Soe Win journeyed twice to China in July and October 2005 to attend Second Greater Mekong Subregion Summit and ASEAN-China Business and Investment Summit.

Soe Win paid his first official visit to China in February 2006. During his meeting with Soe Win on 14 February, Wen Jiabao stated that "China would like to jointly advance bilateral cooperation in the economic and trade area with Myanmar in the spirit of equality and mutual benefits". To this end, while emphasizing the role of "equality and mutual benefit", the Chinese side put forward four concrete suggestions. First, to make full use of the preferential tariff treatment offered by China to expand the scale of bilateral trade. Second, to implement key cooperative programmes defined by both sides so that the cooperation in the areas of energy, resources exploitation and infrastructure construction could register achievements at the earliest date possible. Third, to develop closer mutual coordination within ASEAN Plus China, ASEAN Plus Three (China, Japan and South Korea), the Greater Mekong Subregion (GMS) and other multilateral cooperation frameworks, and push for regional economic cooperation in a bid to spur the economic and social development of the respective countries. Fourth, to encourage more businesses of the two countries to directly engage with each other and strengthen personnel training and technological exchanges. Soe Win generally agreed with these suggestions. Wen went on to discuss the issue of narcotics control and said that "currently the spread of narcotics in the boundary area between both sides has severely damaged the local society, as well as people's life and health and it must be attached great importance to and controlled through severe measures". He stated that China hoped to strengthen bilateral and multilateral cooperation with

Myanmar in narcotics control and sign an agreement on narcotics control cooperation at an early date.

For the first time since the mid 1970s, the overseas Chinese in Myanmar became a point of discussion in this official bilateral meeting. The issue was raised by the Chinese side. Wen Jiabao noted that the Chinese government had always encouraged overseas Chinese to observe the local laws, mix with the people of the country where they lived and actively participate in local social and economic development. Yet he also stated, more assertively, that: "It is hoped that Myanmar will show care for overseas Chinese in Myanmar, adopt a more loose policy, attach great importance to their demand and provide more facilitation for their work, life and education".[43] Turning to the domestic situation in Myanmar, he added: "As Myanmar's neighboring country, China sincerely hopes that Myanmar could continue to push forward reconciliation at home and realize economic development and social progress".[44] Clearly the Chinese government wished to demonstrate its continuing interest in political reform in Myanmar. Again on 31 October 2006, when he met Soe Win on the sidelines of the China-ASEAN Commemorative Summit, marking the 15th anniversary of the establishment of Dialogue Relations between China and ASEAN, Wen observed that China hoped Myanmar would achieve political stability, economic development and national reconciliation. While he promised that China was ready to strengthen cooperation with Myanmar in infrastructure development and other areas, based on the principle of mutual benefit, the Chinese Premier once again stressed cooperation with Myanmar in fighting drug trafficking, urging that the two sides should strengthen cooperation within both bilateral and multilateral frameworks, actively develop substitute planting and completely eliminating the drug menace for the benefit of both peoples.[45]

Political relations were further cemented by China's cultural diplomacy. This included frequent exchanges of visits between members of writers' and journalists' associations, cultural troupes and sports teams. Since all social organizations were either sponsored or controlled by the state, China sent formal invitations through official channels only so that there would be no misunderstanding between the two governments. Between 1991 and 1994, Myanmar sent four writers' and journalists' delegations and eight cultural delegations to China while China sent five writers' and journalists' delegations and nine cultural delegations. Moreover, in the same period, Myanmar and China exchanged two educational delegations each.[46] Perhaps the most significant cultural events during these years were the journeys of the Buddha's Tooth Relic from China. The "Dethasari (sacred journey)" of the Buddha's Tooth Relic was extremely important since it was a well publicized state event.

The sacred tooth relic had already come to Myanmar three times, in 1955, 1994 and 1996. The first time coincided with the Sixth Buddhist Synod, held in commemoration of the 2,500 years of Buddhism. The second and third journeys took place during the SLORC period. The Exchange of Buddhist Delegations between China and Myanmar had preceded the first journey of the tooth relic. A Myanmar Buddhist delegation led by the Vice-Chairman Sayadaw (monk) of the State Sangha Maha Nayaka Committee went to China in November 1993. It was reciprocated by a Chinese Buddhist delegation headed by the Vice-Chairman of the All China Buddhist Association in December 1993. These visits were forerunners of the tooth relic's journey. All necessary preparations for a countrywide journey having been completed, the tooth relic finally arrived in Myanmar on 20 April 1994. During the public obeisance in Myanmar, which lasted for about 45 days, the tooth relic was conveyed from Yangon to Mandalay. The event was widely reported in the Myanmar media. Then on 5 December 1996, the tooth relic made its second journey to Myanmar. While the tooth relic was at the Kaba Aye Pagoda in Yangon, an unexpected explosion occured, killing four people, although the relic itself was unscathed. The government accused dissident elements and Karen insurgents for the explosion. This was promptly denied by the accused parties. Nevertheless, the "Dethasari" was a great success and China played "tooth relic diplomacy" rather well in Myanmar.

While there exists a close and cordial Sino-Myanmar relationship at the government-to-government level, anti-Chinese sentiments can be found among certain segments of Myanmar's people. Politically, dissidents feel China is responsible for prolonging the military rule in Myanmar by supporting the military regime. For a wider general public, the main issue has been the growing affluence of Chinese in Myanmar and alleged Chinese migration into the country. The growing number of people interested in learning Chinese is an indication of China's economic clout in Myanmar. Nowadays, many job advertisements require applicants to be fluent in Chinese.

Some observers have pointed out that there has been an influx of Chinese migrants in upper Myanmar since the late 1980s. In fact, the social landscape, physical character, and ethnic composition of Mandalay was profoundly transformed by two major fires, the first on 12 May 1981 and the second on 24 March 1984. The former razed about 6,000 houses and public buildings and rendered 36,000 people homeless. The latter destroyed 2,700 buildings and made 23,000 people homeless.[47] Since many of the original ethnic Myanmar occupants were unable to afford the cost of reconstruction, huge swaths of land blackened and left vacant by the fires were later purchased by ethnic Chinese who had lived in Myanmar for sometime. It is, however, important to note that, due to the war between the government and the BCP in the northeast border area, illegal migration had been practically halted since 1968. Nevertheless, many cities in the Shan State, by then, had been heavily populated by immigrants from Yunnan.[48] Beginning in the mid 1980s, while open and straight forward printed media discussion about growing Chinese influence in Myanmar, and the increasing wealth of many ethnic Chinese residents was either censored or discouraged by the authorities, short stories occasionally appeared, discreetly drawing public attention to the issues. Fictional accounts, too, sometimes portrayed the changing social landscape that had resulted from influx of Chinese immigrants in Upper Myanmar or in Mandalay.[49] Despite the emergence of some anti-Chinese sentiment in the early 1990s that might possibly lead to social tension between ethnic Myanmar people and overseas Chinese or ethnic Chinese, the Myanmar government has so far successfully managed to control the situation. The resentment was most strongly felt in Mandalay, where new Chinese migrants bought up real estates in the city center with huge sums of money, forcing ethnic Myanmar people to resettle in new satellite towns. The government policy of relocating squatter settlements in new satellite towns also accelerated the tendency for the city center to become populated with rich Chinese families and new migrants.

There was some confusion over the so-called Chinese immigrants from Yunnan. Although there were some illegal migrants, who had obtained their status through bribing Myanmar immigration officials and buying Myanmar citizenship cards, there were also many who were entitled to hold Myanmar citizenship since they belonged to the Kokang and Wa national minorities who lived in the border region. In the aftermath of a series of ceasefire agreements between the government and various ethnic insurgent groups operating along the Sino-Myanmar border, Mandalay and other major cities in Upper Myanmar witnessed an influx of Chinese looking immigrants, many of whom were actually Kokang, Wa and A-khar, officially recognized national races of Myanmar. While many newcomers were from towns in the Shan State and the border areas, including towns and villages in Yunnan province, some were believed to be from as far away as Sichuan province. Some observers believed that 30 per cent–40 per cent of the million people who inhabited the city in 2008 were new immigrants or settlers.[50]

The influx of these so-called Chinese migrants in Mandalay shocked the local people since the city's Chinese population had been relatively stagnant for at least twenty years since 1968 due to the prevalence of Communist insurgency in the border area and the government's strict control on population movement. The ceasefire agreements with various armed national groups and the opening of border trade, as well as deregulation of business activities, have generated a massive movement of human being and capital from the Sino-Myanmar border region into upper and central Myanmar. The commercial and cultural life of Mandalay, historically dominated by native Myanmar people, is now heavily penetrated by ethnic Chinese, a process which Mya Maung has called "Sinonization".[51] The problem centers around the issue of assimilation of these new migrants into mainstream Myanmar culture. Mandalay had a rather large Chinese population even before 1990, most of whom lived harmoniously with the native Myanmar people. However, many of the new Chinese migrants seemed arrogant and rude. Their vast financial assets, it was popularly believed, derived from their involvement in drug trafficking and other illegal businesses. The problem was exacerbated by the Myanmar government's extraordinary tolerance toward the new migrants, the majority of whom were Wa and Kokang and belonged to the ceasefire groups. Nevertheless, the anti-Chinese sentiment did not go beyond resentment and failed to develop into genuine racial tension. The problem of the lawless nature of some new migrants was more or less resolved when the government took strong action against them in the late 1990s. However, the government needs to be vigilant about any sign of racial tension in Myanmar.

The Myanmar government was careful to avoid projecting a bad image about China in its local media, state-owned or otherwise. Nor will it permit local private media to carry any news about China detrimental to Chinese national interests. One example is the strict censorship on news about "Made in China Products" in August 2007. In July and August 2007, the issue of tainted food stuffs and toiletries, counterfeit goods, pirated products, and harmful toys and garments occupied the headlines in much of the world press. The Chinese government was naturally sensitive about this increasingly bad image and negative publicity of Chinese made products. The Chinese Ministry of Foreign Affairs even summoned the Vietnamese Ambassador in Beijing and lectured him about the Chinese government's unhappiness over how the Vietnamese media had highlighted the issue. Beijing felt that Vietnam should direct its state-controlled press to downplay the issue and indicated that a recurrence could lead to action against Vietnamese exports to China.[52] The Myanmar government imposed censorship on reporting the issue in local media.

In the meantime, on 15 March 2005, Myanmar Ministry of Foreign Affairs issued a statement with regard to the ratification of the Anti-Secession Law by the NPC of the PRC on 14 March. The statement read as follows: "Myanmar welcomes the ratification of the Anti-Secession Law by the NPC of the PRC unanimously on 14 March 2005. As a friendly nation which has steadfastly nurtured good-neighborly relations with the PRC, the Union of Myanmar maintains that Taiwan is an integral part of China. Myanmar has consistently adhered to the One-China policy and supports China's inalienable right to safeguard its sovereignty and territorial integrity".[53] The Myanmar government stood by China on the Taiwan issue, the bombing of the Chinese embassy in Belgrade, and the spy plane incident with the US air force off Hainan Island. Whenever an occasion arises, Yangon quickly moves to reconfirm its position on the "One China" policy. For its part, Beijing provides much needed diplomatic support for Myanmar on almost all occasions. When Myanmar's chairmanship of ASEAN became an issue, the Chinese government supported Yangon's position.[54] Political consultation has also become part of Sino-Myanmar relations since 1992.

Meanwhile, with security considerations in mind, among several other factors, the SPDC leadership decided to move Myanmar's capital from Yangon to Naypyitaw in November 2005.[55] Some ASEAN countries openly expressed their disappointment with the Myanmar government's failure to consult them about this matter. From the point of view of the SPDC leadership, however, this was a domestic affair and consultation with any other country was not necessary. Despite the claim by some people that the Chinese government also found the failure of Yangon to "notify Beijing in advance" unacceptable,[56] China subsequently financed the construction of the Myanmar International Convention Center (MICC) in Naypyitaw. The stake-driving ceremony for the construction of MICC, attended by three Myanmar ministers and Chinese Ambassador Mr. Guan Mu, on 15 February 2008 was widely reported in Myanmar newspapers.[57] Considering the sheer scale of construction work in Naypyitaw by the government, the Chinese contribution for the MICC was financially negligible, but it was politically very significant since it clearly demonstrated China's support for the new capital.

One of the most important tests of Sino-Myanmar friendship was the Chinese stand on Myanmar in the United Nations (UN). During the Bush presidency, the U.S. ambassador at the UN, John Bolton, persistently attempted to bring the Myanmar issue before the United Nations. On 1 September 2006, Ambassador Bolton submitted a resolution on Myanmar to be put on the Security Council agenda, arguing that Myanmar's domestic situation posed a threat to regional and international peace and security. On 15 September 2006, a draft resolution was put to the vote at the United Nations Security Council (UNSC), and was approved by 10 votes to four, with one abstention; China, Russia, Qatar and Democratic Republic of Congo voted against the resolution while Tanzania abstained. The Chinese Ambassador at the UN, Wang Guangya, told the procedural meeting that neither Myanmar's neighbours nor most Asian countries considered the situation in the country as posing any threat to regional peace and security. As a result of majority voting, a resolution was passed to put Myanmar on the UNSC agenda under the title of "Situation in Myanmar". When a U.S drafted resolution was submitted at the UNSC, on 12 January 2007, China, along with Russia, vetoed it.[58] The Chinese Ambassador to the UN, Wang Guangya, once again argued that "the situation in Myanmar does not constitute or pose a threat to regional or international peace and security".[59] At the same time, he said: "It cannot be denied that Myanmar is now facing many political, economic and social challenges and that some of its problems are quite serious. But no country is perfect and every country has to go through a process of constant improvement".[60] Moreover, referring to the "many constructive recommendations" made by ASEAN, Ambassador Wang declared that, "China sincerely hopes and expects that the Myanmar government will give due consideration to those recommendations, listen to the call of its own people, learn from the good practices of others and speed up the process of dialogue and reform, so as to achieve prosperity for its nation, bring benefits to its people and contribute to peace, stability and development in Southeast Asia".[61] One scholar noted that this represented "a key shift in Beijing's policy" toward Myanmar for it was probably the first time since 1988 that China had publicly criticized the Myanmar government.[62] Nevertheless, the Myanmar government thanked China for its stand at the UNSC. To demonstrate Beijing's continued support for the Myanmar government and to explain China's overall foreign policy objectives, and also China's international obligations, State Councilor Tang Jiaxuan (唐家璇) travelled to Naypyitaw on 26 February 2007 and held talks with Myanmar leaders, including Senior General Than Shwe, during his three-day visit. He also seems to have advised the SPDC to speed up the "National Convention" and to proceed with the promised "national reconsolidation" process.

As a result of this visit, during his journey to Beijing as acting Prime Minister in June 2007, Lieutenant General Thein Sein informed the Chinese leadership on the progress of the ongoing National Convention and its deadlines. On the same occasion, he apparently enlisted Chinese assistance in arranging a meeting with representatives from the U.S. State Department. A meeting between three Myanmar ministers and U.S. Deputy Assistant Secretary of State Eric John took place in Beijing on 28 June. The Myanmar government's decision to meet the U.S. Deputy Assistant Secretary of State in Beijing was a shrewd move that assured the Chinese government that it would not do anything behind China's back. Giving Beijing a leading role in this diplomatic initiative indicated that Yangon/Naypyitaw understood

China's strategic interests in Myanmar and would not do anything to jeopardise them.

In September 2007, monk-led anti-government demonstrations broke out on the streets of Yangon and a few other towns. The international media quickly began to refer to this movement as the "Saffron Revolution", following the style of the other "colour-revolutions". In the early days of the demonstrations, on 13 September, the SPDC Chairman sent Foreign Minister Nyan Win to Beijing as his special envoy to explain the situation in Myanmar and to confirm that "the government of Myanmar was committed to maintaining domestic stability, national solidarity and economic growth and that [it] would advance the process of democratization according to the already established guidelines". During his meeting with Nyan Win, Tang Jiaxuan said that "China, as a friendly neighbor of Myanmar, sincerely hoped that Myanmar could resume domestic stability in the earliest time possible, properly address related issues, vigorously promote national reconciliation, and unswervingly advance the process of democratization suited to the national realities of Myanmar".[63] Despite the fact that it exhibited a considerable degree of tolerance, at least in terms of its own previous record, the government's crackdown on the demonstrations on 26–27 September drew widespread international condemnation and calls for international intervention. The issue was tabled at the UNSC by the United States and Britain for a resolution. However, due to the possibility of veto by both China and Russia, a compromise was reached to issue a non-binding "UNSC Presidential Statement". After nearly a week of negotiations on the details and terms of this document, to be issued by the United States as the rotating President of the UNSC, Beijing eventually agreed to the final version of the "Presidential Statement", which was duly released on 11 October 2007. This non-binding and ambiguously worded statement "emphasized the importance of the early release of all political prisoners and remaining detainees" and "stressed the need for the Government of Myanmar to create the necessary conditions for a genuine dialogue with Daw Aung San Suu Kyi and all concerned parties and ethnic groups".[64] The Chinese government continued its diplomatic support for the SPDC government while at the same time playing a crucial role in helping Secretary-General's Special Adviser Ibrahim Gambari to visit Myanmar and to hold meetings with a wide range of leaders and political figures, including Senior General Than Shwe and Daw Aung San Suu Kyi. The Chinese government's special envoy, Vice Minister of Foreign Affairs Wang Yi (王毅), came to Myanmar for three days, 14–16 November 2007, and held talks with the country's leaders on the subject of further cooperation with the

Secretary-General's Special Advisor. Throughout this period, the Myanmar government coordinated efforts with the Chinese government to quieten and overcome the international pressure. Prime Minister General Thein Sein, who became Prime Minister on 24 October 2007 after the death of Soe Win on 12 October, sent his special envoy, Deputy Foreign Minister Maung Myint, to Beijing in January 2008 for political consultation. Maung Myint met Tang Jiaxuan on 21 January 2008 and briefed China on situation in Myanmar.

In the meantime, the SPDC speeded up the National Convention process and, on 9 February 2008, the government announced a timeline for implementation of the Seven-Step Roadmap, which featured a nationwide referendum for the draft constitution to be held in May and then multi-party general elections in 2010. Beijing welcomed this announcement and viewed the move as a viable way to cool down international pressure for political change in Myanmar.

When China had to deal with the "Tibetan unrest" in March 2008, Naypyitaw issued a statement in support of Beijing, couched in tones reminiscent of the statements made by Chinese authorities in connection with Myanmar issues in the past. The statement read:

> The Government of the Union of Myanmar ... views the recent occurrences in the Tibet Autonomous Region as purely the internal affairs of the People's Republic of China. *Myanmar is fully confident that the Chinese Government with all its wisdom and far-sightedness will overcome the challenges successfully and will be able to maintain the domestic peace and stability.* Moreover, the Government of the Union of Myanmar also joins the international community in voicing its opposition to any move to link the incidents in Tibet with Beijing Olympic Games.[65]

A few days later, Prime Minister Thein Sein journeyed to Laos to attend the third Greater Mekong Subregion (GMS) summit. However, his planned meeting with Premier Wen Jiabao, on the sidelines of the summit in Vientiane, never took place. A leaked document that listed a number of points for discussion at the meeting included a request for Chinese financial and technical assistance for the RMB3,700 million tagged Shweli-Lashio railway project. In addition, the Prime Minister planned to thank Chinese leaders for "their kind attention and friendly advice on the political developments in Myanmar by dispatching a special envoy" as well as for their "understanding and support extended to Myanmar at the international forums". He also hoped to enlist Chinese help "in preventing the UNSC from adopting any statement or decisions with regard to the issue of Myanmar".[66]

It was during this period that the SPDC government became increasingly concerned about the prominent role being played by China in Myanmar's affairs. There were fears that Myanmar was becoming too dependent on Beijing. To redress the balance, Vice Senior General Maung Aye travelled to New Delhi on 2 April 2008. During his four-day trip to India, Maung Aye signed a framework agreement and two related protocols for facilitation of the US$130 million [Rs. 536 crore] Kaladan project with the Indian government. Maung Aye's Indian visit was also viewed by some observers as an attempt to remind Beijing of New Delhi's significance in China's strategic calculus. The SPDC leaders were increasingly aware of China's international obligations and its desire to project and maintain a positive image in the eyes of the international community. This was by no means risk-free for Naypyitaw. Although China continued its political support, it began to criticize the Myanmar government, which made the SPDC uncomfortable.

On 2 May 2008, Cyclone Nargis struck Myanmar, leaving more than 100,000 dead and 1.5 million people "severely affected", according to the United Nations. The inadequate and slow response by the government, as well as its reluctance to accept international agencies and NGOs to assist in disaster relief operations provoked a global outrage. The international community approached China, urging it to play a crucial role in convincing the SPDC government to accept international relief aid and to receive Admiral Timothy J. Keating, Commander of U.S. Pacific Fleet Command, in Yangon. In fact, China sent its Foreign Minister, Yang Jiechi (杨洁篪), to Yangon to attend ASEAN-UN International Pledging Conference on Cyclone Nargis, held on 25 May. In the early days of the post-Nargis relief operations, a U.S. led flotilla, including the aircraft carrier *Essex* and three amphibious vessels, carrying 22 heavy-lift helicopters and a small fleet of landing craft, and HMS *Westminster* from the Royal Navy, suddenly appeared near Myanmar waters with the announced intention of engaging in relief operations, against the background of debate on "humanitarian intervention". The Myanmar government, always suspicious of Anglo-American hidden agenda centering on forceful "regime change", refused to allow any direct aid delivery from the warships to the disaster areas, although it did permit airlifts of relief goods to Yangon airport.

When he met Premier Wen Jiabao on 8 August 2008, during his trip to Beijing for the opening ceremony of the Beijing Olympics, Prime Minister General Thein Sein thanked him for the help rendered by the Chinese government for the disaster relief operations and aid for Cyclone Nargis victims. His fifty-minute meeting with Wen Jiabao did not appear to take up matters of bilateral cooperation in detail, but he explained the "measures taken for relief, rehabilitation and reconstruction after the Cyclone Nargis, constitutional referendum, and bilateral economic and social cooperation". Similarly, Thein Sein's meeting in Naypyitaw on 19 November 2008 with Mr Zhang Gaoli (张高丽), Member of Central Committee of the Political Bureau of the Communist Party of China and Secretary of the CPC Tianjin Municipal Committee, did not dwell too much on major bilateral issues.

It would seem that since early 2008, the Sino-Myanmar bilateral relationship began to enter a difficult phase. Naypyitaw was uneasy with Beijing's increasing contacts with anti-government activists and organizations. The SPDC was aware that Chinese authorities, mostly from Yunnan, held a series of meetings with Myanmar dissidents in Maesot and Chiang Mai (Thailand) and Ruili (Yunnan): some of these dissidents were invited to tour Kunming and Beijing. Naypyitaw did not show any enthusiasm for the proposed construction of oil and gas pipelines from the Myanmar port of Kyaukphyu to Kunming, where China plans to build refineries. The pipelines are of considerable strategic significance to energy hungry China. The pipelines are intended to carry about 85 per cent of China's energy imports from the Middle East and Africa. China plans to invest about US$2.5 billion in the pipelines project. China is aware of its vulnerability in the Malacca Straits area.

Chinese Foreign Minister Yang Jiechi's two-day visit to Naypyitaw in December 2008 was perhaps intended to fine-tune bilateral relations and to clear up any misunderstandings that might have existed between the two countries. During his meeting with Foreign Minister Nyan Win on 4 December, Yang Jiechi "stressed that the Chinese government attached great importance to the relations with Myanmar and [would] follow the principle of 'treating its neighbors well and as partners', in continuously pushing forward the China-Myanmar good-neighborly and friendly ties on the basis of the Five Principles of Peaceful Coexistence".[67] The ministers also agreed to maintain frequent communications and consultations and exchanges of views on bilateral ties and issues of common concern between foreign ministries of both countries in a timely manner, to closely coordinate and further implement the China-aided projects, and to enhance cooperation in jointly combating cross-border criminal activities such as drug trafficking. Yang Jiechi also "expressed China's willingness to render assistance within its ability for Myanmar's national construction".[68] On the next day, Senior General Than Shwe told Yang Jiechi that "the Myanmar government appreciates the Myanmar-China traditional friendship, and expressed willingness to maintain exchange at high level and expand the mutually beneficial cooperation in all sectors, so as to enable the Myanmar-China friendship to be passed on from generation to generation". He further said: "the government would continue to promote the country's stability, democratic process and economic development based on the principle of independence and self-determination, conduct foreign exchange and cooperation and oppose outside interference".[69] With regard to Yang Jiechi's points of discussion, the Chinese Ministry of Foreign Affairs reported:

> At the meeting, Yang said China and Myanmar are friendly neighbors with deep 'Paukphaw [fraternal]' friendship. The two sides always pay respect to each other, treat each other as equals and cooperate sincerely with mutual trust. Recalling that the cause of friendly relations between China and Myanmar was forged and fostered by leaders of elder generations of the two countries, Yang reaffirmed that the policy of adhering to China-Myanmar friendship would not change. He also expressed China's willingness to enhance exchange and cooperation in all sectors to jointly push ahead with the development of China-Myanmar good-neighborly and friendly ties.[70]

However, ICG reported that Yang Jiechi had urged Senior General Than Shwe "to do more for his own country" and said that "Beijing would not be in a position to provide endless support to Myanmar".[71] According to the report, Yang Jiechi told Than Shwe that "China was concerned about Myanmar's spending on non-priority programmes, and warned that the government would face problems in failing to ensure economic growth and the delivery of social services".[72] However, the present writer is doubtful about the authenticity of this account, which was never reported officially in the media of either country. It is always possible, of course, that the Chinese Foreign Minister used very polite and diplomatic language to express his point of view, without violating the much cherished norm of non-interference in internal affairs. Nevertheless, Yang Jiechi's visit paved the way for Li Changchun (李长春), member of the Standing Committee of the Political Bureau of the CPC Central Committee, to pay an official visit to Myanmar on 26 March 2009, during which the two governments signed three agreements and one Memorandums of Understanding (MoU) on bilateral cooperation, which included an agreement to build oil and gas pipelines from Kyaukphyu to Kunming.

During his meeting with Prime Minister Thein Sein on 17 April 2009, on the sideline of the Boao Forum for Asia, held on Hainan Island, Premier Wen Jiabao confirmed "that being a good neighbour of Myanmar the PRC stands by Myanmar in its drive for stability, economic development and national unity; that as Myanmar affairs is an internal affairs it will be dealt with by the government and Myanmar people only; and that since the PRC has already realized the current development in Myanmar it will continue to support Myanmar in the international arena with full understanding".[73] Wen Jiabao called for both countries to enhance cooperation in energy and transportation network building and to provide sound infrastructure for bilateral trade and investment.[74]

Finally, Vice Chairman of the SPDC, Vice Senior General Maung Aye, went to Beijing in June 2009. His visit was to smooth bilateral relations and to seek Chinese understanding on the government's policy towards the ethnic-based ceasefire groups that exist along the Sino-Myanmar border. [This issue is discussed in a later section.] During his meeting with Vice President Xi Jinping (习近平) on 16 June, Maung Aye explained that the aim of his visit is "to enhance the existing bilateral friendship as well as to scale up the economic cooperation between the two countries".[75] For his part, Xi Jinping told Maung Aye that "only the people and the government of Myanmar can solve the internal affairs of Myanmar, and foreign countries should not interfere in internal affairs of Myanmar and should not impose sanctions against Myanmar; China will continue to support Myanmar in the international sphere, and China will stand by the interests of Myanmar".[76] More importantly, Xi assured his counterpart that "China will maintain peace and stability of China-Myanmar border by adopting the non-interference policy in the internal affairs of Myanmar".[77] Xi Jinping also assured Maung Aye that "China is always a good friend of Myanmar and will uphold the *fair interests of Myanmar*"[78] and that "China would like to join with Myanmar to promote comprehensive, stable and lasting relations".[79]

On the same day, Maung Aye met Premier Wen Jiabao. Interestingly, as reported on the front page of the national press, when he met Wen Jiabao on 16 June, Maung Aye told the Chinese Premier that "he has visited China many times and *he is the one who has always given priority to strengthening the relationship between China and Myanmar*".[80] This point is particularly important since the international media and many observers have frequently classified Maung Aye [and Than Shwe] as having strong anti-China views and sentiments. Maung Aye also recalled:

> The relationship between the two countries is based on Paukphaw relations. China and Myanmar have been good neighbourly nations for many years based on mutual understanding, respect and friendship. This is the third time he has arrived in China and the aim of the visit is to scale up friendly ties and economic cooperation between the two nations.[81]

Maung Aye further stated that "Myanmar is ready to work with China to push forward bilateral ties".[82] For his part, Wen Jiabao reportedly declared that "China always considers the relations with Myanmar important under the China's foreign policy [and] China would protect the *fair interests* of Myanmar in the international community".[83] During his stay in China, Maung Aye witnessed the signing of various agreements and MoUs. These included an agreement on economic and technical cooperation, an agreement on Development, Operation and Transfer of the Hydropower Projects on Ayerwaddy River, and a Memorandum of Understanding on the Development, Operation and Management of the Myanmar-China Crude Oil Pipeline Project.

The Chinese Vice-President's assurance of China's interest in maintaining peace and stability in the Sino-Myanmar border region and his promise of non-interference in Myanmar's internal affairs has pleased the SPDC leadership and made them more confident in their policy towards ceasefire groups along the Sino-Myanmar border. Myanmar leaders were satisfied with China's "appropriate response in the Kokang Affair of August 2009". When Xi Jinping reciprocated with a visit to Myanmar in December 2009, the SPDC government expressed its satisfaction by signing a total of 16 documents, including five agreements on trade, economic matters, transport infrastructure, technical cooperation and purchase of machinery; seven financial agreements, three agreements on hydroelectric power; and one agreement on the energy sector and oil and natural gas pipelines.[84] Xi Jinping put forward a four-point proposal to upgrade China's relations with Myanmar during talks with Maung Aye on 20 December 2009. This proposal centered around maintaining high-level contact, deepening reciprocal cooperation, safeguarding the peace and prosperity of the border area, and strengthening coordination on international and regional affairs.[85] Myanmar was more than happy to accept these proposals.

To commemorate the 60th anniversary of China-Myanmar diplomatic ties, Chinese Premier Wen Jiabao paid a state visit to Myanmar in June. On 3 June 2010, Wen Jiabao met with Senior General Than Shwe in Naypyitaw. During his meeting with the Senior General, Wen reportedly stated that "China and Myanmar are linked by mountains and rivers and enjoy deep connections, and the two peoples share traditional Pauk-Phaw friendship".[86] Wen Jiabao also noted that "the consensus and agreements China reached with Myanmar" during his visit would enhance bilateral cooperation and safeguard peace and tranquility in border areas, and it would constitute "a step forward in the development of relations between the two countries".[87] Moreover, Wen stated that "China values friendly and good-neighbourly relations with Myanmar *from a strategic perspective*".[88] During his meeting with Prime Minister Thein Sein, Wen suggested that both countries "should make proper planning of key areas and projects for cooperation, speed up the interconnection of the two countries' infrastructure, and complete the agreed major cooperation projects in energy, transportation and other areas in a timely manner and with good quality".[89] Both leaders also discussed issues pertaining to the stability along the Sino-Myanmar border. They reached a broad understanding on the issues and agreed to make "concerted efforts to maintain peace and stability along the common borders between the two countries and turn the borders into a bridge for friendly cooperation between the two countries".[90] Wen Jiabao attended the handing over ceremony of the Myanmar International Convention Center, fully financed and built by the Chinese government in Naypyitaw, and witnessed the signing of 15 MoUs and agreements for cooperation in economic development and technology sectors, rail transportation, trade, hydropower, energy and mining. He also attended the opening ceremony for the Sino-Myanmar oil and natural gas pipelines projects. Soon after Wen Jiabao left Myanmar, Foreign Minister Nyan Win went to Beijing to commemorate the 60th Anniversary of China-Myanmar diplomatic ties. During his meeting with Chinese Foreign Minister Yang Jiechi on 8 June 2010, Nyan Win briefed Yang on the preparatory work for Myanmar's general elections.

A month later, General Tin Aung Myint Oo, Secretary-1 of the SPDC, paid a 10-day visit to China, from 3 to 12 July 2010, at the invitation of Li Keqiang (李克强), Vice Premier and member of the Standing Committee of Politburo. Tin Aung Myint Oo's visit came only one week after a visit to Naypyitaw by Chinese Vice Premier Zhou Tienong (周铁农), Vice chairman of the Standing Committee of the National People's Congress and president of the Chinese Association for International Understanding. During his visit, on 28 June, Zhou Tienong held discussions with Prime Minister Thein Sein, which reportedly included the 2010 elections and ethnic issues along the Myanmar-China border. While in Beijing, Tin Aung Myint Oo was received by Li Changchun (李长春), the 5th ranked member of the Politburo Standing Committee. Tin Aung Myint Oo visited several industrial plants and transport facilities and he held discussions with various business firms.

After nearly 15 years since his last visit, Senior General Than Shwe travelled to China on 7 September 2010. It was interesting to note that Than Shwe's visit to China took place a month after his visit to India. His visit seemed to be aimed at securing Beijing's support for Naypyitaw's policy of transforming ceasefire groups into Border Guard Forces and for the general elections to be held on 7 November 2010, which had been criticized by the

West and anti-SPDC activists. Than Shwe held discussions with three highest ranking political figures in China: Hu Jintao, Wu Bangguo and Wen Jiabao. During his meeting with Than Shwe on 8 September, President Hu Jintao was quoted as saying that "China-Myanmar relations have seen consolidation and growth ever since [the establishment of diplomatic ties between the countries] thanks to the bilateral strategic cooperations. China has been consolidating Myanmar-China friendship based on its policy of maintaining friendly relations with neighbouring countries, and it was an unswerving policy of China".[91] According to state-owned newspapers in Myanmar, making headlines on the first page, Hu Jintao reportedly told his counterpart that "China would not accept and support any groups who would carry out anti-Myanmar government movements in border areas to damage the bilateral relations".[92] This statement was politically significant since some ceasefire groups along the China-Myanmar border areas refused to comply with the government policy. In official Chinese press, *Xinhua*, however, it was mentioned that "Hu called on both sides [Myanmar and China] to jointly safeguard peace and stability of the frontier and boost economic and social development of the border areas, and China respects sovereignty and territorial integrity of Myanmar, understands and supports the Myanmar government's efforts for national reconciliation".[93] Although what Hu Jintao actually said in Chinese was neither readily available nor subject to different interpretations, one could safely assume that Beijing did not want any armed conflict and violence taking place along the Myanmar-China border areas. China would have attempted to convince Naypyitaw to settle the differences between the government and ceasefire groups in peaceful ways; however, it was not prepared to allow any anti-Myanmar government troops to station on its soil.

In his conversation with Wu Bangguo on 9 September, Than Shwe reconfirmed Naypyitaw's stand on China and told Wu that "Myanmar will be, as always, committed to developing strategic relations with China". Than Shwe's discussions with Premier Wen Jiabao centered around cooperation in the areas of Myanmar's economic and industrial development, maintaining peace and tranquility and law and order along Myanmar-China border, and construction of Shweli-Kyaukphyu road and railway. With regard to the general elections in Myanmar, just a few hours before Than Shwe's arrival in Beijing, during a regular press conference on 7 September, Chinese Foreign Ministry official spokeswoman Jiang Yu clarified Beijing's stand on the issue. She said: "The general election in Myanmar is its internal affairs. We always uphold the principle of non-interference in others' internal affairs. It is hoped that the international community will provide constructive help for Myanmar's general election and refrain from any negative impact on its domestic political process as well as regional peace and stability.[94] It can be safely concluded that Than Shwe has secured Beijing's support for the SPDC's key policy initiatives.

It appeared that, by late 2008, both China and Myanmar understood the rules of the game and the emerging framework of Sino-Myanmar bilateral relations. Beijing also seemed to realize the parameters of its influence on Myanmar. Naypyitaw was also increasingly aware of China's international obligations as a responsible major power. It is in this context, while it would continue to press the Myanmar government to promote good governance, political transition and national reconciliation, and even other good advice and constructive criticism at the private level or in informal discussions, at various bilateral meetings, China would defend and protect Myanmar's *"fair interests"* to prevent international interference in Myanmar's internal affairs, as China undeniably has strategic interest in the country.

SECURITY COOPERATION ALONG THE BORDER

Security cooperation along the Sino-Myanmar border area is another important aspect of the bilateral relations. Both countries are concerned with security along the porous fronter and want to ensure the stability in the border region. The Sino-Myanmar border area is notorious for various types of transnational crimes, including the drug trade and human trafficking. The lawless nature of the Sino-Myanmar border area, particularly on the Myanmar side, has been a major security concern. This was partly due to the lack of state security apparatus on the Myanmar side and to the existence of [substantially] autonomous "peace groups" which entered into ceasefire agreements with the Myanmar government. As mention earlier, in 1989, ethnic groups, such as the Kokang, Wa, Akher and Shan, which constituted the BCP troops, revolted against the BCP leadership and negotiated ceasefire agreements and peace settlements with the SLORC. As part of the deal, these "ceasefire groups" were allowed to retain their arms and exercise full administrative authority over their "special regions", designated by the government. Out of several "special regions", five are prominent along the Sino-Myanmar border area. These are the Northern Shan State Special Region (1) largely inhabited by the Kokang [Myanmar National Democracy Alliance Army with its HQ in Laukai], the Northern Shan State Special Region (2) inhabited by the Wa [United Wa State Army with its HQ in Panghsaung], the Eastern Shan State Special Region (4) dominated by the Akhar and the Shan [National Democratic Alliance Army with its HQ in Mongla], the Kachin State Special Region (1) dominated by the Kachin [New Democratic Army — Kachin with its HQ in Pangwa], and the Kachin State Special Region (2), also dominated by the Kachin [Kachin Independence Organization with its HQ in Laizar]: the first four groups comprise former BCP members. Among these groups, the United Wa State Army (UWSA) and the Kachin Independence Organization (KIO) are particularly strong.

The Myanmar government has sought cooperation from Chinese authorities in managing the ceasefire groups along the Sino-Myanmar border, especially in the case of the Wa, Kokang and Akher minorities, since Chinese influence in the Myanmar border region has been substantial. Chinese officials and the state intelligence apparatus have long maintained informal but regular contacts with these ceasefire groups. In fact, China pressured some of these groups to enter ceasefire agreements with the government in 1989 and during the early 1990s. A recently released International Crisis Group's (ICG) report entitled *China's Myanmar Dilemma* claimed that "China maintains a balance of power between these ethnic groups and the SPDC government to ensure neither side gains the upper hand".[95] It also argues that "China uses its relationship with these groups as a buffer and a lever in managing its relationship with the government".[96] China surely has a clear interest in preventing these ceasefire groups from gaining full autonomy because it fears that this would stimulate nationalist sentiment among ethnic minorities on its side of the border. Yet China would not gain any particular long term benefit from the perpetuation of such a potentially explosive situation and from the continued existence of ceasefire groups, some of which are notorious for drug production and trafficking and are involved in transnational crimes. China wants to maintain peace and stability around its periphery and wants to prevent the emergence of either interstate or intrastate conflicts, which could invite interference by major powers and undermine its own national security.

The Myanmar government appeared to believe that China was not enthusiastic about supporting its attempt to solve the problems posed by these groups by transforming them into paramilitary forces under the command of the Tatmadaw.[97] Naypyitaw occasionally expressed its displeasure with China's perceived stance. ICG reported that, during his visit to China in November 2008, General Thura Shwe Mann had asked Chinese authorities for help in persuading the ceasefire groups to comply with the Myanmar government's policy of transforming them into "Border Guard Forces (BGF)" under the Tatmadaw, but "the Chinese reportedly feigned ignorance and skirted the issue".[98] It was also reported that Senior General Than Shwe had expressed his displeasure about the lack of Chinese support for the Myanmar government's policy towards these ceasefire groups when he met

Chinese Foreign Minister Yang Jiechi in Naypyitaw in December 2008. Beijing, however, apparently wished to do more than encourage both the Myanmar government and the ceasefire groups to find a common ground and a mutually acceptable solution.

As a preparation for the upcoming 2010 general elections, the Myanmar government pressured ceasefire groups to comply with the constitutional requirement that "all the armed forces in the Union shall be under the command of the Defence Services",[99] which meant that all [ceasefire] groups carrying weapons should either disarm or transform themselves into smaller, lightly armed Border Guard Forces under the command of the Tatmadaw. This placed China in a difficult position. The Myanmar authorities argued that there would be no guarantee for the security and safety of the proposed oil and gas pipelines that passed through the border area if these armed groups were not under the command of the Tatmadaw, and that they could even constitute a threat to the border area peace and stability. During his visit to Beijing in June 2009, Chinese leaders told Vice Senior General Maung Aye to handle the ceasefire group issue carefully. At the same time, China indicated that the ceasefire groups could not expect any backing from Beijing or permission to use Chinese soil to launch attacks on the Myanmar government if the Tatmadaw moved against them. The reality of China's policy was clearly demonstrated when the Tatmadaw launched an attack on the Kokang ceasefire group and took control of Laukai, in an attempt to search a facility believed to be an illegal arms factory, acting on the information given by Chinese authorities, in August 2009.

The Kokang incident of August 2009 left an unknown number of dead and other casualties on both sides and triggered an outflow of about 37,000 Kokang refugees into China. Some 700 Kokang troops loyal to Pheung Kya-shin crossed the border into China while 300 others joined a splinter group led by Bai Xuoqian. The Pheung loyalists were immediately disarmed by the Chinese authorities. The Myanmar government issued arrest warrants for Pheung Kya-shin, his brother Pheung Kya-fu and their associates who were allegedly involved in illegal drug production and illegal arms manufacture. Pheung Kya-shin himself went into hiding. After the outbreak of the incident, China issued an unusual public statement, calling on the Myanmar government to "properly handle domestic problems and maintain stability in the China-Myanmar border region" and "to protect the security and legal rights of Chinese citizens in Myanmar". Meanwhile, the Chinese authorities provided temporary shelter and food to refugees and encouraged them to return to Myanmar. This incident sent a clear signal to other ceasefire groups that the Tatmadaw was prepared to take military action if its demands were not met. In Naypyitaw, the SPDC leadership watched Chinese government's response very carefully. In the post-incident period, the SPDC appeared to become more confident in handling the ceasefire groups and even the staunch opponents of the government plan for the BGF, such as the Wa and the Kachin, became more conciliatory in tone while some groups accepted the transformation.

When he met the Myanmar Prime Minister in Thailand on 15 October, during the 12th ASEAN-China Summit, Chinese Premier Wen Jiabao told his counterpart that "he believed Myanmar could properly handle problems and safeguard peace and stability in the China-Myanmar border region so as to make it a bond for friendly cooperation and harmonious coexistence between the two countries". He also reminded Thein Sein that "friendly China-Myanmar relations with mutually beneficial cooperation conforms to the fundamental interests of the two countries and will be conducive to regional peace and development [and] China sincerely hopes Myanmar will realize stability, reconciliation and development".[100] The issue of maintaining peace and stability along the Myanmar-China border region has been a recurrent theme in high level talks between leaders from the two countries. As mentioned earlier, during his visit to China in September 2010, Senior General Than Shwe discussed the matter with Chinese leaders and he appeared to solicit Beijing's support for the Myanmar government's policy of transforming ceasefire groups into Border Guard Forces.

Other important issues that could destabilize the border area are production and trafficking of illegal drugs, human trafficking, transnational health problems and gambling. It is widely reported that almost 95 per cent of the heroin sold in China comes from this area. Some ceasefire groups are notorious for involvement in the illegal drug business. Since the early 2000s, there has been a marked increase in the production and trafficking of Amphetamine-Type Stimulant (ATS) into China from the Myanmar border region. By the mid 2000s, Yunnan province already had more than one million registered drug users. There has been a rise in social problems and transnational crime. Armed confrontations between drug dealers, who carry automatic rifles and grenades, and Chinese police have become common in the border area. The problem became so serious that when he met Prime Minister General Soe Win on 14 February 2006, the Chinese Premier Wen Jiabao said that the China-Myanmar border area was flooded with drugs and asked Soe Win to take serious measures to address the issue. The Myanmar government argued that the country itself did not produce any precursor chemicals used in the ATS production and that some ceasefire groups were behind all these activities. Cooperation with Chinese authorities is necessary to deal with the ceasefire groups and to address the illegal drug issue. Drug abuse leads to a transnational health issue in the spread of HIV/AIDS in Yunnan, which has become a leading cause of death in province. It is estimated that Yunnan currently hosts about 85,000 HIV positive people and China needs the Myanmar government's help to control this epidemic on its territory. Human trafficking is another issue that relates to transnational crimes. Women and children are trafficked into China. Due to the shortage of brides in China's rural areas, many Myanmar girls are trafficked into China for forced marriage. For example, in 2006, a total of 73 cases of human trafficking were reported, 74 Myanmar girls were rescued by the Chinese authorities, and 18 more were rescued by the China-Myanmar joint task force. Gambling along the Myanmar-China border is yet another problem that Beijing has tried to eliminate but without any success. Some ceasefire groups operate casinos themselves or allow Chinese businessmen to run casinos along the Myanmar side of the border. One prominent site of such activities is Mongla, the capital of Shan State Special Region (4), dominated by the Akher/Shan ceasefire group. On 26 August 1998, Mongla authorities legalized up to ten varieties of gambling, such as Mah-jong and dominoes. Mongla subsequently became a booming gambling town with a capacity to generate up to US$830 million annually in total gambling revenues. By the end of 2004, it was reported that Mongla had accumulated up to US$5 billion in total gambling revenue.[101] Chin Shwe Haw in the Kokang region had reportedly operated some casinos in the past but Chinese authorities pressured the Chinese operators and local Kokang leaders to close them down a few years ago. A recent ICG report vividly described Beijing's effort to address the gambling issue:

> Efforts by Beijing to close them down have been unsuccessful. Gambling has led to the kidnapping, torture and murder of gamblers unable to repay their debts, including businessmen and the sons of high-ranking government officials. A series of such abductions made headlines in early 2009. The Yunnan government responded by cutting off water, telecommunications, power and roads to the Myanmar town of Maijayang to pressure the local authorities to shut it down. Chinese troops have closed border crossings to casino towns and raided casinos across the border, arresting and firing all Chinese, including casino operators and gamblers. The foreign ministry in Beijing has also taken the unusual measure of issuing a statement warning Chinese nationals against going to Myanmar to gamble due to the risk of scams and kidnapping.[102]

China undoubtedly needs the Myanmar government's cooperation in addressing these cross-border issues.

A range of agreements on bilateral cooperation is already in place. The Sino-Myanmar bilateral cooperation mechanism on control and suppression of drug trafficking was negotiated as early as 1990. A six-member Chinese delegation led by Yuan Yong Yuan from Ministry of Public Security came to Myanmar in August 1990 to discuss the drug trafficking issue. The second meeting, which lasted 20 days, was held in Beijing in May 1990 between Myanmar Foreign Minister Ohn Gyaw and Vice Minister of Public Security Gu Lin Fang. An agreement for drug control was then signed between Myanmar, China and the United Nations International Drug Control Programme. Bilateral cooperation on control of drug trafficking developed smoothly but with limited results. There were only a few exchanges of criminals. In 1997, the two countries agreed to set up "Border Representative Agencies" headed by local battalion commanders, "Contact Stations" and "Contact Points" along the border. During the visit of State Councilor Mr. Luo Gan (罗干) to Myanmar, both countries signed the "Agreement on Myanmar-China Border Areas Management and Cooperation" on 25 March 1997. It was aimed "to promote efficiency and enhancing management at border gates, to repair boundary demarcation markers, to ensure the rule of law and order and prevalence of peace and stability, to control arms smuggling and drug trafficking in the border area, to carry out transgression management at the border, to carry out management of territorial affairs, and to establish communication links and liaison offices between authorities of both sides at the border".[103]

To facilitate implementation of the agreement, the two countries held senior official level meetings four times between 1999 and 2002 in Beijing and Yangon. These meeting also discussed matters concerning border passage and tax rates. The fourth meeting on Implementation of Agreement on the Management and Cooperation in China-Myanmar Border Areas, held in Yangon in December 2002, reached wide ranging agreements in many fields such as strengthening the construction and management of border posts. At this meeting it was agreed that the two nations would cooperate in ensuring the rule of law & order in border areas; for allowing the peoples in border areas of both nations are to cross border only with border passports; for both sides to co-operate in fixing tax rates at border entry gates; and that the authorities of both sides would set up a liaison system to arrange occasional meetings. The eighth meeting was held in Yangon in January 2008. Under the Agreement on Myanmar-China Border Areas Management and Cooperation, moreover, both countries signed the "Border Security Cooperation Agreement between the Ministry of Home Affairs of Myanmar and the Ministry of People's Security of China", which became effective as of 17 June 2002.

This agreement was intended to promote joint action against cross-border crimes such as illegal border crossing, gambling, arm smuggling and drug trafficking. During the visit of Myanmar Prime Minister General Khin Nyunt to China in July 2004, the Chinese government raised the issue of border security cooperation between the two countries and measures to speed up the implementation of the agreement. General Khin Nyunt subsequently called a coordination meeting to address these issues.

This was followed by the signing of the Memorandum of Understanding (MoU) on the establishment of the Border Defense Talks Mechanism and the Management of Border Affairs between the Ministry of Defence of the Union of Myanmar and the Ministry of National Defense of the People's Republic of China by General Thura Shwe Mann and General Ge Zhenfeng on 5 December 2004 in Yangon. The MoU, initially valid for five years, was to be renewable automatically every successive five years unless either party requested its termination by serving a written notice on the other party six months prior to the date of expiration. It remains in force at the time of writing. The MoU covered coordinating positions on various cross-border issues and sharing or exchange of information conducive to maintaining law and order in the border areas. This included situation of boundary markers, transnational crimes, terrorist activities, natural disaster or epidemic diseases and advanced information on troop movements and military operations along the border. Both side also agreed to set up "Border Representative Agencies" headed by local battalion commanders, "Contact Stations", and "Contact Points" along the border.[104]

In the second week of January 2005, Myanmar and China agreed to increase cooperation against drug trafficking and the violation of immigration rules along their shared border. The agreement was reached at a meeting of officials from the two countries headed by Myanmar's Deputy Minister for Home Affairs and China's Deputy Minister of Public Security, which took place between 12 and 15 January 2005. This meeting was first of its kind. The agreement included measures to increase intelligence sharing to curb drug trafficking and to work together to standardize regulations on the entry of tourists as well as on border trade.[105] At the meeting, the Chinese side pledged to provide 3 million Yuan to Myanmar for both equipment and technical assistance to strengthen its capacity to combat transnational crimes. The two sides also agreed to establish a 24-hour hot line. The opening of police liaison offices to strengthen bilateral cooperation was also considered. Myanmar and China have already established border liaison offices at the Muse, Lejwe and Chin-shwe-haw crossings with the assistance of UNODC.[106] To date, however, these agreements have yielded only limited success. While

China appears to be disappointed with the Myanmar government for the slow pace of progress in addressing issues that could potentially undermine the stability in the border region, the Myanmar government holds the view that it cannot deal with these problems effectively unless it exercises real power over the ceasefire groups, for which active cooperation on the part of the Chinese authorities is necessary.

BILATERAL MILITARY COOPERATION

One of the most prominent features in the Sino-Myanmar relationship since 1988 has been a closer cooperation between the Tatmadaw and the PLA. The exchange of high level visits between the two armed forces testifies that military relations have become increasingly significant. Since 1989, China has become a major supplier of weapons for Myanmar. Faced with Western sanctions, particularly the arms embargo, Myanmar lost access to traditional weapons suppliers at a time when its military forces were embarking on a large scale modernization programme. It has been estimated that nearly US$4 billion worth of weapons have been supplied by China. These included combat aircraft, warships, main battle tanks, armoured personnel carriers, small arms, anti-aircraft guns, and so on. Moreover, China has supplied trucks of various sizes and capacities. Training packages have accompanied the arms procurement program. In addition to specific training programs for weaponry, China has offered places to Myanmar officers at the PLA's Staff College and Defence College. Arms supply has clearly been one of the Chinese strategies to engage Myanmar.

Lieutenant General Than Shwe's visit to China in October 1989, as the Commander-in-Chief (Army), heralded the beginning of the new era of closer military ties between the two armed forces. This seems to have been the first Myanmar military delegation to visit China since 1978. It consisted of 24 members and lasted altogether 12 days. The delegation was received by State Councilor and Minister of National Defence General Qin Jiwei (秦基伟), the Chief of General Staff General Chi Haotian (迟浩田), and the Deputy Chief of General Staff General Xu Xin (徐信). It was also received by Premier Li Peng. The delegation was provided with a military aircraft and it visited Shijiazhuang of Hebei Province, Nanjing, Shanghai and Guangdong. It also went on study tours of the Defence (Army) Academy, the Nanjing Radio Factory and the Shanghai Naval Base.[107] According to the Myanmar Information Committee, "the Myanmar delegation headed by Commander-in-Chief (Army) Lieutenant General Than Shwe paid a goodwill visit to the People's Republic of China and studied about the People's Liberation

Army with keen interest".[108] During the visit, Premier Li Peng declared that "PRC pays serious consideration to friendship between the two nations and cooperation between the two armed forces". Two months later, in December 1989, Major General Tin Oo, Chief-of-Staff (Army), also went to China leading a military delegation. This delegation proved to be a milestone in the relations between the two countries in general and the two armed forces in particular, signing the purchasing contract for an estimated US$1.2 billion worth of Chinese military hardware, the largest and most important weapons contract ever signed by the Tatmadaw. Soon after the visit, observers began to witness the appearance of Chinese made military aircraft, naval vessels, tanks and military trucks in Myanmar.

Another important, yet unpublicized, Myanmar military delegation, headed by Major General Tin Oo, went to China in November 1994. This delegation was believed to be a follow-up mission to procure more Chinese military hardware from Beijing. The shopping list appeared to include six naval vessels. From 28 April to 3 May 1996, General Zhang Wannian (张万年), Vice-Chairman of the Central Military Commission, paid a friendly visit to Myanmar. He held discussions with Senior General Than Shwe and General Maung Aye. The agenda appears to have included matters relating to the defence policies of both countries and international issues of common concerns. General Zhang's visit was reciprocated by the visit of a high level military delegation led by General Maung Aye to China in October 1996. This delegation was comprised of the Chief of Staff (Army) Lieutenant General Tin Oo, the Commander-in-Chief (Navy) Vice Admiral Tin Aye, the Commander-in-Chief (Air) Lieutenant General Tin Ngwe, the Quarter-master-General Lieutenant General Tin Hla, the Chief of Armed Forces Training Major General Saw Lwin, and the directors of Signals, Ordnance, and Procurement. They visited PLA, PLA Navy, and PLA Air Force bases during their stay in China, which extended from 22 to 31 October.

In May 2000, Lieutenant General Tin Oo led another military delegation to China for further negotiations on the terms of arms purchases. The Myanmar delegation was offered a soft loan for arms procurement. In addition, it apparently received US$1 million worth of weapons as goodwill present from the PLA. It was at this very time, however, the Tatmadaw decided to diversify its procurement patterns. Myanmar subsequently began to show more interest in Russian and Eastern European weaponry. This led to the procurement of Russian MiGs and Bulgarian anti-aircraft missiles.

Lieutenant General Tin Oo died in a helicopter crash on 19 February 2001.[109] Meanwhile, Lieutenant General Thura Shwe Mann was appointed as the Joint Chief of Staff (Army, Navy, and Air Force), a newly created position within the Ministry of Defence. Thura Shwe Mann led a seven-member military delegation to China in December 2002. During his visit to China, which extended from 4 to 12 December, the General called on General Liang Guanglie (梁光烈), Chief of the General Staff of the PLA and a member of the Central Military Commission. The delegation also held talks with the Deputy Chief of the General Staff. Vice Senior General Maung Aye's follow up visit to China in August 2003 took place at the invitation of General Cao Gangchuang (曹刚川), the Vice-Chairman of the Central Military Commission and Minister of Defence. Maung Aye held talks with President Hu Jintao, General Cao Gangchuang, General Guo Boxiong (郭伯雄), and State Councilor Mr. Tang Jiaxuan. Maung Aye and his party visited Beijing, Kunming and Dalian. Subsequent high level military delegations to China included a visit by the Chief of Air Defence, Lieutenant General Soe Win, in July 2004 and a visit by the Commander-in-Chief (Air), Lieutenant General Myat Hein, in April 2005. Vice Senior General Maung Aung made another visit to China in June 2006. He was followed by the Joint Chief of Staff, General Thura Shwe Mann, in January 2007. Other minor Myanmar delegations went to China on goodwill visits and to oversee the delivery of weapons and equipment. These included the visits of Lieutenant General Thein Win and Major General Myint Swe (both Commanders-in-Chief of Air Force at different times) in September 1994 and September 2001 respectively. Chinese military delegations to Myanmar included those led by General He Qizong (何其宗), Deputy Chief of General Staff, in November 1991, by General Li Jiulong (李九龙), Commander of the Chengdu Military Region, in June 1994, by General Chi Haotian, the Minister of Defence, in July 1995, by General Zhang Wannian (张万年), Vice-Chairman of the CMC, in April 1996, by General Fu Quanyou (傅全有), Chief of Staff Headquarters of the PLA, in April 2001, by General Ge Zhenfeng (葛振峰), Deputy Chief of General Staff, in December 2004, and by Lieutenant General Sun Zhiqiang (孙志强), Deputy Chief of the General Logistics Department, in December 2004. It has become customary for either the Deputy Chief of the Chinese General Staff or the Chief of Staff to pay regular visits to Myanmar. Moreover, as a gesture of the high regard in which the Chinese military is held, PLA anniversary celebrations are always honored by the presence of senior members of the SLORC/SPDC. Since early 2000s, such receptions have usually been attended by General Thura Shwe Mann, No. 3 in the military regime.

During his unpublicized visit to China in November 2008, General Thura Shwe Mann held discussions with the Chief of Staff General Chen

TABLE 3.1

Military Delegations Exchanged between Myanmar and China

Sr.	Name	Position	Year
		From Myanmar	
1	General Than Shwe	Deputy Commander-in-Chief; Commander-in-Chief (Army)	October 1989
2	Major General Tin Oo	Chief of Staff (Army)	December 1989
3	Major General Thein Win	Commander-in-Chief (Air Force)	April 1992
4	Lieutenant General Tin Oo	Chief of Staff (Army)	November 1994
5	General Maung Aye	Deputy Commander-in-Chief; Commander-in-Chief (Army)	October 1996
6	Lieutenant General Tin Ngwe	Commander-in-Chief (Air Force)	September 1997
7	Lieutenant General Tin Oo	Chief of Staff (Army)	May 2000
8	Major General Myint Swe	Commander-in-Chief (Air Force)	September 2001
9	Vice Admiral Kyi Min	Commander-in-Chief (Navy)	May 2002
10	Lieutenant General Thura Shwe Mann	Chief of Staff	December 2002
11	Vice Senior General Maung Aye	Deputy Commander-in-Chief; Commander-in-Chief (Army)	August 2003
12	Lieutenant General Soe Win	Chief of Air Defence	July 2004
13	Lieutenant General Myat Hein	Commander-in-Chief (Air Force)	April 2005
14	Vice Senior General Maung Aye	Deputy Commander-in-Chief; Commander-in-Chief (Army)	June 2006
15	General Thura Shwe Mann	Chief of Staff	January 2007
16	General Thura Shwe Mann	Chief of Staff	November 2008
17	Lieutenant General Myat Hein	Commander-in-Chief (Air Force)	November 2009
		From China	
1	Lieutenant General He Qizong	Deputy Chief of General Staff	November 1991
2	General Li Jiulong	Commander, Chengdu Military Region	June 1994
3	General Chi Haotian	Minister of Defence	July 1995
4	General Zhang Wannian	Vice Chairman (CMC)	April 1996
5	Lieutenant General Li Jinai	Political Commissar, GAD	June 1999
6	General Fu Quanyou	Chief of General Staff	April 2001
7	General Wu Quanxu	Deputy Chief of General Staff	December 2003
8	Lieutenant General Sun Zhiqiang	Deputy Chief of General Logistic Dept	December 2004
9	General Ge Zhengfeng	Deputy Chief of General Staff	December 2004
10	General Liang Guangli	Chief of General Staff	October 2006
11	General Liu Dongdong	Political Commissar, Jinan Military Region	August 2007
12	General Zhang Li	Deputy Chief of General Staff	October 2008
13	General Chen Bingde	Chief of General Staff	March 2009
14	General Fan Changlong	Commander, Jinan Military Region	June 2010

Bingde (陈炳德) and the Minister for Defence General Liang Guanglie (梁光烈) on 29 November and 1 December respectively. Two years later, in September 2010, as a member of Myanmar delegation led by Senior General Than Shwe, Thura Shwe Mann once again met with General Chen Bingde in Beijing. During his meeting with Shwe Mann, Chen Bingde "hailed the stable growth of bilateral ties between the two militaries" and called for the "two militaries to work together to carry forward the traditional friendship".[110] Shwe Mann, on his part, pledged his host "pragmatic cooperation between the two militaries".[111]

In terms of weapons procurement from China, the Myanmar armed forces have bought a huge quantity of Chinese military hardwares. Trainees have also been sent to various PLA institutions, including the Defence College, the Staff College and other Service Schools, such as Armor and Artillery and Electronic Warfare. Between 1990 and 1999, 389 army personnel, 98 navy personnel and 455 air force personnel were sent abroad for training.[112] Out of the total of 942 persons, 615 were dispatched to the PRC: 330 from the air force, 79 from the navy and 206 from the army.[113] According to another set of data, between 1990 and 2005, the Tatmadaw sent 665 officers and 249 other ranks to China for 163 different courses. Many PLA-trained officers now occupy influential positions within the Tatmadaw. However, since the early 2000s, the Tatmadaw has sent more and more trainees to Russia.[114] According to one scholar, Russia has trained 4,185 Myanmar military officers in nuclear sciences over the past decade.[115]

Some speculations about the nature of military cooperation between the two armed forces centered around alleged signal intelligence stations along the coastal regions of Myanmar and on Great Coco Island. This has been one of the most intriguing stories concerning Sino-Myanmar military cooperation. For almost 15 years, a steady stream of newspaper stories, scholarly monographs and books have referred *inter alia* to the existence of a large Chinese signals intelligence (SIGINT) station on Great Coco Island, in the Andaman Sea. Both the Myanmar and Chinese governments have consistently denied that any such listening post exists. Indian sources, in contrast, have persistently claimed that there is a Chinese SIGINT post on Coco Island. However, in August and October 2005, the Indian Chief of Naval Staff publicly announced that there is no such base on this island, nor has there ever been. However, port calls of Chinese warships to Myanmar in early May 2001 caused concern among Myanmar watchers.[116] Only in August 2010, did the Chinese Navy make another port call at Yangon's Thilawa Port. On 29 August 2001, two Chinese destroyers from the 5th Escort Task group, "Guanhzhou" and "Caohu", arrived at Thilawa Port.

Meanwhile, Myanmar has established closer military contacts with the Indian Armed Forces. General Ved Prakash Malik visited Myanmar twice in January and July 2000. To reciprocate his first visit, in January 2000, General Maung Aye, the Commander-in-Chief (Army), made a day trip to Shillong, the capital of Meghalaya state in north-eastern India. In November, Maung Aye journeyed to New Delhi, not as the Commander-in-Chief (Army) but as the Vice Chairman of the SLORC. General J.J. Singh and General Deepak Kapoor, the Chiefs of Army Staff, also visited Myanmar in November 2005 and October 2009 respectively. Other senior Indian Army officers also came to Myanmar. On Myanmar side, General Thura Shwe Mann, the Chief of Staff, travelled to New Delhi in December 2006. Myanmar's Air Force Chief Lieutenant General Myat Hein's visit to India in September 2003 was reciprocated by his counterpart Air Chief Marshal S. Krishnaswamy's in November 2004. The Indian navy is an active player in the defence cooperation between the two countries. The Indian warships made port calls in Myanmar in December 2002, in September 2003 and in May, August and December 2005. During some of these port calls, joint naval maneuver with Myanmar warships were conducted on their way back to the Indian Waters. Myanmar navy also participated in India-led MILAN multinational joint naval exercises in 2003, 2006 and 2010. Admiral Madhvenndra Singh, the Indian Naval Chief, visited Yangon in September 2003. His visit was followed by Admiral Arun Prakash in November 2005 and January 2006 and Admiral Sureesh Mehta in May 2007. To reciprocate these visits, Vice Admiral Soe Thein travelled to India in March 2005 and April 2007, followed by Vice Admiral Nyan Tun in February 2010. During his visit to Myanmar in January 2006, Admiral Prakash presented the Myanmar Navy with a US$3 million worth Shiphandling Simulator. It was also reported in some media that the admiral had also discussed with his counterpart on the transfer of two BN-2 Defender Maritime Surveillance Aircraft; the actual transfer appeared to take place in August 2006. During his meeting with Admiral Nirmal Verma, the Indian Chief of Naval Staff, on 22 February 2010, Vice Admiral Nyan Tun reportedly requested the Indian Navy for inshore and offshore patrol boats — running into two digit figures — for the Myanmar Navy.

For the army, the Myanmar government purchased nearly 190 Type 69-II Main Battle Tanks, over 100 Type 63 Light Tanks, a dozen of Type 59D Main Battle Tanks, about 250 Type 85 Armoured Personnel Carriers, over 50 Type 90 Armoured Personnel Carriers, a large quantity of man-portable anti-aircraft missiles, and more than 100 artillery pieces of various types and calibers. In addition, the Myanmar army benefited from Chinese transfers of technology and technical assistance in building a domestic arms industry.

For military transport, too, the Myanmar army bought various vehicles from China.

Under the terms of the arms deal package negotiated in 1989, the Myanmar navy was to receive a number of patrol craft from China. In 1991, the navy placed an order of ten 59-metre *Hainan*-class Type 037 Sub-chasers from the PRC. The first batch of six craft arrived Yangon in January 1991 and the second batch of four in May 1993 (UMS 441 to 450).[117] In March 1994, the Myanmar navy signed a procurement contract with the PRC for a delivery of six 63-metre *Houxin*-class (1G Missile Escort) Fast Attack Crafts-Missile (UMS 471 to 476).[118] The first two units were delivered in November 1995 and the rest arrived in 1996 and 1997. These missile escorts were armed with Chinese made YJ-1 (C-801) missiles. Moreover, with technical assistance and weaponry from the PRC, the Myanmar navy also locally built six 50-metre long Fast Patrol Crafts — Gun (UMS 551–556) between 1995 and 2006.[119] It also built two corvettes with the assistance of the PRC in its Naval Dockyard.[120] Since 1995, according to some observers, the Myanmar navy has built about twenty 50-metre Fast Attack Crafts, three 77-metre corvettes [UMS 771–773] and one 108-metre frigate [F-11 Aung Zeya]; three more frigates are reported to be under construction. While the Myanmar navy has continued to build warships in its own dockyard, it begins to acquire technical assistance from the Indian navy. It is believed among observers that recently commissioned warships are fitted with Indian-supplied radars, weapon systems, and sonars. In May 2008, the Myanmar navy had suffered severe damages and lost several warships during the Cyclone Nargis. The navy also needs to replace its aging warships. While the Myanmar Navy is interested in procuring inshore and offshore patrol crafts from the Indian navy, it has negotiated the purchase of two Type 053H frigates, reconditioned and fitted with newer missile complexes, from the PLA Navy in mid 2010.

Since 1990, according to some observers, the Myanmar air force has purchased 146 aircraft of various types from China, including F-7 IIK interceptors, FT-7K trainers, A-5 ground attack aircraft, FT-6M trainers, K-8 trainers and Y-8 transport aircraft. In December 1990, the air force took the first delivery of 10 *Chengdu* F-7IIK fighters and two GAIC FT-7 twin-seat trainers. In May 1993, it received another batch of 12 F-7IIK fighters. According to various sources, further deliveries of F-7IIK squadrons were made in 1995, 1998 and 1999. It was estimated by some knowledgeable observers that, between 1990 and 2000, the Myanmar air force had received altogether 58 F-7IIK fighters from the PRC. It was also estimated that the Myanmar air force received 36 A-5C aircraft from the PRC between 1992 and 2000. In addition, the air force has bought a number of air-to-air missiles from China.

In terms of trainers, the air force received four FT-7 twin seat aircraft, two FT-6 trainers and 30 PT-6 trainers from the PRC during the 1990s. In 1998 and 1999, it was reported that the air force bought 12 K-8 Karakorum jet trainers from the PRC.[121] It was also reported that the air force bought 4 SAC Y-8s from China to strengthen the existing fleet of transport aircraft.

However, the Tatmadaw was not happy with Chinese weapons because of their poor quality. In addition, there were some problems with spare parts and other follow-up services. For example, Y-8 aircraft were grounded for about a year due to the lack of spare parts. Anti-Aircraft missile simulators were faulty. Even for technical training the PLA did not provide full courses; thus pilots had to learn supersonic flying by themselves only when they were back to Myanmar. As noted earlier, for both political reasons and practical purposes, the Tatmadaw began to procure more advanced Russian weapons and sent more trainees to Russia in the early 2000s. For example, out of the total of 198 aircraft procured by the Myanmar air force between 1990 and 2000, 74 per cent or 146 aircraft were from China. However, among 154 aircraft purchased by the air force in the period between 2000 and 2010, only 50 K-8 Karakorum jet trainers, acquired in late 2009, were from China; the rest were from Russia. The Myanmar air force purchased 12 MiG-29B combat aircraft in 2001, another 20 more MiG-29D and 10 Mil Mi-24/35 helicopter gunships in 2009 and 50 more Mil Mi-24/35 and 12 Mil Mi-2 armed transport helicopters in 2010 from Russia. The defence contact between Myanmar and China has remained mostly at the level of exchanges of visits between the two armed forces and training facilities for Myanmar officers.

SINO-MYANMAR ECONOMIC RELATIONS

Another important feature of the Sino-Myanmar relationship since 1988 has been the growing bilateral cooperation in the areas of trade, aid or development assistance, and investment. Since the coming of the SLORC to power on 18 September 1998 in Myanmar China has become one of the principal trading partners and most important sources of development assistance for Myanmar. The bilateral trade, especially the border trade, is also important in China's policy of developing western provinces, Yunnan Province in particular, since Myanmar is geographically the "back door" of China. In this regard, sub-state actor played an increasingly important role in bilateral relations. Moreover, Myanmar can also serve a central link in the transit trade between China and other South and Southeast Asian countries. A hallmark of Chinese investment in Myanmar, though the total amount remains small, is its heavy concentration in a few strategic sectors.

Sino-Myanmar bilateral trade has been growing steadily since 1988. Towards the end of 1988, the Myanmar government liberalized its trade policy and lifted the restrictions on private sector trading. This greatly increased the volume of trade. In addition, with the introduction of market economy, which has stimulated the role of the private sector in the national economy, Chinese made machinery and parts have made inroads into the Myanmar markets. Since then China has become a major supplier of consumer and capital goods to Myanmar. According to Chinese statistics, the total value of bilateral trade in 1989 was just US$313.72 million: China enjoyed a trade surplus of US$61.60 million. By 1995, bilateral trade reached a total value of US$767.40 million and the Chinese surplus had risen to

TABLE 3.2
Myanmar's Trade with China
(US$ million)

Year	Export	Import	Value	Balance
1988	137.10	133.61	270.71	+3.49
1989	126.06	187.66	313.72	−61.60
1990	104.08	223.54	327.62	−119.46
1991	105.92	286.17	392.09	−180.25
1992	131.27	259.04	390.31	−127.77
1993	164.83	324.70	489.53	−159.87
1994	143.34	369.11	512.45	−225.77
1995	149.55	617.85	767.40	−468.30
1996	137.41	521.12	658.53	−383.71
1997	73.41	570.09	643.53	−496.68
1998	62.04	518.86	580.90	−456.82
1999	101.68	406.53	508.21	−304.85
2000	124.82	496.44	621.26	−371.62
2001	134.19	497.35	631.54	−363.16
2002	136.89	724.75	861.64	−587.86
2003	169.52	910.22	1079.74	−740.40
2004	206.94	938.44	1145.38	−731.50
2005	274.40	934.85	1209.25	−660.45
2006	252.65	1207.42	1460.07	−954.77
2007	378.14	1699.70	2077.84	−1321.56
2008	647.55	1977.77	2625.32	−1330.22
2009	646.13	2253.99	2900.12	−1607.86
2010*	675.xx	2752.xx	3427.xx	−2077.xx

Source: China Statistical Yearbook (Various Years); *Bi-Weekly Eleven (3:41, 7 January 2011)

US$468.30 million. In 2008, China reported that the total value of bilateral trade had reached US$2,625.32 million and that the Chinese surplus stood at US$1,330.22 million. Between 1989 and 2008, China accumulated a total of US$10,046.62 million surplus in trade with Myanmar. In 2009 and 2010, China further accumulated a trade surplus of US$3,684 million in Sino-Myanmar bilateral trade. Some observers have speculated that this trade surplus could flow back into Myanmar in the form of investments in property and other assets or through the illegal drug trade.

While Myanmar's exports to China increased about five times, during this period, from US$126.06 million in 1989 to US$647.55 million in 2008, its imports from China grew over ten fold, from US$187.66 million in 1989 to US$1,977.77 million in 2008. The bilateral trade figures also showed a chronic trade deficit on the part of Myanmar.

It is generally agreed among Myanmar scholars that the Myanmar trade statistics are notoriously unreliable. The figures are, indeed, completely distorted. Chinese data is by no means accurate concerning Sino-Myanmar trade. It is nevertheless more reliable than that of Myanmar. With regard to Sino-Myanmar trade, Myanmar data shows a different picture. Generally, Myanmar trade data is undervalued. This is not only due to different methods of calculation, but also, more importantly, to widespread corruption among trade and customs offices as well as among border security authorities.[122] Myanmar data show smaller deficits or even a surplus.

Perhaps the most significant component of bilateral trade is the border trade. During his trip to China in 1984, President San Yu made a stop over in Yunnan and invited Yunnan authorities to visit Myanmar. President San Yu noted that Kunming was much closer to Yangon than Beijing and believed that it was important to nurture friendly relations between Myanmar and Yunnan authorities. As a result, a delegation led by the Yunnan Governor paid a visit to Yangon in May 1986. During the visit, the Yunnan Governor discussed the issue of border trade with the Myanmar Deputy Minister for Trade. This initiative was followed up by the Chinese authorities and, in August 1986, the *Charge d'Affairs* at interim from the Chinese Embassy in Yangon called on the Deputy Minister for Trade for further discussions. On the Myanmar side, the issue was submitted for further discussions at the cabinet meeting held on 5 January 1987. In March 1987, the Chinese government invited Myanmar's Minister for Trade to Beijing for negotiations on the border trade. The ministerial delegation left for Beijing on 4 April and returned 12 days later. During the trip, the delegation reached a 15-point agreement on border trade with the Chinese authorities. Meanwhile the Myanmar government conducted a preliminary survey. As a result of the survey, the

TABLE 3.3
Sino-Myanmar Trade
Kyat in Million

Year (Apr–Mar)	Export	Import	Value	Balance
1988–89	942.56	929.18	1771.74	+13.38
1989–90	800.85	517.97	1318.82	+282.88
1990–91	396.29	1205.39	1601.68	−809.10
1991–92	438.34	894.97	1333.31	−456.63
1992–93	338.60	945.96	1284.56	−607.36
1993–94	209.82	1261.43	1471.25	−1051.61
1994–95	277.48	1019.38	1296.86	−741.90
1995–96	195.14	1433.82	1628.96	−1238.68
1996–97	336.14	1116.29	1452.43	−780.15
1997–98	836.98	1524.42	2061.40	−687.44
1998–99	570.62	1744.34	2314.96	−1173.72
1999–00	846.99	1568.17	2415.16	−721.18
2000–01	1143.00	1855.20	2998.20	−712.2
2001–02	1545.17	2068.14	3613.31	−522.97
2002–03	3070.48	2349.99	5420.47	+720.49
2003–04	1343.24	2816.74	4159.98	−1473.50
2004–05	1658.80	2818.95	4477.75	−1160.15
2005–06	2125.19	2716.01	4841.20	−590.82
2006–07	3530.37	4185.75	7716.12	−655.38
2007–08	3832.52	5472.54	9305.06	−1640.02
2008–09	3352.27	6578.14	9930.41	−3225.87

Source: Statistical Yearbook of Myanmar

Myanmar government found out that average annual exports from Myanmar through the border were valued at K341.42 million while imports totaled K799.92 million, in addition to illegal exports of about K458 million. In total, therefore, according the survey, Myanmar's annual export was K799.42 million. The result of survey was reported at the Burma Socialist Programme Party's 84th CEC (Central Executive Committee) meeting held on 11 July 1988. Subsequently, the CEC subsequently authorized border trading.

The border trading agreement concluded was in line with the Myanmar-China Trade Agreement signed in Beijing on 19 November 1970. To implement the border trading agreement, a Chinese delegation led by the then Deputy Governor of Yunnan Province came to Yangon in July 1988. After the resumption of negotiations, the Agreement for Sale and Purchase of Goods between Myanma Export Import Corporation (MEIC) and Yunnan Provincial

Import Export Corporation (YPIEC) was finally signed on 5 August 1988. In addition to a Banking Arrangement between Bank of China (Kunming Branch) and the Myanma Foreign Trade Bank (MFTB) was concluded on the same day. According to the plan outlined in the agreement, border trading offices were to be opened in Lashio and Muse in August 1988 and to begin trading on 1 October 1988. However, due to the subsequent political upheavals in Myanmar the implementation of this border trade agreement was temporarily suspended. Finally, on 2 December 1988, the MEIC opened border trade offices in Muse, Kyukok, Namkham, Lashio and Kunlone.

In the initial stage, 25 per cent of the export earnings from cooperative societies and 40 per cent of the export earnings from private firms were required to import items prescribed by the MEIC. This percentage was changed to 20 per cent and 30 per cent respectively as of 15 June 1989. Between December 1988 and July 1989, the MEIC imported K214.409 million worth of commodities under this arrangement. In August 1989, the Myanmar government stopped border trading of private firms and cooperative societies. Only the MEIC and YPIEC were permitted to continue border trading, on a government-to-government basis. Thus, in the 1989–1990 fiscal year, the MEIC exported K17.020 million worth of goods and imported K13.128 million. However, private firms and cooperative societies were allowed to trade all goods except for 16 items restricted under state monopoly, by following the normal procedure at the customs department.[123] A new system was introduced on 1 October 1991 to supplement the existing one. Under the new system, border trading was carried out by both normal trade procedures and border trade procedures. Border trading posts were opened in Muse-105 Mile, Laizar, Lweje and Chinshwehaw. According to Myanmar statistics, the border trade at these centres occupies over 60 per cent of Myanmar's total border trade and approximately 50 per cent of overall Sino-Myanmar trade. To facilitate the Sino-Myanmar border trade, Foreign Minister Ohn Gyaw, during his visit to China in May 1991, negotiated construction of two bridges across the Shweli River on the Sino-Myanmar border, linking Muse, Wantin and Ruili. The first bridge was completed and opened in October 1992. It later became known as the "Gun Bridge" as Chinese military equipment was transported across it. The construction of the second bridge, linking Wantin and Kyukok, began in 1992. This bridge was opened on 30 May 1993.

Chinese statistics shows a slightly different picture. We can assume that Yunnan's trade with Myanmar has basically centered around the border trade. Although the value of trade that appears in Chinese Statistics is much higher than that presented in the Myanmar figures, the percentage of Yunnan's trade with Myanmar is about the same, that is about 50 per cent of overall

TABLE 3.4
Myanmar's Border Trade with China
(US$ million)

Year (Apr–Mar)	Export	Import	Value	Balance	TBT	Percentage
1991–92	52.52	54.47	106.99	–1.95	139.27	76.82
1992–93	58.50	131.24	189.74	–72.74	257.93	73.56
1993–94	27.04	90.23	117.27	–63.19	248.04	47.28
1994–95	29.96	65.08	95.04	–35.12	231.87	40.99
1995–96	22.03	229.31	251.34	–207.28	335.95	74.81
1996–97	29.82	158.68	188.50	–128.86	357.13	52.78
1997–98	86.44	59.37	145.81	–27.07	257.06	56.72
1998–99	94.88	99.41	194.29	–4.53	300.27	64.71
1999–00	96.39	94.90	191.29	+1.49	344.39	55.54
2000–01	124.38	100.11	224.48	+24.28	411.74	54.52
2001–02	133.12	115.85	248.96	+17.27	505.83	49.22
2002–03	158.17	132.57	290.74	+25.60	460.57	63.13
2003–04	177.26	163.84	341.10	+83.42	531.80	64.14
2004–05	246.46	176.37	422.83	+70.09	687.88	61.47
2005–06	315.02	203.63	518.66	+111.39	716.73	72.36
2006–07	453.12	296.64	749.76	+156.48	1092.61	68.62
2007–08	555.48	421.95	977.43	+133.53	1329.53	73.52
2008–09	490.85	495.75	986.60	–4.9	1348.48	73.16
2009–2010	500.16	576.65	1076.81	–76.49	1383.68	77.82

Source: Ministry of Commerce (Myanmar)   TBT (Total Border Trade)

Sino-Myanmar trade. The Myanmar-Yunnan border trade accounts for about 55 per cent of the total value of the overall Sino-Myanmar trade. Over 80 per cent of Myanmar's exports to China and about 40 per cent of Myanmar's imports from China are accounted for by the border trade. Myanmar is the largest trading partner for Yunnan, followed by Hong Kong, Vietnam and Japan in term of export destinations and Hong Kong, Germany and Canada in term of origin of imports.

While Myanmar exports raw materials, agricultural produces, livestock, fishery products, and forest products to China, China has flooded the Myanmar market with its cheap finished products ranging from foodstuffs to electronics. The trade imbalance will continue to grow. According to customs data, the top Myanmar export items to China are beans and pulses, timber, textiles and garments, gems and jewelry, prawns, fish and rubber. In 2000 and 2001, exports of timber stood at the top of the list but beans and pulses have taken

TABLE 3.5
Sino-Myanmar Bilateral Trade (1996–2005)
(US$ million)

Year (Apr–Mar)	Export	Import	Volume	Balance	Border	Percentage
1996–97	56.87	188.87	245.74	−132.00	188.50	76.71
1997–98	134.51	244.98	379.49	−110.47	145.81	38.42
1998–99	91.37	279.31	370.68	−187.94	194.29	52.41
1999–00	135.68	251.20	386.88	−115.52	191.29	49.44
2000–01	175.44	285.12	460.56	−158.33	224.48	48.74
2001–02	229.40	307.91	537.31	−78.51	248.96	46.33
2002–03	472.23	362.89	835.12	+109.34	290.74	34.81
2003–04	224.87	471.23	696.10	−246.36	341.10	49.00
2004–05	290.90	489.65	780.55	−198.75	422.83	54.17
2005–06	367.91	465.18	833.09	−97.28	518.66	62.26
2006–07	972.84	754.35	1727.19	+218.49	749.76	43.41
2007–08	1345.57	1016.70	2362.27	+328.87	977.43	41.38
2008–09	1130.42	1240.62	2371.04	−110.20	986.60	41.61
2009–2010	1582.68	1268.77	2851.45	+313.91	1076.81	37.76

Source: Directorate of Trade (Myanmar)

this position since 2004. Top import items from China since 2000 have been machines and machinery equipment, garment accessories, construction materials, electronic and electrical product, and consumer goods. Yet it is important to remember that serious illegal logging and export of timber to China has been going on at various points on the Sino-Myanmar border. The extent and value of this trade cannot be properly calculated. Nevertheless, Chinese customs data revealed that timber accounted for 69 per cent of all China's import from Myanmar in 2004 and 71 per cent in 2005. Nearly 90 per cent of this timber is imported via Yunnan province. Thus, timber remains at the top of China's import list, contrary to the Myanmar data. In terms of imports, there has been a shift away from heavy dependence on consumer goods in 1990s to capital and intermediate goods in years since 2000.[124] However, since capital and intermediate goods are mostly for import-substitution industries, this trend cannot have had a major immediate impact on Myanmar's export revenues.

Sino-Myanmar bilateral trade accounts for about 10 per cent of Myanmar's total trade according to Myanmar statistics. Myanmar's imports from China account for nearly 25 per cent of its total imports while exports account for just 10 per cent of Myanmar's total exports. In the 2005–06 fiscal year, Myanmar's imports from China were valued at US$468 million, out of a total

TABLE 3.6

Yunnan's Share of China's Trade with Myanmar

(US$ million)

Year	Export			Import			Value		
	Yunnan	China	%	Yunnan	China	%	Yunnan	China	%
1999	245.99	406.53	60.51	53.53	101.68	52.65	299.52	508.21	58.94
2000	293.01	496.44	59.02	69.93	124.82	56.02	362.94	621.26	58.42
2001	251.51	497.35	50.57	97.22	134.19	70.21	348.73	631.54	55.22
2002	296.08	724.75	40.85	110.70	136.89	80.87	406.78	861.64	47.21
2003	356.83	910.22	39.20	135.96	169.52	80.20	492.79	1079.74	45.64
2004	386.61	938.44	41.20	164.71	206.94	79.59	551.32	1145.38	48.13
2005	410.63	934.85	43.92	221.02	274.40	80.55	631.65	1209.25	52.23
2006	521.13	1207.42	43.16	170.95	252.65	67.66	692.08	1460.07	47.40
2007	640.68	1699.70	37.69	232.89	378.14	61.59	873.57	2077.84	42.04
2008	727.69	1977.77	36.79	465.10	647.55	71.82	1192.79	2625.32	45.43

Sources: China Statistical Yearbook; Yunnan Yearbook

of US$1.95 billion worth of goods imported. Singapore stands at the top of the list with US$558 million worth of goods being imported from that country to Myanmar. However, the share of Myanmar's exports to China in its overall export performance has declined in recent years due to more exports of gas to Thailand. This trend might be reversed once Myanmar begins to export gas to China in near future. At present, China occupies the position of Myanmar's second largest trading partner after Thailand.

Naypyitaw has also facilitated the China's transit trade with Thailand via Myanmar: Xishuangbanna to Maesai via Tachileik. The value of this trade was about US$75 million a year in the early 2000s. The Myanmar government has allowed the crossing of 20 convoys per day. Chinese authorities have tried to boost this trade three to four times the present value.[125]

Chinese investment in Myanmar is driven by both geopolitical and economic factors. Official Chinese FDI (Foreign Direct Investment) in Myanmar is rather small. Nevertheless, there are a large number of hidden individual Chinese investments and business ventures, most of which are registered in the names of ethnic Chinese relatives who hold Myanmar citizenship. Many businesses, both large and small, in almost all major cities in Myanmar, have some form of Chinese investment. According to official FDI figures, as of 30 November 2005, China had invested only US$194.221 million in 26 projects in Myanmar. They were mostly in some strategic sectors like energy and mining. By the end of 2009, China's

TABLE 3.7

Myanmar's Share in Yunnan Trade

(US$ million)

Year	Export			Import			Value		
	Yunnan	Myan	%	Yunnan	Myan	%	Yunnan	Myan	%
1999	1034.43	245.99	23.78	625.24	53.53	8.56	1659.67	299.52	18.05
2000	1175.16	293.01	24.93	637.67	69.93	10.97	1812.83	362.94	20.02
2001	1244.12	251.51	20.22	744.94	97.22	13.05	1989.06	348.73	17.53
2002	1429.65	296.08	20.71	796.70	110.70	13.89	2226.35	406.78	18.27
2003	1676.58	356.83	21.28	991.09	135.96	13.72	2667.67	492.79	18.47
2004	2238.82	386.61	17.27	1508.95	164.71	10.92	3747.77	551.32	14.71
2005	2641.58	410.63	15.54	2096.64	221.02	10.54	4738.22	631.65	13.33
2006	3391.43	521.13	15.37	2840.31	170.95	6.02	6231.74	692.08	11.11
2007	4736.12	640.68	13.53	4043.63	232.89	5.76	8779.75	873.57	9.95
2008	4986.96	727.69	15.59	4612.40	465.10	10.08	9599.36	1192.79	12.43

Sources: China Statistical Yearbook; Yunnan Yearbook

official investments in Myanmar reached US$1,347.437 million, involving a total of 29 projects. In 2006 China invested US$281.22 million in power generation. In July 2008, China invested US$855.996 million in the mining sector and, again in December 2009, another US$15 million in the same sector. Chinese firms have invested heavily in nickel and copper mines. By the end of July 2010, according to the Myanmar government figures, China has invested US$6,415.058 million in 32 projects, ranking second among the foreign investors.

Another investment area of interest to China is the energy sector, especially oil and gas. By February 2007, three China-based companies had signed contracts for oil and gas exploration in 14 blocks. As noted earlier, in November 2008, Myanmar and China agreed to construct a US$1.5 billion crude oil pipeline and a US$1.04 billion natural gas pipeline. These agreements were finalized in March 2009 and in June 2009. The pipelines are to be constructed from Kyaukphyu to Kunming.[126] Kyaukphyu port is also to be used as a deep water seaport. These projects are part of the so-called Kyaukphyu-Kunming Corridor. In connection with the gas pipeline, Petro China will buy 6.5 trillion cubic feet of Myanmar's natural gas for over a period of 30 years starting from 2009.[127] The gas pipeline will initially supply 600 million cubic feet of gas a day and this will eventually increase to 1 billion cubic feet a day. The oil pipeline will have an annual capacity of 20 million metric tons. The oil for the pipeline will be mainly imported from the Middle East and

TABLE 3.8
Yunnan's Trade with Mainland Southeast Asia
(US$ million)

Year	Export				Import			
	Myanmar	Vietnam	Thailand	Laos	Myanmar	Vietnam	Thailand	Laos
1999	245.99	62.52	18.56	10.22	53.53	9.69	5.93	5.39
2000	293.01	92.64	23.56	13.36	69.93	7.66	8.02	5.90
2001	251.51	142.32	36.39	14.08	97.22	18.67	6.88	4.25
2002	296.08	133.71	37.66	10.53	110.70	28.95	5.94	6.02
2003	356.83	192.99	77.11	14.58	135.96	28.15	10.18	6.53
2004	386.61	286.82	110.32	26.63	164.71	51.76	19.05	7.13
2005	410.63	264.04	129.52	28.77	221.02	54.70	14.94	13.39
2006	521.13	374.63	109.19	34.69	170.95	132.80	21.05	34.63
2007	640.68	777.73	156.80	35.91	232.89	193.94	63.41	47.48
2008	727.69	493.31	228.88	57.12	465.10	151.60	20.87	53.34

Source: Yunnan Yearbook

Africa. The gas pipeline may speed up efforts by China to tap gas reserves in Myanmar to meet strong domestic demand, while the oil pipeline will boost security for China's oil imports from the Middle East and Africa by reducing the country's exclusive reliance on the Malacca Straits.[128] The inauguration ceremony marking the start of construction was held on 31 October 2009 on Maday Island, off Kyaukphyu. China also plans to build a refinery near Kunming to process crude oil piped from Myanmar.

More Chinese companies were expected to invest in Myanmar. In recent years, some Chinese companies began to invest in power generation plants in Myanmar. For example, Sinohydro will be a major investor as well as a

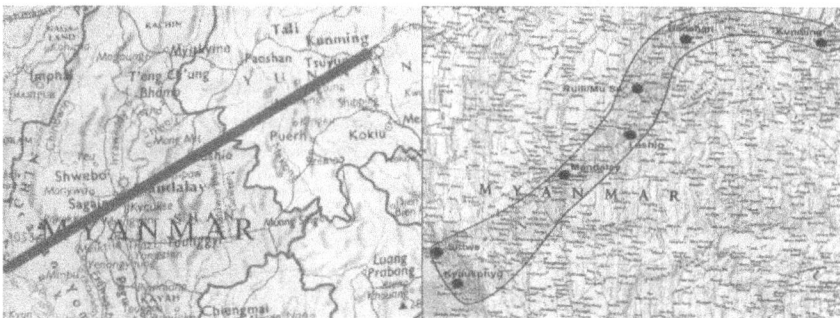

Source: Ministry of Construction

TABLE 3.9

The Share of Sino-Myanmar Trade in Myanmar's Overall Trade

(US$ million)

Year	Sino-Myanmar Trade				Myanmar's Overall Trade			
	Export	Import	Value	Balance	Export	Import	Value	Balance
2000–01	111.79	270.62	382.41	−158.83	1595.88	2291.24	3887.12	−695.36
2001–02	229.40	307.90	537.31	−78.51	2439.33	2631.95	5071.28	−192.62
2002–03	472.23	362.89	835.12	+109.34	3062.87	2299.64	5362.51	+763.23
2003–04	224.87	471.23	696.10	−246.36	2356.82	2239.97	4596.79	+116.85
2004–05	290.90	489.65	780.55	−198.75	2927.83	1973.28	4901.11	+954.55
2005–06	367.91	465.18	833.09	−97.28	3558.03	1984.41	5542.44	+1573.62
2006–07	972.84	754.35	1727.19	+218.49	5232.68	2936.73	8169.41	+2295.95
2007–08	1345.57	1016.70	2362.27	+328.87	6401.71	3353.42	9755.13	+3048.29
2008–09	1130.42	1240.62	2371.04	−110.20	6778.85	4543.45	11322.30	+2235.40
2009–10	1582.68	1268.77	2851.45	+313.91	7586.95	4181.40	11768.35	+3402.55

Source: Directorate of Trade (Myanmar)

major contractor for the design, procurement and implementation works of the Hutgyi project.[129] On 31 December 2006, the Myanmar Ministry of Electric Power No (1) and China's Yunnan United Power Development signed an MoU to build a hydroelectric power plant on the Shweli River on the Build-Operate-Transfer (BOT) basis. This is China's first hydropower BOT project in a neighbouring country and the first in Myanmar. The company will run the power station for 40 years after its completion, and then transfer it to the Myanmar government. The plant will have an installed capacity of 600 megawatts but the actual power supply will be 174.8 megawatts and the annual power output is 4,022 GWh.[130] During Vice Senior General Maung Aye's visit to China in June 2009, the Myanmar government singed an MoU with the China Power Investment Corporation for the Development, Operation and Transfer of the Hydropower Projects, in Maykha, Malikha and Upstream of Ayeyawady-Myitsone River Basins, with a combined capacity of 5.6 gigawatts. Moreover, according to China's State Asset Supervision and Administration Commission, a consortium of three Chinese firms will invest in a US$9 billion worth hydroelectric project on the Thanlwin River that could generate 7.1 gigawatts.

Like any other country, China uses development assistance as an instrument to win friends and influence people. Chinese development assistance usually comes in the forms of grants, interest free loans, concessional loans and debt relief. Since 1988, international donors have halted all developmental assistance to Myanmar. The Western Powers, led by the United States, have also imposed economic sanctions on Myanmar. Against this background, China has become a major source of development assistance. Between 1966 and 2000, Myanmar received loans equivalent to US$138.7 million from China.[131] Before 1988, the Chinese government loaned for the construction of the Yangon-Thanlyin Rail cum Road Bridge, the construction of the Hmawbi rubber ball factory, a tyre factory, the Belin sugar mill, the Shwedaung textile mill, the Meikhtila textile mill, and the Thuwana national indoor stadium.

Major development assistance from China followed in the wake of the state visit of Senior General Than Shwe to Beijing in January 1996. Although the amount of Chinese development assistance is not really great, it is significant for the Myanmar government. According to the Myanmar government, between 1989 and 2010, the PRC government provided over RMB46.67 billion and US$474.08 million in various forms of loans. There was also an agreement on debt relief to the extent of RMB15 million and RMB520 million in grant aid. Under the grant aid, the Myanmar government received 85 tractors in 1996; an electric generator manufacturing plant, railway materials, medical equipments for the traditional medicine department, electrical equipments

TABLE 3.10
Chinese Development Assistance to Myanmar
US$/RMB in million

No.	Year	Grant	Loan	Debt Relief
1	1989	—	RMB 50	
2	1990	—	—	
3	1991	—	RMB 50	
4	1992	—	—	
5	1993	—	RMB 50	
6	1994	—	—	
7	1995	—	—	
8	1996	RMB 10	RMB 150	
9	1997	—	RMB 100	RMB 5*
10	1998	—	—	
11	1999	—	RMB 50	
12	2000	—	RMB 50	
13	2001	RMB 80	RMB 150	
14	2002	RMB 30		
15	2003	RMB 50	RMB 300; US$200	RMB 5**
16	2004	RMB 50	RMB 200	RMB 5***
17	2005	RMB 130	RMB 1000; US$74.08	
18	2006	RMB 70	RMB 170; US$200	
19	2007	RMB 85	RMB 350	
20	2008	—	—	
21	2009	—	RMB 14000	
22	2010	—	RMB 30000	

(*) for the renovation of the National Theater in Yangon; (**) for the purchase of sports materials; (***) for crop substitution in drug eradication program
Source: the Author's compilation from various government sources

and spare parts for three hydroelectric power plant projects, and scholarships for aerospace and maritime universities in 2001; a technical training school in Mandalay in 2002; equipments for three small hydroelectric power plants and a combine harvester plant in 2003; several number of Audi cars for office use, scholarships for trainees, and the expenditure for drafting of master plans for the Lashio-Muse railway, an industrial zone and a convention center in 2004; and scholarships for PhD candidates, a biotech center, twenty water pumps, a mobile X-ray machine for Muse border trading zone and a rice mill in 2006. The grant also included a convention center in Naypyitaw, completed in 2010, with the price tag of RMB210 million for building and an extra RMB5 million for security equipments.

The Chinese government loaned RMB50 million for the completion of Yangon-Thanlyin Rail cum Road Bridge in 1989, RMB50 million for installation of satellite communication earth station and satellite TV ground station, the building of the a steam power station in Mawlamyaing, and the renovation and procurement of turbine generator for Sittaung paper mill in 1991, RMB300 million for an agricultural machinery plant in 1993, 1996 and 1997, RMB116 million for a hand-tractor and harvester plant in 1999, 2000 and 2001, RMB100 million for extension and replacement of auto-telephone exchange switches in 2001, RMB84 million for the procurement of railway tracks in 2001 and 2003, RMB250 million for telecommunication equipments in 2003, US$200 million for Yeywa hydro-electric power plant in 2003, RMB200 million for 10 projects (procurement of water pumps, renovation of various factories, and construction of three hydroelectric power plants) in 2004, US$74.08 million and RMB1,000 million for a chemical fertilizer plant in 2005, US$200 million for 11 projects (new factories, construction of national power grid, procurement of a drilling rig, 20 locomotives and 200 miles of railway tracks, and a hydroelectric power plant) in 2006, RMB170 million for the extension of national power grid in 2006, and RMB300 million for telecommunication equipments in 2007. Latest loans from China are for the procurement of passenger aircrafts, construction of hydroelectric power plants, highways and, more importantly, Naypyitaw-Yangon high-speed railway and train, and Information Technology infrastructure, among others.

Moreover, the Chinese government also helped the Myanmar government secure private financial loans from Chinese banks and business firms. China has provided financial and technical assistance for industrial and infrastructural developments in Myanmar. Without official data from both sides, it is difficult to distinguish genuine development assistance from commercially-based operations. Most development projects have been tied to Chinese state-owned economic enterprises (SEE). Although the Chinese government and the Chinese SEEs have charged either no or very low interest on commercial loans and suppliers' credits, according to some observers, they have in reality added the cost to the plants or parts they export to Myanmar. Moreover, some observers believe that the machines themselves are outdated and of poor quality. There are naturally reports about bribery and corruption during the loan negotiation process. Nevertheless, low priced machinery, equipment and services, long-term and low-interest loans, and export credits by Chinese public financial institutions have made it possible for Chinese firms possible to play an important role in Myanmar's economy. It has also helped the Myanmar government achieve a massive expansion of SEEs. Through bilateral development assistance, by the end of 2007, China helped the Myanmar government build eight sugar mills [US$158 million], 20 hydroelectric power plants [US$269 million], 13 new factories under the Ministry of Industry-1 [US$198 million], and 12 new plants under the Ministry of Industry-2 [US$137 million]. In addition, China also upgraded six factories under the Ministry of Industry-2 [US$346 million], supplied six ocean-going vessels and built a dry dockyard [US$25 million]. In 2007 alone, Chinese firms were building seven hydroelectric plants in Myanmar [US$350–400 million]. According to the Chinese government, the turnover of China's economic cooperation with Myanmar in the period between 1998 and 2008 amounts to US$3,914.36 million, including US$3,783.49 million for contracted projects.

However, the Myanmar government has changed its approach to the loan negotiation for industrial development projects. In the past, loans were negotiated for SEE projects and, once they were approved, Chinese firms supplied machinery. Now, loans are negotiated for joint venture projects with Chinese firms. This is to ensure that the Chinese firms have stakes in the plants so that they will supply quality products and maintenance services.

The transport sector is another important area of Sino-Myanmar development cooperation. Since 1988, the Myanmar government has bought a total of six vessels from China with a total DWT of 31,092 tons. Although the number of ships and the total tonnage is relatively small, it is extremely significant since it constitutes 86 per cent of the ships and 92 per

TABLE 3.11

Turnover of China's Economic Cooperation with Myanmar (1998–2008)
(US$ million)

Year	Contracted Project	Labor Cooperation	Design Consultation	Total
1998	491.83	29.71	1.78	523.32
1999	192.69	4.29	0.85	197.83
2000	178.48	6.28	1.96	186.72
2001	249.09	5.52	1.90	256.51
2002	288.05	8.17	3.98	300.20
2003	370.74	6.43	1.61	378.78
2004	331.20	1.93	2.44	335.57
2005	286.72	1.66	1.38	289.76
2006	277.89	0.45	3.24	281.58
2007	434.02	0.18	27.65	461.85
2008	682.78	0.25	19.21	702.24

Source: China Statistical Yearbook (various years)

cent of the tonnage that the government procured in the period between 1988 and 2006. More importantly, it represents a major break with the past since all 18 vessels, with a total DWT of 108,061 tons plus, purchased between 1962 and 1988 were from European countries: nine from the FRG, five from Norway, and two each from Denmark and Poland. All the new ships were bought under low interest commercial loans agreements. The PRC also helped Myanmar build a dry dockyard at Simaleik at the cost of US$25.45 million and K16 billion in 2001. The Shandong Agricultural Industry and Commerce Group Corporation provided the loan and technical assistance.[132] Between June 2006 and October 2010, the Chinese government also presented 35 locomotives, 150 passenger coaches and 200 freight coaches for the Myanmar Railways.[133] The Lashio-Muse railway project is another infrastructure development project to be implemented with financial and technical assistance from China. A Memorandum of Understanding was signed during Prime Minister Soe Win's visit to China in February 2006. As part of China's plans to build the Kunming-Singapore rail-link, the Chinese government is constructing a 690 kilometres long Kunming-Ruili [Muse] railway. This comprises a 340 kilometres Kunming-Dali section and a 350 kilometres Dali-Ruili section.[134] Myanmar will build the 132 kilometres long Lashio-Muse [Ruili] railway.

The Ayerwaddy Transportation project, which has been in the process of negotiation since the late 1990s, will provide a transport link between Yangon and Kunming, mostly by the Ayerwaddy River. In October 1999, the then Secretary-1 of the SPDC, Lt. Gen Khin Nyunt and a high level Chinese delegation visited the northernmost port city Bhamo, which is about 30 miles from the China border, to help materialize the project. The project included building a container port near Bhamo, upgrading the road from Bhamo to the Chinese border town of Lweje [then to Zhangfang], and dredging the waterway of the Ayerwaddy river. The project will allow transport of up to two million containers per year in the future. However, details for project funding and management arrangements have still not been finalized. The total cost of the project, moreover, has yet to be revealed. In February 2005, a 500-GRT container barge was built with financial assistance from China. This will ply the route regularly. During his visit to China in February 2006, the Prime Minister General Soe Win discussed the dredging of the Yangon River with his Chinese counterpart. In connection with this project, two cross border road-links were constructed. Local county governments in Yunnan Province built 95-kilometre long Tengchong-Myitkyina road [via Kanpeikti] at the cost of RMB192 million [US$23.2 million] and upgraded the Zhangfeng-Bhamo road at the cost of RMB28 million [US$3.38 million]. Another infrastructure project is the Kyaukphyu-Kunming corridor project. No details are yet known about it. While Senior General Than Shwe was in Beijing in September 2010, Chinese leaders raised the issue of the Kyaukphyu-Kunming corridor, including the construction of the Shweli-Kyaukphyu corridor. As a result, Beijing sent the Deputy Minister for Transport Feng Zhenglin (冯正霖) to Naypyitaw to speed up the process. The first Shweli-Kyaukphyu corridor project meeting was held in Naypyitaw on 13 September 2010. At the meeting, Naypyitaw and Beijing agreed to draw up a master plan and to conduct a pre-feasibility study.[135]

In the telecommunication sector, too, Chinese firms play increasingly important role in wireless communication and fixed lines. Chinese firms have supplied auto-exchanges, mobile telecommunication systems, and fiber optics to the state-owned Myanma Post and Telecommunication.

The PRC government encourages Chinese businessmen to invest in Myanmar. China has helped establish at least two industrial zones in Myanmar: Yangon-Thanlyin and Kyaukphyu. The Yangon-Thanlyin special industrial zone, built on 1,000 acres, has been set up with 100 per cent foreign investment with export concentration. The Myanmar government will lease the land to Chinese investors. The location of the zone, which is next to Thilawa seaport, is convenient for international trade. The industrial zone project is related to the "Ayerwaddy Transportation Project". In July 2003, during the visit of Prime Minister General Khin Nyunt to China, the two governments signed an MoU for the establishment of the Yangon-Thanlyin Industrial Zone. Another industrial zone project is the Kyaukphyu industrial zone on the west coast of Myanmar. Details have not yet been revealed.

The China-Myanmar border trade has thrived and low-priced but poor quality consumer goods have literally flooded the Myanmar market.[136] In fact both countries had been planning the expansion of border trade even before the collapse of the BSPP government in September 1988. Sino-Myanmar trade has witnessed the growing importance of sub-state actors in bilateral relations. The Sino-Myanmar border trade remains a lifeline for the Myanmar economy. However, high dependency on primary product exports to China will pose serious problems in long term bilateral trade relations once these natural resources are depleted. Myanmar needs to export more value-added products. Since early 2005, Naypyitaw has been planning a "balanced trade" policy which will eventually impose restrictions on the value of imports, unless Myanmar's exports can be increased. One way of addressing this issue is to attract more foreign investment and technological transfer into Myanmar so that it can export value-added products, which will, in turn, increase the value of exports.

Beijing's development assistance has also been related to Chinese business interests in Myanmar. Commercially-based loans have been made available to the Myanmar government so that Chinese firms can also benefit from the Chinese development programme. Moreover, this strategy also helps China secure a supply of semi-finished materials for its growing economy. In addition, it serves China's geopolitical interests in Myanmar by securing access to the Indian Ocean. Since 1988, as a result of the sanction imposed by the Western governments, Chinese development assistance has constituted the largest source of foreign assistance for the Myanmar government.

As noted earlier, China made strategic investment in critical sectors, such as oil and gas, mining and energy. This has reflected China's growing concern for energy security in the long term. China has been accused of practicing a modern version of mercantilism, buying oil in stead of gold with trade surpluses. China's plans to build oil and gas pipelines are driven by both geopolitical and economic factors. Geopolitically, China appears to realize that it is vulnerable to the imposition of a naval blockade in the Malacca Straits by anti-China forces. Besides, pipelines are more economical in the long term. Chinese interest in building special industrial zones in Myanmar will also help Chinese business interests. Cheap labor and raw materials will benefit Chinese businesses too. This could turn Myanmar into a semi-finished goods producer and exporter for the Chinese market. In any case, Chinese capital, and other foreign capitals as well, will flow into Myanmar though these industrial zones. This will inevitably help facilitate the regime survival in Myanmar.

Notes

1. *Working People's Daily* (3 September 1991).
2. Hla Min, *Political Situation of Myanmar and Its Role in the Region* (Yangon: News and periodical Enterprises, 2001), p. 36 — internet version.
3. International Crisis Group, *China's Myanmar Dilemma*, Crisis Group Asia Report No. 177 (14 September 2009), p. 3.
4. *Kyemon* Newspaper (18 September 2009); *NLM* Newspaper (18 September 2009).
5. Ministry of Foreign Affairs (Myanmar). *Background Paper on China-Myanmar Relations*, 1994.
6. When the military authorities lodged a complaint and sought explanation from the US embassy, the latter explained that it was for the evacuation of US embassy staff in Myanmar. Myanmar authorities, in fact, pointed out that 276 people, including some US embassy staff, had been evacuated on the evening of 11 September on a chartered flight. Indeed, the US embassy had repeatedly

requested the Myanmar authorities' permission for a C-130 military aircraft to land in Yangon for evacuation. The Myanmar authorities rejected the request, explaining that such activity might lead to further confusion among the general public and send the wrong signal to regional neighbors. On 13 September, the US embassy issued a statement that the US fleet in Myanmar territorial water was just a rumor.

7. In September 2003, there were rumors that US paratroops had infiltrated northeastern Myanmar to establish an air force base there. As a precautionary measure, the PLA sent reinforcements into the Myanmar-China border area and deployed the Sichuan-based 13th Group Army in Xishuangbanna Autonomous Region where the PLA also maintains No. 7701 and 7702 military units. Moreover, the PLA also alerted the Yunnan-based 14th Group Army. Both 13th and 14th army groups are under the Chengdu Military Region.

8. Ministry of Foreign Affairs (Myanmar). *Background Paper on China-Myanmar Relations*, 1994.

9. Testimony given by Sai Aung Win (29 June 1990).

10. တောႏိုကျောင်းသားပောင်းများ၊ ထို့ကြောင့် ... ဤသို့ [Former Underground Students. *Therefore — It is*], p.

11. Testimony given by Sai Aung Win (29 June 1990).

12. တောႏိုကျောင်းသားပောင်းများ၊ ထို့ကြောင့် ... ဤသို့ [Former Underground Students. *Therefore — It is*], p.

13. Testimony given by Sai Aung Win (29 June 1990).

14. His visit was preceded by a number of lower level Chinese delegations. These included a 13-member delegation led by the Governor of Yunnan, He Zhiqiang, in November 1989, Vice Minister for foreign Trade and Economic Cooperation Wang Wendong in December 1989, Vice Minister for Culture Liu Deyou in April 1990, Vice Minister for Radio, Film and Television Ma Qingxiong in April 1990, Vice Minister for Machine-building and Electronic Industry Zhang Xuedong in May 1990, Vice Minister for Machine-Building and Electronic Industry Tang Zhongwen in November 1990, and Vice Minister for Railways Sun Yongfu in December 1990.

15. Ministry of Information. *China-Myanmar Goodwill Visits of Great Historic Significance* (Yangon: News and Periodical Enterprises, 1991), p. 21.

16. See Renaud Egreteau. *Wooing the Generals: India's New Burma Policy* (New Delhi: Authorspress, 2003), pp. 90–91.

17. *Bangkok Post* (27 December 1994)

18. Jiang's Myanmar Visit Successful: Chinese FM (<http://english.people.com. cn/200112/16/ eng20011216_86800.shtml>).

19. See <test.fmprc.gov.cn/eng/wjb/zzjg/yzs/gjlb/2747/2749/t16088.htm>.

20. President Jiang Zemin held Talks with Chairman Than Shwe <http://.fmprc. gov.cn/ce/ceee/eng/ dtxw/t111289.htm> (accessed on 24 August 2007).

21. Ibid.

22. Ibid.

23. Vice President Hu Jintao met with Than Shwe <http://fmprc.gov.cn/ce/ceee/eng/dtxw/ t111290.htm> (accessed on 24 August 2007).

24. When a meeting was organized to discuss the "Bangkok Process" in mid-December 2003, diplomats from 12 countries, including China, Japan, and India, participated.

25. *The Myanmar Times Journal*, Vol. 11, No. 210 (29 March 2004) pp. 1, 4.

26. Chinese Vice-Premier meets Myanmar top leader, *Xinhua*, People's Daily Online <http://english. peopledaily.com.cn/ 25 March 2003> (accessed date 24 August 2007, 20:00 hours Singapore Times).

27. *The Myanmar Times Journal*, Vol. 11, No. 210 (29 March 2004) p. 3.

28. Premier Wen Jiabao Holds Talks with Prime Minister Khin Nyunt of the Union of Myanmar — 2004/07/12 — <http://fmprc.gov.cn/eng/zxxx/t143049.htm> (accessed on 24 August 2007).

29. Ibid.

30. Ibid.

31. Hu Jintao Meets with Prime Minister of Myanmar <http://fmprc.gov.cn/eng/zxxx/t143132.htm — 13 July 2004> (accessed on 24 August 2007).

32. *New Light of Myanmar* (20 July 2004) p. 1.

33. Ibid.

34. Ibid.

35. Wu Bangguo Meets with Prime Minister of Myanmar <http://fmprc.gov.cn/eng/zxxx/t143131.htm — 13 July 2004> (accessed on 24 August 2007).

36. *Foreign Ministry Spokesperson's Press Conference on July 13th, 2004* <http://fmprc.gov.cn/eng/ xwfw/2510/t143120.htm> (accessed on 24 August 2007).

37. *New Light of Myanmar* (22 February 2004).

38. *New Light of Myanmar* (24 July 2004).

39. *New Light of Myanmar* (27 July 2004).

40. *New Light of Myanmar* (2 October 2004).

41. For more detail of this issue, please see Maung Aung Myoe, *Building the Tatmadaw: Myanmar Armed Forces since 1948* (Singapore: ISEAS, 2010), pp. 64–70.

42. *NLM* (6 November 2004).

43. Premier Wen Jiabao Holds Talks with Prime Minister of Myanmar Soe Win <http://chineseembassy.org/eng/zxxx/t235759.htm> (accessed on 24 August 2007).

44. Chinese, Myanmar PMs hold talks, vowing to further neighborly ties <http://english.people.com.cn/200602/15/eng20060215_242782.html> (accessed 15 February 2006).

45. Wen Jiabao Meets with Myanmar Prime Minister Soe Win (www.fmprc.gov.cn/eng/zxxx/ t278914.htm).

46. *Sino-Myanmar Bilateral Relations*, unpublished report, MOFA, (December 1994), p. 47.

47. Fire continued to plague the city. More recent breakouts of fire occurred on

25 February 2008, destroying 1,428 market shops, 17 offices and 113 other workspaces, and on 10 February 2009, burning 300 houses.

48. In a city like Lashio, where the present author lived for three years after 1977, there were many restrictions on the movement of population.

49. To the best of the present author's knowledge, the first story of such nature appeared in 1984. In December 1984, Thabin Magazine published a short story titled "Frighten (Soe-Kyauk-Mi-Par-Thi)" by Moe Moe (Inya), a prominent novelist in Myanmar. This was a story about two friends, one from Mandalay and the other from the Delta, who became roommates in Yadana Hall at Yangon University. The friend from the Delta paid a second visit to Mandalay about a decade after her last one. She tried to find her friend, with whom she had lost contact for about ten years. On her way, she passed by the swathes of blackened land and ashes of houses burnt down by the devastating fire [of 24 March 1984]. She knew that her friend's house had been spared by the fire, but she was puzzled by the complete change in the environment. She found out that there was now a new building at the address once occupied by her friend and she saw a woman with a very fair complexion there. When she asked about her friend and her family, the woman stared at her and told that they had been living there for a long time. In her speech, the woman employed the pronoun "Wa", a term exclusively used by Chinese in Myanmar. When she tried to look for neighbors of her friend, she discovered that they, too, were gone; instead, she was answered by "a plump man of yellowish complexion dressed in pants", a typical feature of Chinese in Myanmar. Finally, she went to see her cousin who was working in the Mandalay Hotel. The story concluded that Mandalay, after the ravages of the devastating fire, had begun to recuperate and that people were swarming and busy like bees, yet there were many strange faces among them. There were new and luxurious buildings, cars, hotels, and restaurants and many more would sprout on the blackened land. The author, however, wondered where her friend and family had disappeared to in the great city of Mandalay. The story highlighted the loss of land previously owned by native residents to new [Chinese] immigrants, even in the areas not affected by the fire. The traditional professions and trades of the grest majority of indigenous Myanmar citizens did not even allow them to keep up with the rising cost of living in the Socialist Myanmar [though it was rather modest compared to that a quarter of a century later]. The fire devastated most of the original inhabitants of Mandalay and they had no resources to rebuild their lives on the same patch of land they owned. They were thus forced to sell their plots and moving to the city's outskirts.

Another tale of this nature was "The Story of the Golden Mandalay Ratanabon (Ratanabon-Shwe-Mandalay-Wuthtu)" by Nyi Pu Lay, a Mandalay-based writer famous for short stories. The short story first appeared in July 1987 issue of Yinkhone-Pwint Magazine. It was reproduced in the "Thuhtetkae-Shwepyisoe Collected Short Stories", published by the author himself in March

1989. The story was centered on an early morning alms-gathering round of monks and novices. The great fire [of March 1984] "rooted out the heart from the city, the story ran and "new settlers were on the blackened land. Now, monks and novices received [Chinese] sausage from "a lady with yellowish complexion who owned a recently built guesthouse and [Chinese] iû-chiākóe (油炸粿) [or you-tiao (油條)] from "an old lady with gold teeth living in a double-storey house still under construction". Nobody at the monastery, and visitors as well, liked you-tiao and they usually piled up on the table. White-robed deacons (Phothudaw) were rather unhappy with receiving you-tiao in morning alms-gathering rounds. The new settlers in the story were described as having narrow eyes, a feature of typical Chinese. When a deacon joked "the more the deacon feels confused [at seeing new faces during the alms round], the more likely you are to get more you-tiao", the novices, deacons and monastery boys couldn't help but laugh at this. However, the monks were not even moved to smile, let alone laugh. At the end of the story, a deacon wondered: "Why didn't the monks even smile at a joke?" Then he said: "They were senior and learned people and I should ask why they did not even smile or laugh". What was interesting, too, were the illustrations in the story. In the magazine version there was a drawing of novices, deacons, and monastery boys in the early alms round by Artist Maung Maung Theik. Yet, in the "collected short stories" version, the illustration was a Chinese dragon drawn by the author himself. Nowhere in the story, however, did the word "Chinese" appear.

In the October 1987 issue of Moewai Magazine, "Moving Wall (Shawe-shar-nanyan)" by Theik Tun Thet's, another Mandalay-based short story writer, told a story about a [Chinese] businessman, who owned a wheat mill and lived in a yard fenced with high walls, buying a plot of land, next to his mill, from a native Myanmar family in Mandalay. The wall was subsequently moved to further encroach on the land previously owned by the natives. Win Sithu's "A Bicycle and one Yojana of Journey (Setbi-Tasi-Khayi-Tayuzana)", which appeared in the May 1988 issue of the same magazine, was also about a [Chinese] merchant family moving into Mandalay and buying a plot of land from a native Myanmar citizen. Another native Myanmar citizen living in the vicinity was a clerk who earned a salary of K300 for his family of four. While he was struggling for months to assembly a bicycle, the merchant couple, Maung Hoke Sein and Ma Kyin Hmwe — typical names for ethnic Chinese in Myanmar — bought the land for nearly K4 million and spent another K2 million to build a house on it. The couple planned to give away a bicycle in a lucky draw for all the guests coming to their house warming party. Although he was invited, the Myanmar clerk refused to go to vent his displeasure.

Khin Pan Hnin (Myaungmya)'s short story, entitled "Zero Degree Centigrade (Thonnya-degare-sentigarade)", published in the June 1988 issue of Cherry Magazine, was about an ethnic Myanmar girl from central Myanmar who eventually settled in Lashio in Northern Shan State, after the death of her parents, and married a Chinese. The girl's house was described as a typical Chinese house, decorated in the Chinese way, and the girl became thoroughly absorbed into Chinese customs. Her childhood friend, who lovingly called her "jasmine bud", was amazed at her changed personality when he found her, after several years of search. He asked: "Would the jasmine [metaphor for Myanmar girls] be able to withstand the Northeastern wind [metaphor for Chinese] any further?" Two short stories on the same theme, the growing presence of Chinese in Myanmar were published in the June 1988 issue of Thara Magazine. Nu Nu Yi (Innwa)'s "The Sandbank in the water is called an Island (Yaelaegaung-Thaunghtun-Kyunloe-Khawde)" was about the life of watermelon farmer-sellers and their encounters with Chinese pilgrims in Sagaing, the city across from Mandalay. Nyi Pu Lay's "Boa constrictor (Sapargyimwe)" was about a Chinese businessman buying a plot of land from a native Myanmar in Mandalay. The story was filled with emotionally charged narratives, and was told eloquently. Only in the last line, did the author mention that the native people who were counting the payment could not understand the heavily sicinized Myanmar language of the buyer. Ye Shan's "Essays (Sarsi-Sarkone-Laymya)", which appeared in the September 1988 issue of Yokeshin-Aunglan Magazine, was the story of a high school teacher of Myanmar literature and history, who compared his own essays of 15 and 20 years ago about his native town in Southern Shan State, with that of a contemporary student on the same theme. The student described an emerging "China market", which the teacher felt frightening and duty bound to do something. All the above mentioned short stories, except Nyi Pu Lay's "The Story of the Golden Mandalay Ratanabon" were reproduced in a collection carefully arranged and thoughtfully entitled "Handwriting of Wathondare the God of Earth (Wathondare-letye-wuthtu-tomya)", published by a Mandalay-based publisher in November 1989. The phenomenon of growing Chinese affluence in Myanmar was carefully observed in Upper Myanmar and in Mandalay, and Mandalay-based writers were among the most active and prolific in presenting it.

In June 1993 issue of Yin-Khone-Pwint Magazine, there was a short story titled "The Night of Ratanabon (Ratanabon Nyamya)" by Nay Win Myint, a prominent Mandalay-based author. This was about a group of short story writers who drove around Mandalay (Ratanabon City) at night for a couple of days. The author compared and contrasted the historical and cultural landmarks and icons of the city, which is the cultural heartland of Myanmar, with new developments, such as Chinese restaurants — he mentioned two names, 新春園 (Xīn Chūn Yuán) and 桃園 (Táo Yuán), although they were not new — and signboards in Chinese characters. The author wondered who really owned the nights of Ratanabon. The illustration of the story, it should be noted again, showed a Chinese dragon.

50. When the 150th anniversary of the founding of Mandalay was held in 2009, a one-act play was performed by a group of comedians. The play highlighted

the significance of Chinese influence in the city. In the last scene, it was revealed that the main actor, who dressed very much like a Chinese and spoke Myanmar with Chinese accent, was in fact a native Myanmar; but the actor said that since he had not only to work and live among them [Chinese or new immigrants] but also to study their customs and language, although he was a native born in the city, he had now been thoroughly assimilated into the Chinese community.

51. Mya Maung. "On the Road to Mandalay: A case Study of the Sinonization of Upper Burma", *Asian Survey* (Vol. 34, No. 5: May 1994), pp. 447–459.

52. Roger Mitton. "Sino-Viet ties sour over reports on food scandle", *The Straits Times* (28 August 2007), p. 11.

53. *New Light of Myanmar* (16 March 2005).

54. Chinese Foreign Minister Li Zhaoxing arrived in Yangon on 27 July 2005, hoping not only to promote the traditional and friendly ties between China and Myanmar but also to show support for the Myanmar government which had decided to relinquish the ASEAN Chairmanship in 2006, by not attending the ASEAN Regional Forum (ARF).

55. For more details, please see Maung Aung Myoe, "The Road to Naypyitaw: Making Sense of the Myanmar Government's Decision to Move its Capital", *ARI-NUS Working Paper No. 79*, November 2006.

56. Ian Holliday, "Beijing and the Myanmar Problem", *The Pacific Review* (Vol. 22, No. 4, September 2009), p. 489.

57. New Light of Myanmar (16 February 2008).

58. During the voting, South Africa voted against the resolution, Indonesia, Qatar and Congo abstained, and the United States, United Kingdom, France, Italy, Belgium, Slovakia, Ghana, Panama and Peru voted in favour.

59. UNSC, *Security Council Meeting 5619 minute* (dated 12 January 2007).

60. Ibid.

61. Ibid.

62. Ian Holliday, "Beijing and the Myanmar Problem", *The Pacific Review* (Vol. 22, No. 4, September 2009), p. 489.

63. *State Councilor Tang Jiaxua Meets with Special Envoy of SPDC Chairman of Myanmar*, dated 13 September 2007 <http://mfa.gov.cn/eng/wjb/zzjg/yzs/gjlb/2747/2749/t363133.htm>.

64. *Presidential Statement of the Security Council*, S/PRST/2007/37/ 11 October 2007.

65. *New Light of Myanmar* (27 March 2008).

66. Ministry of Foreign Affairs (Myanmar).

67. Ministry of Foreign Affairs, *Yang Jiechi Holds Talks with His Myanmar Counterpart U Nyan Win* <http://www.chinaconsulatesf.org/eng/xw/t525038.htm>.

68. Ibid.

69. Ministry of Foreign Affairs (China), *Chairman of the State Peace and Development*

Council of Myanmar Than Shwe Meets with Yang Jiechi <http://www.fmprc.gov.cn/eng/zxxx/t525350.htm>.

70. Ibid.
71. ICG. *China's Myanmar Dilemma*, Crisis Group Asia Report No. 177 (14 September 2009), p. 9.
72. Ibid., pp. 9–10.
73. *New Light of Myanmar* (21 April 2009).
74. *Chinese, Myanmar premiers meet on bilateral ties* <http://chinaview.cn> (14 April 2009), <http://news.xinhuanet.com/english/2009-06/16/content_11553126.htm>.
75. *New Light of Myanmar* (21 June 2009).
76. Ibid.
77. Ibid.
78. Ibid.
79. *China, Myanmar to boost "comprehensive, stable and lasting relations"* <http://chinaview.cn> (16 June 2009); <http://news.xinhuanet.com/english/2009-06/16/content_11553126.htm>.
80. *New Light of Myanmar* (22 June 2009).
81. Ibid.
82. *Wen Jiabao Meets with Myanmar State Peace and Development Council Vice-Chairman Maung Aye* (MFAPRC, 16 June 2009), <http://www.mfa.gov.cn/eng/wjdt/wshd/t568286.htm>.
83. Ibid.
84. *Myanmar official media hail Chinese vice president's visit* <http://chinaview.cn> (22 December 2009); <http://news.xinhuanet.com/english/2009-12/22/content_12687051.htm>.
85. *China puts forward four-point proposal to further ties with Myanmar* (Chinese Government's Official Web Portal), <http://www.gov.cn/english/2009-12/20/content_1492539.htm>.
86. *Wen Jiabao Meets with Than Shwe, Chairman of the State Peace and Development Council of Myanmar* <http://www.fmprc.gov.cn/eng/zxxx/t706665.htm>.
87. Ibid.
88. Ibid.
89. *Premier Wen Jiabao Holds Talks with His Myanmar Counterpart Thein Sein* <http://www.fmprc. gov.cn/ eng/zxxx/t706667.htm>.
90. Ibid.
91. *New Light of Myanmar* (12 September 2010).
92. Ibid.
93. See <http://news.xinhuanet.com/english2010/china/2010-09/08/c_13485532.htm>.
94. See <http://www.fmprc.gov.cn/eng/xwfw/s2510/t738694.htm>.
95. ICG. *China's Myanmar Dilemma*, Crisis Group Asia Report No. 177 (14 September 2009), p. 10.

96. Ibid., p. 11.
97. As a constitutional requirement and part of the "Seven-Step" Roadmap, the Myanmar government proposed a plan to ceasefire groups to give up their arms, either by surrendering or becoming border guard forces under the Tatmadaw while they could still form political parties to contest in the 2010 General Elections.
98. Ibid., p. 11.
99. Article 338 of the 2008 Constitution.
100. *Wen Jiabao Meets with Prime Ministers of New Zealand and Myanmar* <http://www.fmprc.gov.cn /eng /zxxx/t623106.htm> dated 15 October 2009 (accessed on 22 November 2009)
101. *Joshua Kurlantzick. Raising the Stakes, Foreign Policy* (18 April 2007), online edition, <http://foreignpolicy. com /articles/2007/04/18> (accessed on 25 December 2009).
102. ICG. *China's Myanmar Dilemma*, p. 16.
103. *New Light of Myanmar* (25 July 2004).
104. It appears that it was agreed to set up Border Representative Agencies in Mongyang, Tangyang, Laukkaing, Muse, Myitkyina (Winemaw), and Putao (Machangpaw) on the Myanmar side and in Xishuangbana, Simao, Lincang, Dehong, Baoshan, and Nujiang on the Chinese side of the border. Contact Stations will be in Kengtung, Tangyang, Kunlon, Kutkai, Bhamo, and Myitkyina on the Myanmar side and in Menghai, Menglian, Mengding, Ruili, Tengchong, and Luiku on the Chinese side.
105. *The Myanmar Time*, 24–30 January 2005, Vol. 13, No. 251, p. 4.
106. *The Myanmar Times*, 31 January–6 February 2005, Vol. 13, No. 252, p. 3.
107. 62nd press conference held on 27 October 1989.
108. 64th press conference held on 10 November 1989.
109. To the delight of conspiracy theorists, Tin Oo's helicopter crash on 19 February 2001 has been the subject of various interpretations and rumors. Since there had been a number of attempts on Tin Oo's life in the past, such as two bombs at Kaba-aye Pagoda on 25 December 1996, one of which went off just after Tin Oo left the pagoda, and a parcel bomb at his residence on 6 April 1997 that killed his eldest daughter, this incident naturally stimulated talk of an assassination plot. The latest addition was a claim made by Sein Lwin, a former Foreign Office employee who was close to one of Tin Oo's staff officers, Major Win Naing Kyaw, in his interview with Mizzima News on 10 January 2010. Win Naing Kyaw was a captain at the "Staff Duty" branch of the General Staff Office while Tin Oo was alive. Tin Oo used to employ several junior officers at the General Staff Office as his staff officers wherever and whenever he toured the country. Yet Win Naing Kyaw was not on the helicopter on that fatal day. According to Sein Lwin, a helicopter pilot saved alive at the time of the crash was later shot dead [presumably at the crash site] either by military intelligence or the army, which could be seen an attempt

to cover up a plot that had something to do with power struggles between or among different factions within the Tatmadaw. However, the present author is fortunate to know personally at least two senior officers who survived the crash. Out of 29 people on board, altogether 14 people died in the incident, including Lt. General Tin Oo, Major General Sit Maung, Brigadier Lun Maung (Minister), Colonel Tin Win (Air Force), Captain Kyaw Tin Hla (Navy), Colonel Win Hlaing (Armour), Lt. Col. Hla Paing, Maj. Aung Phone Naing, Maj. Khin Maung Kyaw, Maj. Soe Naing (pilot), and Captain Ne Min Aung (co-pilot). The crash was a result of pilot error and bad weather. According to the survivors whom I know, about the time the helicopter approached Tayoke Hla village near a bridge across the Thanlwin River, Major General Sit Maung told Lt. General Tin Oo about new plantation along the river. Because of the mist and low visibility, Brigadier General Lun Maung asked the pilots to lower the helicopter. Since the pilots were inexperienced with Russian-made MI-17, they brought down the helicopter so low that by the time they saw the bridge and tried to lift the machine up again, it was too late. The helicopter blades struck the steel cables of the bridge and the aircraft crashed into the Thanlwin River.

110. See <http://news.xinhuanet.com/english2010/china/2010-09/07/c_13483487. htm>.

111. Ibid.

112. This figure does not include armed forces personnel who went abroad for training under directorates other than Military Training. The most obvious case is the medical officers studying abroad for advanced degrees.

113. Directorate of Military Training showroom (Defence Services Museum).

114. Since 2001, the Tatmadaw has sent between 400 and 600 graduates to Russia every year in various fields of graduate studies, including nuclear science and technology, computer science, medical science, and aeronautical engineering. In the ninth batch, sent to Russia in 2009, there were altogether 639 military officers and five civilians.

115. See <http://www.earthtimes.org/articles/news/338306,nuclear-officers-academic-says.html>.

116. *Far Eastern Economic Review* (10 May 2001).

117. These coastal patrol crafts (Sub-chasers) were numbered and named: 441-Yan Sit Aung, 442-Yan Myat Aung, 443-Yan Nyein Aung, 444-Yan Khwin Aung, 445-Yan Min Aung, 446-Yan Ye Aung, 447-Yan Paing Aung, 448-Yan Win Aung, 449-Yan Aye Aung, and 450-Yan Zwe Aung.

118. These Fast Attack Craft are named after astrologically significant stars. (Seik-hta, Mar-ga, Han-tha, Ze-Hta, Ban-Na, and Du-wa).

119. UMS-551 was commissioned on 2 January 1996.

120. *Strategic Affairs* (16 November 2000).

121. It was also reported that the Pakistani air force would also replace its JJ-7s and CJ-6s trainers with K-8s.

122. At the press conference held on 24 October 2004, General Thura Shwe Mann mentioned a wide spread corruption at the Muse trading zone. The amount involved was said to have been over 3 billion kyat within three months. Action was taken against 186 service personnel in connection with the corruption. [*New Light of Myanmar*, Special Pamphlet 31 October 2004] For example, over 500 officers from the Customs Departments were dismissed in 2005.

123. မြန်ကြားရေးဝန်ကြီးဌာန၊ *တိုင်းကျိုးပြည်ပြုမှတ်တမ်းများ*, အတွဲ (၁) (ရန်ကုန်၊ သတင်းနှင့်စာနယ်ဇင်း လုပ်ငန်း၊ ၁၉၉၁) [*Nation-Building Records*, Volume -1 (Yangon: News and Periodical Enterprises, 1991)], pp. 229–231 ။ မြန်ကြားရေးဝန်ကြီးဌာန၊ *တိုင်းကျိုးပြည်ပြုမှတ်တမ်းများ* — အတွဲ (၂) (ရန်ကုန်၊ သတင်းနှင့်စာနယ်ဇင်းလုပ်ငန်း၊ ၁၉၉၅)) [*Nation-Building Records*, Volume -2 (Yangon: News and Periodical Enterprises, 1995)], pp. 158–159.

124. For example, in the 1990s Chinese medicines, Chinese beer, and Chinese cigarettes were very common. But in 2000s, Indian medicines have been more common.

125. *Myanmar News Gazette Journal*, Vol. 1, No. 9 (13 July 2004) p. 1.

126. The oil pipeline, which will eventually terminate in Kunming, capital of Yunnan province, will be 771 km (479 miles) long. The natural gas pipeline will extend further from Kunming to Guizhou and Guangxi in China, running a total of 2,806 km (1,700 miles).

127. *The Myanmar Times*, Vol. 15, No. 300 (16 January 2006), pp. 1, 4; *Weekly Eleven News Journal*, Vol. 1, No. 15 (18 January 2006), p. 3.

128. Dow Jones Energy Service (29 January 2007).

129. See <http://chinaeconomy.ce.cn/no2/newsmore/200606/27> (accessed on 27 June 2006).

130. *New Light of Myanmar* (1 January 2007); *Xinhua Net-Yunnan Channel* (31 December 2006).

131. Myanmar received loans equivalent of US$1,889 million from Japan in the period between 1970 and 2000 and loans equivalent of US$365.6 million from West Germany in the period between 1970 and 1987.

132. *Myanmar Times* (Vol. 11, No. 203; 9–15 February 2004).

133. *Kyemon* Newspaper (20 October 2010).

134. China completed the 340 km long Kunming-Dali railway in 1998 and started construction of 350 km long Dali-Ruili railway in 2007. This is scheduled to be completed by the end of 2010.

135. *New Light of Myanmar* (14 September 2010).

136. Here I would like to give an example of Myanmar's fruit export to China. In 1990s, for example, Myanmar exported plums and water melons to China. Four or five years later, China exported these items back to Myanmar but with higher qualities. Moreover, Chinese made preserved fruits are much cheaper than the local ones.

5

CONCLUSION

Since the nation regained its independence in January 1948, the Myanmar government has tried to find a way to deal with (at one time) an ideologically hostile and traditionally chauvinistic China, which pursued a foreign policy aimed at restoring its perceived historical influence in Myanmar. Countering the Chinese goal of influencing Myanmar's foreign policy options has always been a challenge for the Myanmar government. Since the 1950s, the Myanmar government has realized that bilateral relations with China can best be conducted in the context of promoting the Five Principles of Peaceful Coexistence, the Bandung spirit and the "Pauk-Phaw" friendship.

By bringing China into the Bandung process, promoting the Chinese image and allowing Beijing to play an important role in regional security, the Myanmar government believed that it could cultivate good relations with its great neighbour. Myanmar confirmed that it maintained a "One-China" policy and decided to resolve outstanding bilateral issues in a friendly manner. In fact, the Sino-Myanmar relationship became a model that the PRC government would like to promote in developing its ties with other countries. Sino-Myanmar relations therefore helped to consolidate China's international image. This fairly stable and correct relationship was also founded on the personal diplomacy between leaders of the two countries. By signing the Treaty of Mutual Non-Aggression and Friendship in 1960, the Myanmar government duly recognized Chinese strategic interests in Myanmar. Myanmar did not join any military alliance targeting China and continued to conduct its foreign relations on the basis of a neutralist philosophy. In this way, the Myanmar government made it known to Beijing that Myanmar would neither balance against nor bandwagon with China.

During the 1950s, there were three closely interrelated issues in Sino-Myanmar relations: the undemarcated boundary; the aggression of KMT remnant forces; and the incursion of PLA troops. While these issues were at the top of its agenda, the Myanmar government was shrewd enough to bring China, along with India, to inaugurate the so-called Bandung Era. This certainly increased moral pressure on the Chinese government to resolve bilateral issues in a peaceful and friendly manner. U Nu duly recognized China's important role in assuring regional peace and stability and accordingly accepted it. While assuring Myanmar's strict neutrality in international issues, particularly during the Cold War era, U Nu cultivated a personal friendship with the Chinese leadership in the name of "Pauk-Phaw" relations. The year 1954 could be considered a watershed year in Sino-Myanmar relations. First, Zhou Enlai came to Yangon in June and, then, U Nu, for the first time, journeyed to Beijing in December. Both leaders succeeded in nurturing warmer relations between the two countries through frank discussions; they confirmed their commitment to the Five Principles of Peaceful Coexistence. The Myanmar government assured China that it would resolve the KMT issue through diplomatic and military means.

However, the Myanmar government was rather uneasy about alleged PRC support for left wing political forces in Myanmar, especially during the 1956 elections, although no details were provided and no references to China were made in the press. Nevertheless, when U Nu went to China in October 1956 to discuss the boundary demarcation, he was completely silent on the subject, and concentrated his effort on reaching a settlement of the matter in hand. China also promised to settle the issue of PLA troops in Myanmar. As a result of mutual understanding and accommodation a tentative agreement on the settlement of the boundary question was reached, although concrete details remained to be discussed. On numerous occasions, Zhou Enlai stressed China's commitment to the Five Principles of Peaceful Coexistence. Despite her close relations with China, Myanmar tried to maintain stable and correct relations with the West and non-Communist countries. It decided to participate in the U.S. Military Assistance Programme and procured weapons from Western sources. The Myanmar government condemned Soviet aggression in Hungary and British, French and Israeli aggression in Egypt. Myanmar Prime Minister called the Soviet action in Hungary the "most despicable form of colonialism" while he was at the Asian Socialist Conference in Bombay in November 1956. Myanmar was to show that it had no bias towards the Socialist camp despite its close relations with Communist China. This was about the time Myanmar was negotiating with China for the withdrawal of PLA troops from Myanmar.

Meanwhile, in the context of the Sino-Indian border conflict issue and China's earning a bad reputation as an "aggressive neighbour", Beijing desired to take emergency measures to save its international prestige, above all in the eyes of the non-aligned Afro-Asian countries. Taking advantage of China's interest in settling the Sino-Myanmar border demarcation issue in a way that would demonstrate her "flexibility, generosity, and spirit of compromise" in boundary negotiations, the Myanmar government decided to push ahead and reach a settlement of the issue. Initially, the PRC was strongly against the idea of accepting the "1941 Line" drawn by the British as it viewed the line as a legacy of the unequal treaties. Later, however, Beijing agreed to incorporate the "1941 Line" into the final settlement, together with some natural and historical boundary lines. The process was further speeded up when both the Chinese and Myanmar governments decided to settle the issue through negotiations based on the principles of "give-and-take" and friendship, rather than on legal processes. Negotiations on border demarcation continued and finally, on 28 January 1960, General Ne Win, as the Prime Minister of the Caretaker Government, signed a "package deal" with the Chinese government that included an agreement on the question of the boundary and a treaty of friendship and mutual non-aggression between the two countries. In accordance with the agreement, both parties worked on the detailed boundary demarcation and the final agreement was signed on 1 October 1960. For Yangon, the successful settlement of the border issue removed anxiety about any future Chinese incursion into Myanmar territory. With the exchange of a few square kilometers, the Sino-Myanmar boundary was peacefully demarcated. Premier Zhou Enlai subsequently held up the Sino-Myanmar boundary agreement to the Indian government as a model, for it was necessary to substantiate its claim that China had no territorial ambition against neighboring countries, as outlined by Premier Zhou Enlai on 23 April 1955 at the Bandung Conference.

As a result of changes in personality and policy style since 1962, the activism of Myanmar's foreign policy has become less pronounced. Preoccupied with domestic issues, the Myanmar government under the Revolutionary Council was determined to eliminate outside interference at all costs. The government also took a number of measures that to some extent damaged Chinese interests in Myanmar. In this process, China lost instruments of political control over the Chinese Community in Myanmar. At the same time Myanmar tried to maintain her neutralist foreign policy. Yet the Chinese government became increasingly dissatisfied with Myanmar's failure to demonstrate socialist solidarity in her international relations. Nevertheless, Sino-Myanmar relations in the early 1960s were characterized by closer ties between the two countries. Chinese leaders frequently made trips to Yangon. This relatively trouble-free relationship was interrupted by the Chinese decision to export revolution abroad. With the eruption of the Cultural Revolution in China in 1966, Beijing abandoned its pragmatic approach to foreign affairs and decided to pursue a revolutionary foreign policy, championing Third World Revolutionary movements. Against this background, Beijing decided to actively and openly support the revolutionary movements throughout Southeast Asia and the BCP was perhaps the most important client and beneficiary of this new policy. The Sino-Myanmar relationship in this way became a casualty of the Chinese Cultural Revolution. Anti-China riots erupted in Yangon, disrupting normal diplomatic business and the bilateral relationship plunged its lowest point in post-colonial history. Myanmar's decade-old China policy, based primarily and ceremoniously on the Five Principles of Peaceful Coexistence, came close to bankruptcy with the radicalization of Chinese foreign policy and Chinese decision to actively support the BCP.

Beijing's effort to aggressively export Mao Zedong Thought and the Cultural Revolution to Myanmar apparently ended in failure. This made Myanmar a primary target of Beijing's new assertive policy. The International Liaison Department (ILD), established in 1951 and headed by Wang Jiaxang as director, was responsible for handling Communist parties in other countries and directly answerable to the Central Committee. It operated behind and above the government. By 1963, Kang Sheng, godfather of the Cultural Revolution, had removed Wang from the ILD and took charge of the ILD's operations himself. Kang Sheng now became the chief mentor of the BCP and the BCP was ready to play along with the new militant policy line. The CCP subsequently provided massive overt assistance to the BCP to open up a new military front.

The Chinese attempt to export the Cultural Revolution to Myanmar had at least three major impacts on Myanmar politics in general and the Sino-Myanmar relations in particular. First, since it encouraged a mini Cultural Revolution in the BCP, the party committed serious mistakes which finally led to its downfall. Second, the political activities of the Overseas Chinese community were placed completely under the control of the Myanmar government and a process of assimilation was begun. Third, since the Myanmar government allied neither with "American Imperialism" nor with "Soviet Revisionism", after nearly four years of mutual frustration, Beijing and Yangon realized new rules of the game. The Myanmar government tacitly recognized China's role as the champion of Third World revolution by accepting the *de facto* existence of dual track diplomacy — state-to-state and party-to-party — while China realized that pushing too hard on "neutral"

Myanmar could be counter-productive in the long term and would not serve Chinese strategic interests.

After the 1967 anti-Chinese riots, China downgraded state-to-state relations with the Myanmar government in favour of party-to-party relations with the BCP. The PRC's use of a two-pronged policy to exert political leverage in Myanmar became increasingly apparent after the rupture of friendly relations in 1967. Myanmar learned to live with China's two-pronged policy throughout the 1970s and 1980s. From the late 1960s through the 1970s, Ne Win, while managing domestic political pressures for more drastic action, founded his China policy on efforts to convince Beijing that no matter how hard it tried to pressure the Myanmar government, he would not deviate from the established foreign policy orientation of strictly "positive neutralism". In the post-Mao period, Ne Win understood that unless the Myanmar government followed a foreign policy line that accommodated the Chinese strategic interests in the country, Beijing, even under a "pragmatic leader" such as Deng Xiaoping, could decide to throw much more weight behind the BCP, just as it supported the Khmer Rouge in Cambodia. China, in late 1970s and early 1980s, was concerned with the BCP's possible shift of allegiance towards the Soviet Union, which would establish a Soviet Hegemonist presence on its doorstep. The Myanmar government understandably turned a blind eye on Beijing's low level support for the BCP. At the same time, Myanmar took measures to curtail any contact between the BCP and Communist parties in Laos and other parts of Indochina.

Despite serious security threats, Myanmar maintained its neutralist foreign policy and tried to restore normal diplomatic relations with China. By the time normal diplomatic relations were reestablished in the early 1970s, the Myanmar government had learnt to live with Chinese dual-track diplomacy and recognized Beijing's preferred role in international Communist armed struggles. By the mid-1980s, as a new geopolitical situation emerged, China decided to correct its past mistakes and Myanmar's strictly neutralist policy began to bear fruit. In 1985, the CCP cut off support to the BCP and the Chinese government openly promised to make amends with the Myanmar government for its past errors. Moreover, the Chinese government offered friendly advice on economic reform in Myanmar and extended some development aid. At the time of the political upheaval that shook Myanmar in 1988, China studiously avoided involvement in Myanmar's internal affairs, though there were some serious concerns about possible external military intervention. By then, the PRC had apparently realized that official state-to-state relations with the Myanmar government would better serve Chinese [strategic] interests in Myanmar and beyond.

By the time the SLORC came to power, the bilateral relationship was back on the right track.

Myanmar's China policy since 1988 has been effective and had achieved its principal goal, which is to secure and consolidate China's support for the SLORC/SPDC government. China's political and diplomatic support has helped the SLORC/SPDC regime to strengthen its hold on power and its development assistance has also alleviated the impact of sanctions imposed by the West and Japan. Myanmar has been able so far to construct its China policy on the basis of "mutual benefit" while it still enjoys considerable freedom of action in its overall conduct of international relations. Myanmar's China policy in the post Cold War period should be placed in the context of the changing regional and international political and security environments. The Sino-Myanmar relationship since 1988 has witnessed ever closer cooperation between the two countries in several areas, and the direction in which the relations have developed in recent years has certainly had implications for regional security. In particular, the closer military cooperation between the two countries has caused alarm in some quarters. There are views that Myanmar's China Policy since 1988, unlike its previous cautious and balanced approach, has seen the country being drawn closer to China in the context of changes in the domestic and external environment. Myanmar is seen by some as falling into the Chinese strategic orbit. Viewing the region primarily through the prism of the "China Threat" or "China's Rise" discourse, some scholars conclude that Myanmar has become a "strategic pawn" for China. This has, in fact, tended to become an established self evident truth among many Myanmar observers. Yet there is no reason to believe that there has been a major shift in Myanmar's traditional foreign policy of neutrality. One could reasonably argue that there exists a general misunderstanding about Myanmar's closer relations with China. In reality, the government in Yangon has always been concerned about foreign influence and external interference in Myanmar and has always attempted to diversify its foreign relations. It has always subtly maneuvered to maintain its foreign policy based on strict neutrality and this has become, in a sense, possible only in the late 1990s.

The most significant changes in China's foreign policy during this period were triggered by the collapse of the Soviet Union and the Tiananmen Square incident. Despite the diminishing threat from Russia, the regional security environment did not necessarily change in favor of China. The Tiananmen incident resulted in wide ranging sanctions and pressures from the West. In the view of many Chinese strategists, the United States was shifting to a new containment of China Policy. In the wake of the Soviet disintegration, China became increasingly concerned with the emergence of the United States as the sole superpower, at least in political and strategic terms, dominating a unipolar world. This new global distribution of power and the political realities of post Cold War period as well as its desire to demonstrate that its rise will be peaceful and that it harbors no hegemonic designs, despite the expansion of its strategic frontiers, have pushed China to follow what has been known since the early 1990s as the "policy of good neighborliness", the chief hallmarks of which are accommodation and restraint in relations with neighboring countries. Despite different assessments of the impact of the rise of China, the Myanmar government is aware of the expansion of the Chinese strategic frontiers and its sphere of interests, if not influence. By repeating the Chinese rhetoric concerning United States containment of China, Myanmar hops to highlight its own geopolitical significance to the government in Beijing. Since China desires to assure all that its rise will be a peaceful one, the Myanmar government has realized that it will have more space for diplomatic maneuver. Thus, Naypyitaw has been able to cultivate closer relations with other great powers like Russia and India and regional organizations like ASEAN, without jeopardizing her relations with China.

Myanmar's China policy in the SLORC/SPDC period can be better understood in the larger context of Naypyitaw's relations with other major powers and regional countries. Since the early 1990s, the United States and other Western countries have imposed an increasingly harsh sanctions regime on Myanmar. Myanmar has thus been forced to look elsewhere for friends. China has taken advantage of the opportunity offered. Strategic cooperation between Myanmar and China has been made possible because both countries have been criticized by the West for suppression of "mass movements for democracy". The diplomatic isolation and economic sanctions imposed on Myanmar by the West, including the arms embargo have given a perfect opportunity for China to advance its strategic interests in Myanmar in the emerging post Cold War regional security environment. Diplomatic isolation and economic necessity have inevitably drawn Myanmar closer to China. Yet Sino-Myanmar relations can be best understood in the wider regional geopolitical framework, especially in the context of strategic competition between China and India. Both these countries wish to contain each other's influence in Southeast Asia. In the immediate aftermath of the 1988 uprising in Myanmar, the Indian government, under Indian National Congress Party, was sympathetically disposed towards anti-SLORC/SPDC elements. By the mid 1990s, with the change of government in India, increasingly aware of China's strategic gains in Myanmar, and the implementation of the "Look East" policy, among other things, New Delhi began to pursue a policy of engagement towards Yangon. Moreover, concerned that Myanmar might fall into China's strategic orbit and believing that it could persuade Yangon to fully integrate with the international community, despite opposition from the United States and some other Western countries, as well as anti-SLORC groups, ASEAN accepted Myanmar as a member in 1997. Since then, ASEAN has provided an extremely valuable diplomatic shield for the Myanmar government, giving Yangon/Naypyitaw room to manoeuvre its relations with China. Not only that but the Myanmar government has also cultivated a closer relationship with Russia, a country with growing interests in Southeast Asia, as it is fully aware that it needs to secure an additional veto at the UNSC, so that it will not be too much dependent on China for political survival. In this way, taking advantage of its geopolitical and geostrategic position and the changing dynamics of the regional security environment, Myanmar has tried to maintain a delicate balance in its China's policy. The government also realizes that Myanmar is potentially important in the context of Beijing's drive to establish a strategic presence in the Indian Ocean and link Southwest China to this vast region. In the context of China's grand strategy, while Myanmar will continue to tolerate a certain degree of Chinese influence, the government is fully aware that it has room to manoeuvre in order to maintain a proper balance in its foreign policy of non-alignment. There is no reason to believe that Beijing is capable of setting the parameters of Myanmar foreign policy.

As mentioned earlier, the principal thrust of Myanmar's China policy since 1988 has been directed towards securing and consolidating Chinese political support for the government in international and regional forums. One of the instruments to implement this policy objective has been cultivation of closer ties between the two militaries. When the Myanmar government decided to modernize its Tatmadaw (armed forces) in the early 1990s, China offered to supply relatively modern armaments on generous terms, (but not by any means state-of-the-art weapons) as Beijing has used arms provision as a method to extend and sustain its influence in the region. The development of closer military ties between Myanmar and China precipitated a major shift in Yangon's perception of Beijing. China was transformed from a potential enemy to a friend. However, weapons procurement from China brought with it a number of problems since the Tatmadaw was accustomed to NATO standard weapons. Chinese weapons were considered inferior in quality. Thus, closer military and economic cooperation with China, the Myanmar government tried to diversify its procurement pattern. To obtain more reliable and better-quality arms, Myanmar went to Russia and other Eastern European countries. This policy was by and large successful. Since the late 1990s, the Tatmadaw's arms procurement pattern has changed and become more diversified, indicating that Myanmar does not want to rely entirely on China for its force modernization. While military contacts between the countries remain crucial, Myanmar began to look alternative sources for military hardware.

Myanmar has also used its abundant natural resources as an instrument in its diplomacy towards China. Myanmar plays an important role in China's development strategy for its western provinces: it serves the shortest possible outlet to the Indian Ocean for Yunnan Province, providing the best and most cost-effective route for Yunnan products to reach European markets. Myanmar can also serve as a transit trade point for Chinese products, particularly those from the western provinces, bound for Thailand, Bangladesh, India and even other Southeast Asian countries. Sino-Myanmar trade, particularly the Yunnan-Myanmar border trade, will continue to grow. Myanmar will certainly benefit not only from the Chinese market but also from the Indian market. In terms of development assistance, China is likely to continue its support for Myanmar's industrialization and infrastructural development, at least for the foreseeable future, as the West continues to impose sanctions on Naypyitaw. In the area of FDI, China will continue its investment in strategic sectors, especially in energy. In this respect, Myanmar is well placed to engage in energy and pipeline diplomacy with China. The Kunming-Yangon rail link and the Kyaukphyu-Kunming Corridor will serve as key development links for China.

Despite some changes in the Myanmar leadership during the SLORC/ SPDC period, Myanmar's China policy has remained essentially unaltered. Although bilateral relations have been smooth and stable, they have not been without certain discomfitures on both sides. Yet, these difficult moments have never escalated into tensions or conflicts. Naypyitaw seems to have viewed the lack of state visits by Chinese leaders for nearly a decade simply as a manifestation of ignorance of Myanmar's geo-political significance. Jiang Zemin's 2001 visit was the last state visit by a Chinese dignitary of the highest rank until Vice President Xi Jinping appeared in Naypyitaw in June 2009. Premier Zhu Rongji had never visited Yangon. Premier Wen Jiabao finally came to Myanmar in June 2010. The SPDC government was rather unhappy when Zhu Rongji did not approve new loans and refused to reschedule the loan repayments. China also appears to have been disappointed with the SPDC leadership for its unwillingness to address regional and international concerns about Myanmar and the lack of progress in the national reconciliation process. China seems to be rather uncertain about the Myanmar leadership's commitment to genuine political transition and Beijing has increasingly shown its desire to see national reconciliation in Myanmar.

The Myanmar government assured Beijing that its ties with China remain central to the nation's foreign policy. Trade relations, security cooperation and military contacts have all continued. While China has publicly demonstrated its support for the Myanmar government in international forums, such as the United Nations Security Council, it has also pressed Naypyitaw to proceed with the promised political transition. As a responsible member and stakeholder of the international community, China is obliged to show respect for certain international norms and values. The Chinese government thus seems to want Myanmar to fulfil its international obligations. Failure to do so on the part of Naypyitaw would make it difficult for Beijing to defend the Myanmar government publicly and to prevent international interference in the country. Moreover, as various Western intelligence organizations became more active in Myanmar in the wake of the collapse of the country's intelligence apparatus in late 2004, China, too, began to take more active measures in building its own intelligence networks among Myanmar political activitists and dissidents, both at home and abroad. The Chinese government also seems to have signalled Naypyitaw that it is prepared to relax its policy of non-interference in the internal affairs of other states if this policy becomes harmful to Chinese national and strategic interests, that Beijing's continued support cannot be taken for granted and that it may come at a price. China now tells the Myanmar government that it will defend and protect Myanmar's *"fair interests"* at various international forums. Since 2003, the Chinese government has pushed Myanmar to proceed with the promised political transition and national reconciliation. Recently, in September 2007, at the height of renewed political tension between the government and the opposition in Myanmar, Foreign Minister Nyan Win, went to China, as Special Envoy from the SPDC Chairman, and held talks with Chinese Foreign Minister Yang Jiechi and State Councilor Tang Jiaxuan. Both expressed China's hope that Myanmar would push forward with the establishment of a democratic process that was appropriate to the country's circumstances. This, they declared, was "in the fundamental interests of the people of Myanmar and conducive to regional peace, stability and development". China, they said, hoped that the Myanmar government would restore internal stability as soon as possible, properly handle all relevant issues and actively promote national reconciliation.

Neither the Sinocentric world order of tributary relations nor the Westphalian world order of sovereign equality can adequately define the nature of Sino-Myanmar relations. The Sino-Myanmar relationship has and will always be asymmetric as disparity of power between the two nations exists. It is in the context of these asymmetric relations, that Sino-Myanmar relations should be explained. In reality, Myanmar's China policy is to promote the concept of a "Pauk-Phaw" relationship, which acknowledges the asymmetric nature of bilateral ties and incorporates a delicate balance between the logic of consequences and the logic of appropriateness. Sino-Myanmar relations between 1948 and 1967 could safely be characterized as a "normalized asymmetry". This was followed by a brief period of "hostile asymmetry" which lasted for about a decade. The bilateral relationship then moved into another period of "normalized asymmetry", extending from 1979 to 1988. From 1988 up to around 2000, the Sino-Myanmar relationship could be described as one of "dependent asymmetry". Since the early 2000s, it has moved into the direction of re-establishing "normalized asymmetry". In essence, Myanmar has constantly negotiated the asymmetry. In the "Pauk-Phaw" relationship with China, for all practical purpose, Myanmar is the younger sibling.

Sino-Myanmar relations have been enhanced by the personal diplomacy exercised by leaders of both countries. The historical precedents of the friendly relationship in the name of "Pauk-Phaw" have been highlighted by both sides from time to time to ensure that bilateral ties remain on the right track. The importance of the two country's respective security policies and economic development programmes to each other has been emphasized too. Diplomatic rituals have been performed through frequent exchanges of state visits. Ne Win journeyed to China eleven times while Zhao Enlai came to Myanmar for nine times.[1] In the post 1988 period, the performance of these diplomatic rituals continued. The break down of bilateral relations in late 1960s was partly due to the failure of both sides to fulfil their minimum expectations of each other. The Myanmar government appeared to learn the appropriate lessons and accorded China her preferred status. In addition, the Myanmar government also recognized the existence of important Chinese strategic interests in Southeast Asia generally and in Myanmar itself. Hence, Myanmar decided not to join ASEAN (until the 1990s) and to break the diplomatic isolation of Kampuchea in late 1970s. In recent years, issue routinization has been carried out at both the bilateral and multilateral levels, so that the bilateral relationship can be strengthened. The political consultations between the two foreign ministries and Naypyitaw's request for Beijing's assistance in meeting with U.S State Department officials provide clear examples of Myanmar's deference to China. With public adherence to the principle of non-interference in each other's internal affairs and the promise of mutually beneficial cooperation, China acknowledges Myanmar's autonomy.

Under the banner of "Pauk-Phaw" friendship in an apparently asymmetric relationship, Myanmar skillfully plays the "China card" and enjoys considerable space in her conduct of foreign relations. So long as both sides fulfil the obligations that come under "Pauk-Phaw" friendship, the relationship will remain smooth. Myanmar has constantly repositioned her relations with China to her best advantage. Myanmar's China policy has always been placed somewhere in between balancing and bandwagoning, and the juxtaposition of accommodating China's regional strategic interests and resisting Chinese influence and interference in Myanmar internal affairs has been a hallmark of Myanmar's China policy. This is likely to remain unchanged. As long as it recognizes the legitimate strategic interests of China in Myanmar, the Myanmar government will be left to conduct its foreign relations within the context of its non-aligned policy. In addition, against the background of the growing significance of Myanmar to China in geopolitical and geostrategic terms, and of its own drive for modernization and development, Beijing will base its diplomacy on the good neighborliness policy, mutual benefit, and the Five Principles of Peaceful Coexistence. For all the celebratory talk about a mutually beneficial partnership between Beijing and Naypyitaw, much hard work remains to be done by both sides before this relationship meets the expectations of its most enthusiastic proponents. Naypyitaw will also continue to conduct her China policy in the context of the traditional "Pauk-Phaw" friendship that allows Myanmar flexibility in her foreign relations. However, if Myanmar's engagement with China in the past decades offers any lesson for future reference, it is most likely that Myanmar will be very cautious in its dealing with its powerful neighbour, because it is thoroughly convinced that China, like all other countries, will determine her Myanmar policy in accordance with the calculations of her own interest.

Note

1. See Appendix (2) for detail.

APPENDICES

APPENDIX I

SINO-BURMESE AGREEMENT ON
BOUNDARY QUESTION
28 January 1960

The Government of the People's Republic of China and the Government of the Union of Burma,

With a view to promoting an overall settlement of the Sino-Burmese boundary question and to consolidating and further developing friendly relations between China and Burma,

Have agreed to conclude the present Agreement under the guidance of the Five Principles of peaceful co-existence and have agreed as follows:-

Article I

The Contracting Parties agree to set up immediately a joint committee composed of an equal number of delegates from each side and charge it, in accordance with the provisions of the present Agreement, to discuss and work out solutions on the concrete questions regarding the Sino-Burmese boundary enumerated in Article II of the present Agreement, conduct surveys of the boundary and set up boundary markers, and draft a Sino-Burmese boundary treaty, The joint committee shall hold regular meetings in the capitals of the two countries or at any other places in the two countries.

Article II

The Contracting Parties agree that the existing issues concerning the Sino-Burmese boundary shall be settled in accordance with the following provisions:

(1) With the exception of the area of Hpimaw, Gawlum and Kangfang, the entire undelimited boundary from the high conical peak to the western extremity of the Sino-Burmese boundary shall be delimited along the traditional customary line, that is to say, from the high conical peak northward along the watershed between the Taiping, the Shweli, the Nu (Salween) and the Tulung (Taron) Rivers on the one hand and the Nmai Hka River on the other, up to the place where it crosses the Tulung (Taron) River between Chingdam and Nhkumkang, and then along the watershed between the Tulung (Taron) and the Tsayul (Zayul) Rivers on the one hand and all the upper tributaries of the Irrawaddy River, except for the Tulung (Taron) River, on the other, up to the western extremity of the Sino-Burmese boundary. The joint committee shall send out joint survey teams composed of an equal number of persons from each side to conduct surveys along the above mentioned watersheds so as to determine the specific alignment of this section of the boundary line and to set up boundary markers.

(2) The Burmese Government has agreed to return to China the area of Hpimaw, Gawlum and Kangfang which belongs to China. As to the extent of this area to be returned to China, it is to be discussed and determined by the joint committee in accordance with the proposals put forward and marked on maps by the Governments of Burma and China on February 4, 1957 and July 26, 1957 respectively. After determining the extent of this area to be returned to China, the joint committee shall send out joint survey teams composed of an equal number of persons from each side to conduct on-the-spot survey of the specific alignment of this section of the boundary line and to set up boundary markers.

(3) In order to abrogate the "perpetual lease" by Burma of the Meng-Mao triangular area (Namwam assigned tract) at the junction of the Namwan and the Shweli Rivers, which belongs to China, the Chinese Government has agreed to turn over this area to Burma to become part of the territory of the Union of Burma. In exchange, the Burmese Government has agreed to turn over to China to become part of Chinese territory the areas under the jurisdiction of the Panhung and Panlao tribes, which are west of the boundary line from the junction of the Nam Ting and the Nampa Rivers to the Number One marker on the southern delimited section of the boundary as defined in the notes exchanged between the Chinese and the British Governments of June 18, 1941. As to the extent of these areas to be turned over to China, the Chinese and the Burmese Governments put forward proposals marked on maps of July 26, 1957 and June 4, 1959 respectively. The area where the proposals of the two Governments coincide will definitely be turned over to China. Where the proposals of the two Governments differ as to the area

under the jurisdiction of the Panhung tribe, the joint committee will send out a team composed of an equal number of persons from each side to ascertain on-the-spot as to whether it is under the jurisdiction of the Panhung tribe, so as to determine whether it is to be turned over to China. After the extent of the areas under the jurisdiction of the Panhung and Panlao tribes to be turned over to China has been thus determined the joint committee will send out joint survey teams composed of an equal number of persons from each side to conduct on-the-spot survey of the specific alignment of this section of the boundary line and to set up boundary markers.

(4) Except for the adjustment provided for in paragraph (3) of this Article, the section of the boundary from the junction of the Nam Ting and the Nampa Rivers to the Number One marker on the southern delimited section of the boundary shall be delimited as defined in the notes exchanged between the Chinese and the British Governments on June 18, 1941. The joint committee shall send out joint survey teams composed of an equal number of persons from each side to carry out delimitation and demarcation along this section of the boundary line and set up boundary markers.

Article III

The Contracting Parties agree that the joint committee, after working out solutions for the existing issues concerning the Sino-Burmese boundary as enumerated in Article II of the present Agreement shall be responsible for drafting a Sino-Burmese boundary treaty, which shall cover not only all the sections of the boundary as mentioned in Article II of the present Agreement, but also the sections of the boundary which were already delimited in the past and need no adjustment. After being signed by the Governments of the two countries and coming into effect, the new boundary treaty shall replace all old treaties and notes exchanged concerning the boundary between the two countries. The Chinese Government, in line with its policy of being consistently oppose to foreign prerogatives and respecting the sovereignty of other countries, renounces China's right of participation in mining enterprises at Lufang of Burma as provided in the notes exchanged between the Chinese and the British Governments on June 18, 1941.

Article IV

(1) The present Agreement is subject to ratification and the instruments of ratification will be exchanged in Rangoon as soon as possible.

(2) The present Agreement will come into force immediately on the

exchange of the instruments of ratification and shall automatically cease to be in force when the Sino-Burmese boundary treaty to be signed by the two Governments comes into force.

Done in duplicate in Peking on the 28th day of January 1960, in the Chinese and English languages, both texts being equally authentic.

FOR THE GOVERNMENT OF   FOR THE GOVERNMENT OF
THE PEOPLE'S REPUBLIC   THE UNION OF BURMA
OF CHINA

(Signed) Chou En-lai.   (Signed) Ne Win.

TREATY OF FRIENDSHIP AND MUTUAL NON-AGGRESSION BETWEEN THE UNION OF BURMA AND THE PEOPLE'S REPUBLIC OF CHINA
28 January 1960

The Government of the People's Republic of China and the Government of the Union of Burma,

Desiring to maintain everlasting peace and cordial friendship between the People's Republic of China and the Union of Burma,

Convinced that the strengthening of good neighbourly relations and friendly co-operation between the People's Republic of China and the Union of Burma is in accordance with the vital interests of both countries,

Have decided for this purpose to conclude the present Treaty in accordance with the Five Principles of peaceful coexistence jointly initiated by the two countries, and have agreed as follows:

Article I

The Contracting Parties recognize and respect the independence, sovereign rights and territorial integrity of each other.

Article II

There shall be everlasting peace and cordial friendship between the Contracting Parties who undertake to settle all disputes between them by means of peaceful negotiation without resorting to force.

Article III

Each Contracting Party undertakes not to carry out acts of aggression against the other and not to take part in any military alliance directed against the other Contracting Party.

Article IV

The Contracting Parties declare that they will develop and strengthen the economic and cultural ties between the two states in a spirit of friendship and co-operation, in accordance with the principles of equality and mutual benefit and of mutual non-interference in each other's internal affairs.

Article V

Any difference or dispute arising out of the interpretation of the present Treaty or one or more of its articles shall be settled by negotiations through the ordinary diplomatic channels.

Article VI

(1) The present Treaty is subject to ratification and the instruments of ratification will be exchanged in Rangoon as soon as possible.

(2) The present Treaty will come into force immediately on the exchange of the instruments of ratification and will remain in force for a period of ten years.

(3) Unless either of the Contracting Parties gives to the other notice in writing to terminate it at least one year before the expiration of this period, it will remain in force without any specified time limit, subject to the right of either of the Contracting Parties to terminate it by giving to the other in writing a year's notice of its intention to do so.

In witness whereof the Premier of the State Council of the People's Republic of China and the Prime Minister of the Union of Burma have signed the present Treaty.

Done in duplicate in Peking on the 28th day of January 1960, in the Chinese and English languages, both text being equally authentic.

For the Government of the   For the Government of the
People's Republic of China   Union of Burma

(Signed) Chou En-lai   (Signed) Ne Win

BOUNDARY TREATY BETWEEN THE PEOPLE'S REPUBLIC OF CHINA AND THE UNION OF BURMA
1 October 1960

The Chairman of the People's Republic of China and the President of the Union of Burma,

Being of the agreed opinion that the long outstanding question of the boundary between the two countries is a question inherited from history, that since the two countries successively won independence, the traditional friendly and good-neighbourly relations between the two countries have undergone a new development, and the fact that Prime Ministers of the two countries jointly initiated in 1954 the Five Principles of Peaceful Co-existence among nations with different social systems as principles guiding relations between the two countries has all the more greatly promoted the friendly relations between the two countries and has created conditions for the settlement of the question of the boundary between the two countries;

Noting with satisfaction that the Government of the People's Republic of China and the successive governments of the Union of Burma, conducting friendly consultation and showing mutual understanding and mutual accommodation in accordance with the Five Principles of Peaceful Co-existence, have overcome various difficulties, and have eventually reached a successful and overall settlement of the question of the boundary between the two countries; and

Firmly believing that the formal delimitation of the entire boundary between the two countries and its emergence as a boundary of peace and friendship not only represent a milestone in the further development of the friendly relations between China and Burma, but also constitute an important contribution to the safeguarding of Asian and world peace;

Have resolved for this purpose to conclude the present Treaty on the basis of the agreement on the question of the boundary between the two countries signed by Premier Chou En-lai and Prime Minister Ne Win on January 28th, 1960 and appointed their respective plenipotentiaries as follows:

Chou En-lai, Premier of the State Council, for the Chairman of the People's Republic of China, and

U Nu, Prime Minister, for the President of the Union of Burma,

Who, having mutually examined their full powers and found them in good and due form, have agreed upon the following:

Article I

In accordance with the principle of respect for sovereignty and territorial integrity and in the spirit of friendship and mutual accommodation, the Union of Burma agrees to return to China area of Hpimaw, Gawlum and Kangfang (measuring about 153 square kilometres, 59 square miles, and as indicated in the attached map) which belongs to China; and the People's Republic of China agrees to delimit the section of the boundary from the junction of the Nam Hpa and the Nam Ting rivers to the junction of the Nam Hka and the Nam Yung rivers in accordance with the notes exchanged between the Chinese and the British Governments on June 18th, 1941, with the exception of the adjustments provided for in Articles Two and Three of the present Treaty.

Article II

In view of the relations of equality and friendship between China and Burma, the two parties decide to abrogate the "perpetual lease" by Burma of the Meng-Mao triangular area (Namwan assigned tract) which belongs to China. Taking into account the practical needs of the Burmese side, the Chinese side agrees to turn over this area (measuring about 220 square kilometres, 85 square miles, and as indicated in the attached map) to Burma to become part of the territory of the Union of Burma. In exchange, and having regard for the historical ties and the integrity of the tribes, the Burmese side agrees to turn over to China to become part of Chinese territory the areas (measuring about 189 square kilometres, 73 square miles, and as indicated in the attached map) under the jurisdiction of the Panhung and Panlao tribes, which belong to Burma according to the provision in the notes exchanged between the Chinese and the British Governments on June 18th, 1941.

Article III

For the convenience of administration by each side and having regard for the intratribal relationship and production and livelihood of the local inhabitants, the two parties agree to make fair and reasonable adjustments to a small section of the boundary line as defined in the notes exchanged between the Chinese and the British Governments on June 18th, 1941, by including in China Yawng Hok and Lungnai villages and including in Burma Umhpa, Pan Kung, Pan Nawng and Pan Wai villages, so that these boundary-line-intersected villages will no longer be intersected by the boundary line.

Article IV

The Chinese Government, in line with its consistent policy of opposing foreign prerogatives and respecting the sovereignty of other countries, renounces China's right of participation in mining enterprises at Lufang of Burma as provided in the notes exchanged between the Chinese and the British Governments on June 18th, 1941.

Article V

The Contracting Parties agree that the section of the boundary from the high conical peak to the western extremity of the Sino-Burmese boundary, with the exception of the area of Hpimaw, Gawlum and Kangfang, shall be fixed along the traditional customary line, i.e., from the high conical peak northwards along the watershed between the Taping, the Shweli and the Nu rivers and the section of the Tulung (Taron) river above western Chingdam Village on the one hand and the Nmai Hka river on the other, to a point on the south bank of the Tulung (Taron) River and then further along the watershed between the section of the Tulung (Taron) River above western Chingdam Village and the Tsayul (Zayul) River on the one hand and all the upper tributaries of the Irrawaddy River excluding the section of the Tulung (Taron) River above western Chingdam Village on the other, to the western extremity of the Sino-Burmese boundary.

Article VI

The Contracting Parties affirm that the two sections of the boundary from the high conical peak to the junction of the Nam Kha and the Nam Yung rivers to the south eastern extremity of the Sino-Burmese boundary at the junction of the Nam la and the Lanchang (Mekong) rivers were already delimited in the past and require no change, the boundary being as delineated in the maps attached to the present Treaty.

Article VII

1. In accordance with the provisions of Articles I and V of the present Treaty, the alignment of the section of the boundary line from the high conical peak to the western extremity of the Sino-Burmese boundary shall be as follows:

    (1) From the high conical peak (Mu-lang Pum, Manang Pum) the line runs

northwards, then southeastwards and then northeastwards along the watershed between the Taping River (Ta Ying Chiang), the Lung Chuan Chiang (Shweli) and the Nu (Salween) River on the one hand and the Nmai Hka river on the other, passing through Shuei Cheng (Machyi Chet) Pass, Panwa Pass, Tasamin Shan, Hpare (Yemawlaunggu Hkyet) Pass and Chitsu (Lagwi) Pass to the source of the Chu-I Ta Ho (Chu-Iho Ta-Ho).

(2) From the source of the Chu-I Ta Ho (Chu-Iho Ta Ho) the line runs northwestwards along the Chu-I Ta Ho (Chu-Iho Ta Ho) to its junction with its tributary flowing in from the north, thence northwards along this tributary to a point on the watershed between the tributaries of the Hpim (Htang-kyam Kyaung) River on the one hand and the Wang Ke (Moku Kyaung) river and its tributary, the Chu-I Ta Ho (Chu-Iho Ta Ho), on the other, thence westwards along this watershed, passing through Ma Chu Lo Waddy (2,423 metres 7,950 feet), thence northwards till it crosses the Hpimaw (Htang-kyam Kyaung) River west of Hpimaw Village; thence northwards along the ridge, passing through Luksang Bum and crossing the Gan (Kang Hao) River to reach the Wu Chung (Wasok Kyaung) River; thence westwards along the Wu Chung (Wasok Kyaung) River to its junction with the Hsiao Chiang (Ngawchaung Hka) River; thence northwards up the Hsiao Chiang (Ngawchang Hka) River to its junction with the Ta Hpawte (Hpawte Kyaung) River. Thence the line runs north of Kangfang Village generally eastwards and then southeastwards along the watershed between the Hsiao Hpawte (Phawshi Kyaung) river and the Wu Chung (Wasok Kyaung) River on the one hand and the Ta Hpawte (Huawte Kyaung) River on the other, to a point on the watershed between the Nu (Salween) and the Nmai Hka Rivers.

(3) From the above-mentioned point on the watershed between the Nu (Salween) and the Nmai Hka Rivers, the line runs generally by northwards along the watershed between the Nu (Salween) river and the section of the Tulung (Taron) river above western Chingdam Village on the one hand and the Nmai Hka River on the other, passing through Kia Ngo Tu (Sajyang) Pass, Sala Pass, Ming Ke (Nahke) Pass, Ni Chi Ku (Gi Gi Thara) Pass, Jongit L'ka and Maguchi Pass; thence the line continues to run northwards and then generally westwards, passing through Alang L'ka, Mawa L'ka, Pang Tang Shan (Pum-tang Razi), Lonlang L'Ka, Hkora Razi to Tusehpong Razi.

(4) From Tusehpong Razi, the line runs generally northwestwards along the ridge, passing through height 2,892 metres and height 2,140.3 metres, to a point on the south bank of the Tulung (Taron) River west of Western Chingdam Village. Thence it crosses the Tulung (Taron) river to its junction with its tributary on its northern bank, and thence northwestwards along the ridge to Kundam Razi (Lungawng Hpong).

(5) From Kundam Razi (Lungawng Hpong) the line runs generally northwards and northwestwards along the watershed between the section of the Tulung (Taron) river above Western Chingdam Village on the one hand, and the upper tributaries of the Irrawaddy River [excluding the section of the Tulung (Taron) River above Western Chingdam Village] on the other, passing through Thala Pass, Sungya (Amansan) L'ka to Yulang Pass.

(6) From Yulang Pass the line runs generally southwestwards along the watershed between the Tsayul (Zayu) River on the one hand and the upper tributaries of the Irrawaddy River on the other, passing through Gamlang L'ka to the western extremity of the Sino-Burmese boundary.

2. In accordance with the provisions of Article I, II, III, and VI of the present Treaty, the alignment of the section of the boundary line from the High Conical Peak to the southeastern extremity of the Sino-Burmese boundary shall be as follows:

(1) From the High Conical Peak, the line runs generally southwestwards along the watershed between the upper tributaries of the Taping River, the Mong Ka Hka and the upper tributaries of the Ta Pa Chiang (Tabak Hka) river on the one hand and the lower tributaries of the Nmai Hka River on the other, passing through Ta Ya Kuo (Lunghkyen Hkyet), and thence northwestwards to Hsiao Chueh Pass (Tabak-Hku Hkyet).

(2) From Hsiao Chueh Pass (Tabak-Hku Hkyet), the line runs down the Ta Pa Chiang (Tabak Hka), the Mong Ka Hka and up the Shih Tzu (Paknoi Hka) River (the upper stretch of which is known as the Hkatong Hka River) to its source.

(3) From the source of the Shih Tzu (Paknoi Hka) River, the line runs southwestwards and then westwards along the watershed between the Monglai Hka on the one hand and the Pajao Hka, the Ma Li Ka river and the Nan Shan (Namsang Hka) River on the other, to the source of the Laisa Stream.

(4) From the source of the Laisa Stream, the line runs down the Laisa Stream and up the Mu Lei Chiang (Mole Chang) and the Ga Yang Hka (Cheyang Hka), passing through Ma Po Tzu (A-law-Hkyet), and then runs southwards down the Nan Pen Chiang (Nampaung Hka) to its junction with the Raping river; thence eastwards up the Taping to the point River; thence eastwards up the Taping river to the point where the taping River meets a small ridge west of the junction of the Kuli Hka Stream with the Taping River.

(5) From the point where the Taping River meets the above-mentioned small ridge, the line runs along the watershed between the Kuli Hka Stream, the Husa (Namsa Hka) River and the tributaries of the Namwan River west of the Kuli Hka Stream on the other, up to Pang Chien Shan (Pan Teng Shan).

(6) From Pang Chien Shan (Pan Teng Shan), the line runs southwards to join the Kindit Hka, then down the Kindit Hka and the Nam Wa Hka (Pang Ling) River to a point on the south bank of the Nam Wa Hka (Pang Ling) River southeast of Man Yung Hai Village and north of Nawng Sa Village, thence in a straight line southwestwards and then southwards to the Nan Sah (Manting Hka) River; then it runs down the course of the Nan Sah (Manting Hka) River as at the time when the boundary was demarcated in the past, to its junction with the Namwan River, thence down the course of the Namwan River as it was at that time, to its junction with the course of the Shweli River as it was at that time.

(7) From the junction of the courses of the Namwan River and the Shweli River as at the time when the boundary was demarcated in the past, to the junction of the Shweli and the Wanting (Nam Yang) Rivers, the location of the line shall be as delineated on the maps attached to the present Treaty. Thence the line runs up the course of the Wanting (Nam Yang) River as at the time when the boundary was demarcated in the past, and the Weishang Hka, then turns northwestwards along a tributary of the Nam Che Hka (Nam Hse) River to its junction with the Nam Che Hka (Nam Hse) River, thence eastwards up the Nam Che Hka (Nam Hse) River, passing through Ching Shu Pass, and thence along the Monglong Hka and the course of the Mong Ko (Nam Ko) River as at the time when the boundary was demarcated in the past, thence up the Nam Hkai and the Nam Pang Wa Rivers, passing through a pass, and then along the man Hsing (Nam Hpawn) River [Whose upper stretch is known as the Nam Tep (Nam Lep) River] to its junction with the Nu (Salween) river, thence eastwards up the Nu (Salween) River to its junction with the Ti Kai Kou (Nam Men) Stream.

(8) From the junction of the Nu (Salween) River with the Ti Kai Kuo (Nam Men) Stream, the line runs southwestwards along the Ti Kai Kuo (Nan Men) Stream, then southwestwards, then southwards along the watershed between the Meng Peng Ho (the upper stretch of the Nam Peng River) on the one hand and the tributaries of the Nu (Salween) River on the other, up to Pao Lou Shan.

(9) From Pao Lou Shan, the line runs southeastwards along the Wa Yao Kou Stream, the ridge south of the Mai Ti (Mai Ti Ho) river, the Pan Chiao Ho and the Hsiao Lu Chang (Hsin Chai Kou) Stream up to the source of the Hsiao Lu Chang (Hsin Chai Kuo) Stream. From the source of the above stream to the junction of the nam Hpa and the nam Ting Rivers, the location of the line shall be as delineated on the maps attached to the present Treaty. The line then runs eastwards for about four kilometres (about three miles) up the Nam Ting River and thence southeastwards along the

northwest slope of Kummuta Shan (Loi Hseng) to the top of Kummuta Shan (Loi Hseng).

(10) From the top of Kummuta Shan (Loi Hseng), the line runs southeastwards along a tributary of the Kung Meng Ho (Nam Loi-hsa) river to its junction with another tributary flowing in from the southeast; thence up the latter tributary to a point northwest of Maklawt (Ma-Law) Village. Thence, the line runs in a straight line to a point southwest of Maklawt (Ma-Law) Village, and again in a straight line across a tributary of the Yun Hsing (Nam Tap) River to Shien Jen Shan, located east of the junction of the above-mentioned tributary with another tributary of the Yun Hsing (Nam Tap) River; thence along the watershed between the above two tributaries of the Yun Hsing (Nam Tap) River to the source of the one to the west and then turns westwards and southwestwards along the Mong Ling Shan Ridge, up to the top of Mong Ling Shan. Thence it runs eastwards and southeastwards along the Nam Pan River to its junction with a tributary, northeast of Yakaw Chai (Ya Kuo Sai) Village, which flows in from the southwest; thence in a south-westerly direction up that tributary, to a point northeast of Yakaw Chai (Ya Kou Sai) Village, from where it turns southwards passing through a point east of Yakaw Chai (Ya Kou Sai) Village, and crosses a tributary of the Nam Pan River south of Yakaw Chai (Ya Kou Sai) Village, thence westwards to the source of the Nam It River a little east of Chao Pao (Taklyet No) Village. Thence the line runs siuthwards along the Nam It and the Nam Mu Rivers, and then turns eastwards along the Nam Kunglong and the Chawk Hkrak Rivers to the northeast source of the Chawk Hkrak River.

(11) From the northeast source of the Chawk Hkrak River, the line runs southwards and eastwards along the watershed between the upper tributaries of the Nam Kunlong River on the one hand and the southern tributaries of the Chawk Hkrak River and the Nan Tin (Nam Htung) River on the other, to a point on the west side of Umhpa Village. Thence it runs eastwards passing a point 100 metres north of Umhpa Village, and theneastwards up to the source of a small river on the above-mentioned watershed; thence along the ridge eastwards to the source of a tributary of the Mongtum (Nam Tum) river (the upper stretch of which is called the Ta Tung River), which it follows in an easterly and north-easterly direction to its junction with another tributary of the Mongtum (Nam Tum) River flowing in from the southeast; thence it follows this tributary to its source on the watershed between the Mongtum (Nam Tum) and the Lung Ta Hsiao Ho (Nam Lawng) Rivers. It then crosses the watershed in an easterly direction to the source of the Lung Ta Hsiao Ho (Nam Lawang) River which it follows to its junction with its tributary flowing in from the north, thence in a northerly direction along

the above-mentioned tributary, passing through a point on the Kanpinau Ridge, thence generally eastwards along a valley, crossing the junction of two subtributaries of a tributary of the Lung Ta Hsiao Ho (Nam Lawng) River, then northeastwards to the watershed between the Mongtum (Nam Tum) River on the one hand, and the Nam Ma River on the other, until it reaches height 1,941.8 metres (6,370 feet). Thence the line runs eastwards, then southwards and then northwestwards along the watershed between the Mongtum (Nam Tum), the La Meng (Nam Meng Ho), the Ku Hsing Ho (Nam Hka Lam) and the Nam Hka Hkao (Nam Hsiang Ho) Rivers on the one hand and the Nam Ma River on the other, up to a point on this watershed northwest of La Law Village.

(12) From the point on the above-mentioned watershed northwest of La law Village, the line runs down the nearest tributary of the Nam Hka Khao River and thence down the NamHka Hkao River to its junction with a tributary flowing in from the southwest. Thence the line runs generally in from the southwest up that tributary to its course, which is northeast of and nearest to height 2,180 metes (7,152 feet). Thence it crosses the ridge at a point 150 metres (492 feet) southeast of the above-mentioned height and then turns southwards to the source of the nearest tributary of the Nam Lung (Nam Sak) river, from where it proceeds along the Nam Lung (Nam Sak), the Nam Hse and the Nam Hka Rivers to the junction of the Nam Hka and the Nam Yung Rivers, and thence up the Nam Yung River to its source.

(13) From the source of the Nam Yung River the line runs in a south-easterly direction to the watershed between the Na Wu (Nam Wong) and the Nam Pei (Nam Hpe) rivers; thence generally eastwards along the above-mentioned watershed, and then eastwards along the Na Wu (Nam Wong) River, which it follows to its junction with the Nan Lai (Nam Lai) River, thence along the watershed between the Na Wu (Nam Wong) and the Nan Lai (Nam Lai) Rivers to the Anglang Shan (Loi Ang Lawng) river; thence northwards along the ridge to the top of Anglang Shan (Loi Ang Lawng), thence generally eastwards along the ridge, crosses the Nam Tung Chik (Nam Tonghkek) River and then follows the watershed between the tributaries on the west bank of the Nam Lei (Nam Lwe) River at the north of the La Ting (Hwe-Kye-Tai) River and the Nam La Ho [a tributary of the Nan Ma (Nam Ma) River] on the one hand and the tributaries on the west bank of the Nam Lei (Nam Lwe) River at the south of the La Ting (Hwe-Kye-Tai) River on the other, up to the top of Pang Shun Shan (Loi Pang Hsun).

(14) From the top of Pang Shun Shan (Loi Pang Hsun) the line runs generally eastwards along the La Ting (Hwe-Kye-Tai) River, the Nam Lei

(Nam Lwe) River, the course of the Nam Lo (Nam Law) Stream as at the time when the boundary was demarcated in the past, and the Nan Wo (Nambok) River at Nan Wo Kai Nam Shan (Loi Kwainang).

(15) From the source of the Nan Wo (Nambok) river at Nan Wo Kai Shan (Loi Kwainang) the line runs generally eastward along the watershed between the Nan La (Nam Lak) [a tributray of the Nam Lei (Nam Lwe) River], the Nan Pai (Nam Hpe) and the Nan Hsi (Nam Hok) Rivers on the one hand and the Nan Ping (Nam Hpen), the Nan Mau (Nam Mawng) and the Nan Hsi Pang (Nam Hsi Pang) Rivers on the other, up to San Min Po (Loi Hsammong).

(16) From San Min Po (Loi hsammong) the line runs in a general northeasterly direction to a point on the west bank of the Nam Lam River. Thence it descends the Nam Lam river to the foot of Chiu Na Shan (Kyu Nak) on the south bank of the Nam Lam River and then runs in a general southeasterly direction passing through Hue Ling Lang (Hwe Mawk Hkio), La Ti (La Tip), Nan Meng Hao (Nam-mong Hau) to Mai Niu Tung (Mai Niu Tawng); thence the line runs in a general northeasterly direction passing through Lung Man Tang (Long Man Tang) to the Hui La (Hwe La) Stream, which it follows northwards to its junction with the Nam Lam River. Thence the line runs eastwards and southwards along the Nam Lam, the Nan Chih (Nam Se) Rivers and the Nam Chia (Hwe Sak) Stream, to Lei Len Ti Fa Shan (Loi Len Ti Hpa). The line then follows the Nam Mot (Nan Mai), the Nan Tung (Nam Tung) and the Nam Ta Rivers to Hsing Kang Lei Shan (Loi Makhinkawng).

(17) From Hsing Kang Lei Shan (Loi Makhinkawng) the line runs eastwards along the watershed between the Nam Nga River and its upper tributaries on the one hand and the Nam Loi River (including its tributary the Nam He River) on the other, to the top of Kwang Pien Nei Shan (Kwang Peknoi).

(18) From the top of Kwang Pien Nei Shan (Kwang Peknoi) the line runs generally northeastwards along the Hue Le (Nam Luk) river and the course of the Nam Nga River as at the time when the boundary was demarcated in the past, to the junction of the Nam Nga and the Lanchang (Mekong) Rivers; thence down the Lanchang (Mekong) River up to the southeastern extremity of the Sino-Burmese boundary line at the junction of the Nam La and the Lanchang (Mekong) River.

3. The alignment of the entire boundary line between the two countries described in this Article and the location of the temporary boundary marks erected by both sides during joint survey are shown on the 1/250,000 maps

indicating the entire boundary and on the 1/50,000 maps of certain areas, which are attached to the present Treaty.

Article VIII

The Contracting Parties agree that wherever the boundary follows a river, the mid-stream line shall be the boundary in the case of an unnavigable river, and the middle line of the main navigational channel (the deepest watercourse) shall be the boundary in the case of a navigable river. In case the boundary river changes its course, the boundary line between the two countries shall remain unchanged in the absence of other agreements between the two sides.

Article IX

The Contracting Parties agree that:

1. Upon the coming into force of the present Treaty, the Meng-Mao Triangular Area to be turned over to Burma under Article II of the present Treaty shall become territory of the Union of Burma;

2. The area of Hpimaw, Gawlum and Kangfang to be returned to China under Article I of the present Treaty and the areas under the jurisdiction of the Panhung and Panlao tribes to be turned over to China under Article II shall be handed over by the Burmese Government to the Chinese Government within four months after the present Treaty comes into force;

3. The area to be adjusted under Article III of the present Treaty shall be handed over respectively by the Government of one Contracting Party to that of the other within four months after the present Treaty comes into force.

Article X

After the signing of the present Treaty, the Burmese-Chinese Joint Boundary Committee constituted in pursuance of the Agreement between the two Parties on the Question of the Boundary Between the Two Countries of January 28, 1960, shall continue to carry out necessary surveys of the boundary line between the two countries, to set up new boundary markers, and shall then draft a protocol setting forth in detail the alignment of the entire boundary line and the location of all the boundary markers, with detailed maps attached showing the boundary line and the location of the boundary markers. The above mentioned protocol, upon being concluded by the Governments of the two countries, shall become an annex to the present Treaty and the detailed maps attached to the present Treaty.

Article XI

The contracting Parties agree that any dispute concerning the boundary, which may arise after the formal delimitation of the boundary between the two countries shall be settled by the two sides through friendly consultations.

Article XII

The present Treaty is subject to ratification and the instruments of ratification will be exchanged in Rangoon as soon as possible.

The present Treaty shall come into force on the day of the exchange of the instruments of ratification.

Upon the coming into force of the present Treaty, all past treaties, exchanged notes and other documents relating to the boundary between the two countries shall be no longer in force, except as otherwise provided in Article X of the present Treaty with regard to the Agreement between the two Parties on the Question of the Boundary Between the Two Countries of January 28, 1960.

Done in duplicate in Peking on October 1, 1960, in the Burmese, Chinese and English languages, all three texts being equally authentic.

Plenipotentiary of the   Plenipotentiary of the
Union of Burma   People's Republic of China
(Signed) U NU   (Signed) CHOU EN-LAI

APPENDIX II

(A) U Ne Win's Visits to China

Sr.	Date	Designation	Remark
1	November 1955	Commander-in-Chief	
2	January 1960	Prime Minister, Caretaker Government	
3	September 1960	Commander-in-Chief	Member of U Nu's delegation
4	October 1961	Commander-in-Chief	Member of U Nu's delegation
5	July 1965	Chairman, Revolutionary Council	
6	August 1971	Chairman, Revolutionary Council	
7	November 1975	President	
8	April 1977	President	
9	September 1977	President	
10	October 1981	President	
11	May 1985	Chairman, BSPP	

(B) Zhou Enlai's Visits to Myanmar

Sr.	Date	Designation	Remark
1	June 1954	Premier	
2	April 1955	Premier	
3	December 1956	Premier	
4	April 1960	Premier	
5	January 1961	Premier	For the Exchange of Treaty
6	February 1964	Premier	
7	July 1964	Premier	
8	April 1965	Premier	
9	April 1965	Premier	

In the period between 1950 and 2010, 16 Myanmar ambassadors have served in Beijing and 15 Chinese ambassadors in Yangon.

(C) List of Myanmar and Chinese Ambassadors

Myanmar to China		China to Myanmar	
Name	Date	Name	Date
U Myint Thein	08-06-1950	Mr. Yao Zhongming	05-09-1950
U Hla Maung	17-09-1951	Mr. Li Yimang	30-04-1958
U Maung Maung Kyaw Win	17-02-1959	Mr. Geng Biao	20-09-1963
Samar Duwah Sinwah Naung	05-12-1964	Mr. Chen Zhaoyuan	01-04-1971
U Thein Maung	16-11-1970	Mr. Ye Chengzhang	08-06-1973
Thakin Chan Tun	11-11-1974	Mr. Mo Yanzhong	23-11-1977
U Myint Maung	27-12-1976	Mr. Huang Mingda	03-08-1982
U Tha Tun	18-05-1978	Mr. Zhou Mingji	13-08-1985
U Aung Win	30-06-1982	Mr. Cheng Ruisheng	25-08-1987
U Hla Shwe	31-01-1984	Mr. Liang Feng	10-07-1991
U Tin Maung Myint	05-07-1986	Mrs. Chen Baoliu	27-09-1994
U Tin Aung Tun	07-04-1989	Mr. Liang Dong	10-09-1997
U Sett	22-02-1993	Mr. Li Jinjun	13-03-2001
U Ba Htay Chit	01-04-1998	Mr. Guan Mu	31-10-2005
U Sein Win Aung	08-11-2001	Mr. Ye Dabo	22-01-2009
U Thein Lwin	18-06-2003		

BIBLIOGRAPHY

Articles (English)

Ambassador U Thant. "Some Reflections on Burma's Foreign Policy", *The Guardian Monthly Magazine* (Vol. 8, No. 9; September 1961).

Aung Myoe, Maung. "The Road to Naypyitaw: Making Sense of the Myanmar Government's Decision to Move its Capital", *ARI-NUS Working Paper No. 79*, November 2006.

Badgley, John H. "Burma and China" Policy of a Small Neighbor", in A.M. Halpern (ed.) *Policies Toward China: Views from Six Continents* (New York: McGraw-Hill Books, 1965).

Badgley, John H. "Burma's China Crisis: the Choice Ahead", *Asian Survey* (Vol. 7, No. 11; November 1967).

Barrington, James. "The Concept of Neutralism: What Lies behind Burma's Foreign Policy", *The Atlantic Monthly* (Vol. 201, No. 2; February 1958).

Bert, Wayne. "Chinese Policy toward Burma and Indonesia", *Asian Survey* (Vol. 35, No. 9; September 1985).

Bert, Wayne. "Burma, China and the U.S.A.", *Pacific Affairs*, vol. 77, no. 2, Summer 2004.

Chi-shad Liang. Burma's Relations with the People's Republic of China: From Delicate Friendship to Genuine Co-operation" in Peter Carey (ed.) *Challenge of the Change in Divided Society* (London: Palgrave Macmillan, 1997).

Ghoshal, Baladas. "Trends in China-Burma Relations", Verinder Grover (ed.) *Myanmar: Government and Politics* (New Delhi: Deep & Deep Publication PVT. LTD, 2000).

Hak Yin Li and Yongnian Zheng. "Re-interpreting China's Non-intervention Policy towards Myanmar: Leverage, Interest and Intervention", *Journal of Contemporary China* (vol. 18, issue no 61, September 2009).

Holliday, Ian. "Beijing and the Myanmar Problem", *The Pacific Review* (Vol. 22, No. 4, September 2009).

Holmes, Robert A. "Burma's Foreign Policy toward China Since 1962", *Pacific Affairs* (45:2; Summer 1972).

Holmes, Robert A. "China-Burma Relations Since the Rift", *Asian Survey* (Vol. 12, No. 8; August 1972).

Lee, Pak K., Gerald Chan & Lai-Ha Chan. "China's '*Realpolitik*' Engagement with Myanmar", *China Security* (Vol. 5, No. 1; Winter 2009).

Lintner, Bertil. "Burma and Its Neighbours", in Surjit Mansingh (ed.) *Indian and Chinese Foreign Policies in Comparative Perspective* (New Delhi: Radiant Publishers, 1998).

Maung Maung, Dr. "Burma-China Boundary Settlement", *Guardian Magazine* (Vol. 8, No. 3; March 1961).

Mittin, Roger. "Sino-Viet ties sour over reports on food s Lee, Pak K., Gerald Chan & Lai-Ha Chan. "China's '*Realpolitik*' Engagement with Myanmar", *China Security*, vol. 5, no. 1, Winter 2009.

Mya Maung. "On the Road to Mandalay: A case Study of the Sinonization of Upper Burma", *Asian Survey* (Vol. 34, No. 5: May 1994), pp. 447–459.

Selth, Andrew. Burma's China Connection and the Indian Ocean Region, *SDSC Working Paper No. 377* (Canberra: SDSC, 2003).

Silverstein, Josef. "Burma and the World: A Decade of foreign Policy under the State Law and Restoration Council", in Robert Taylor (ed.) Burma: Political Economy under Military rule (New York: Palgrave, 2001).

Singh, Udai Bhanu. "Recent Trends in Relations Between Myanmar and China" *Strategic Analysis* (Vol. 18, No. 1; April 1995).

Thompson, Virginia. "Burma and Two Chinas", in *Foreign Policy Bulletin*, Issue No. 23 (15 May 1953).

Tin Maung Maung Than. "Myanmar and China: A Special Relationship?, *Southeast Asian Affairs 2003* (Singapore: ISEAS, 2003).

Trager, Frank N. "Sino-Burmese Relations: the End of the Pauk Phaw Era", *ORBIS* (Vol. XI, No. 4; Winter 1968).

Unna, Warren. "CIA: Who Watches the Watchman?" *Harper's Magazine*, No. 216 (April 1958).

Books and Monographs (English)

Barnett, Doak. *Communist China and Asia: A Challenge to American Policy* (New York: Random House, 1960).

Brimwell, J. H. *Communism in Southeast Asia: A Political Analysis* (London: Oxford University Press, 1959).

Burma Socialist Programme Party. *1965 Party Seminar* (Yangon: BSPP Press, 1966).

Butwell, Richard. *U Nu of Burma* (Stanford, California: Stanford University Press, 1963).

Central Intelligence Agency (CIA). *Peking and the Burmese Communists: The Perils and Profits of Insurgency* (Report prepared in 1971).

Chinese People's Institute of Foreign Affairs, *A Victory for the Five Principles of Peaceful Co-existence* (Peking: Foreign Language Press, 1960).

Chi-shad Liang. *Burma's Foreign Relations: Neutralism in Theory and Practice* (New York: Praeger Publisher, 1990).

Colbert, Evelyn. *Southeast Asia in International Politics* (Ithaca: Cornell University Press, 1977).

Egreteau, Renaud. *Wooing the Generals: India's New Burma Policy* (New Delhi: Authorspress, 2003).

Gurtov, Melvin. *China and Southeast Asia — The Politics of Survival* (London: Heath Lexington Books, 1971).

Hinton, Harold. *China's Relations with Burma and Vietnam* (New York: Institute of Pacific Relations, 1956).

Hla Min, *Political Situation of Myanmar and Its Role in the Region*, (Yangon: News and periodical Enterprises, 2001).

International Crisis Group, *China's Myanmar Dilemma*, Crisis Group Asia Report No. 177 (14 September 2009).

Johnstone, William C. *A Chronology of Burma's International Relations 1945–1958* (Rangoon: Rangoon University, 1959).

Johnstone, William C. *Burma's Foreign Policy: A Study of Neutralism* (Cambridge, Massachusetts: Harvard University Press, 1963).

Kaznacheev, Alexsandr. *Inside a Soviet Embassy* (Philadelphia: J. P. Lippincott, 1962).

Mao Zedong. *Mao Zedong on Diplomacy* (Beijing: Foreign Language Press, 1998).

Maung Maung, Dr. *Burma in the Family of Nations* (Amsterdam: Djambatan, 1957).

Mende, Tibor. *South-East Asia between Two Worlds* (London: Turnstile Press, 1955).

Min Maung Maung, *The Tatmadaw and Its Leadership Role in National Politics* (Yangon: News and Periodical Enterprise, 1993).

Ministry of Information. *Burma* (Vol. IX, No. 4; October 1960).

Ministry of Information. *China-Myanmar Goodwill Visits of Great Historic Significance* (Yangon: News and Periodical Enterprises, 1991).

Ministry of Information. *From Peace to Stability* (Yangon: Ministry of Information, 1951).

Ministry of Information. *Kuomintang Aggression Against Burma* (Rangoon: Ministry of Information, 1955).

Myo Myint. *China Factor in Burma's Foreign Policy* (unpublished paper, 1987).

Nu, U. *Premier Report to the People* (Rangoon: GUB, 1958).

Pettman, Ralph. *China in Burma's Foreign Policy* (Canberra: Australian National University, 1973).

Royal Institute of International Affairs. *Collective Defence in Southeast Asia — The Manila Treaty and its Implications* (London: Oxford University Press, 1958).

Soong Ching Ling. *Good Neighbours Meet* (Peking: Foreign Language Press, 1956).

Taylor, Jay. *China and Southeast Asia: Peking's Relations with Revolutionary Movements* (New York: Praeger Publishers, Second Edition, 1976).

Taylor, Robert H. *Foreign and Domestic Consequences of the KMT Intervention in Burma* (Ithaca; Cornell University Southeast Asia Program, 1973).

Teiwes, Frederick C. and Warren Sun. *The End of the Maoist Era: Chinese Politics During the Twilight of the Cultural Revolution, 1972–1976* (New York: M.E. Sharpe, 2007).

The Chinese People's Institute of Foreign Affairs (ed.), *A Victory for the Five Principles of Peaceful Co-existence* (Beijing: Foreign Language Press, 1960).

Tinker, Hugh. *The Union of Burma: A Study of the First Years of Independence,* fourth edition (London: Oxford University Press, 1967).

Watson, Francis. *The Frontier of China* (London: Chatto and Windus, 1969).

Wise, David and Thomas Ross. *The Invisible Government* (New York: Random House, 1964).

Woodman, Dorothy. *The Making of Burma* (London: the Cresset Press, 1962).

Xiaolin Guo, *Towards Resolution: China in the Myanmar Issue* (Silk Road Paper, Johns Hopkins University-SAIS, March 2007).

Unpublished Dissertations

Holmes, Robert A. *Chinese Foreign Policy Toward Burma and Cambodia: A Comparative Analysis,* unpublished Ph.D Dissertation, Columbia University, 1969.

Kay Khine, *Sino-Myanmar Relations: Operation Burma Boundary* (M.A Thesis, Department of International Relations, Yangon University, 1996).

Kuo-kong Show, *Communist China's Foreign Policy toward the Non-aligned States,* unpublished Ph.D Dissertation, University of Pennsylvania, 1972.

Books and Articles (Myanmar Language)

ကြည်ညွှန့်၊ *ချစ်ကြည်ရေး ချစ်ကြည်ရေးလှို့ဆိုက္က* (ရန်ကုန်၊ အပေါင်းအသင်းစာပေ၊ ၁၉၆၈) [Kyi Nyunt. *In the Name of Friendship* (Yangon: Apaung-Athin, 1968)].

ကြည်ညွှန့်၊ ချစ်ကြည်ရေး။ *ခေတ်လေးခေတ်တရှက်မြန်မာဆက်ဆံရေး* (ရန်ကုန်၊ မိုးနတ်စာပေ၊ ၁၉၇၆) [Kyi Nyunt, Chitkyiye. *Sino-Myanmar Relations under Four Periods* (Yangon: Moe Nat Press, 1976)].

စစ်သမိုင်းပြတိုက်နှင့်တပ်မတော်မော်ကွန်းတိုက်မှူးရုံး။ *တပ်မတော်သမိုင်း* (ရန်ကုန်၊ စစ်သမိုင်းပြတိုက်နှင့် တပ်မတော်မော်ကွန်းတိုက်မှူးရုံး၊ ၂၀၀၃) [Defence Services Historical Museum and Research Institute (DSHMRI), *History of the Armed Forces* (Yangon: DSHMRI, 2003)].

စာပေဗိမာန်။ *ဂွှလရာဇ်မှတ်တမ်း* (ရန်ကုန်၊ စာပေဗိမာန်၊ ၁၉၅၅) [Burma Translation Society, *Record of China* (Yangon: Burma Translation Society, 1955)].

ဇန်ထားဆင်၊ ဦး။ *ဒီမိုကရေစီပြောင်းပြန်* (ရန်ကုန်၊ အောင်စစ်သည်စာပေ၊ ၁၉၉၀) [U Zan Hta Sin. *Reversed Democracy* (Yangon: Aung Sithi Sarpay, 1990)].

တောခိုကျောင်းသားဟောင်းများ။ ထို့ကြောင့် ... ဤသို့ (ရန်ကုန်၊ ဦးတင်မောင်ဝင်း၊၁၉၉၁) [Former Underground Students. *Therefore — It is* (Yangon: U Tin Maung Win, 1991)].

ပြန်ကြားရေးဝန်ကြီးဌာန၊ တိုင်းကျိုးပြည်ပြုမှတ်တမ်းများ — အတွဲ (၁) (ရန်ကုန်၊ သတင်းနှင့်စာနယ်ဇင်းလုပ်ငန်း၊ ၁၉၉၁) [*Nation-Building Records*, Volume -1 (Yangon: News and Periodical Enterprises, 1991)].

ပြန်ကြားရေးဝန်ကြီးဌာန၊ တိုင်းကျိုးပြည်ပြုမှတ်တမ်းများ — အတွဲ (၂) (ရန်ကုန်၊ သတင်းနှင့်စာနယ်ဇင်းလုပ်ငန်း၊ ၁၉၉၅) [*Nation-Building Records*, Volume -2 (Yangon: News and Periodical Enterprises, 1995)].

ဘခက်၊ ရဲဘော်။ "ငြိမ်းချမ်းပန်းကမ်းခဲ့ပေမယ့်"၊ ပြည်သူတို့နှင့်အတူ (ရန်ကုန်၊ မြရာပင်စာပေ၊ ၁၉၇၀) [Ba Khet, Yebaw. "Although the Peace was Offered" *Together with the People* (Yangon: Myayarpin Press, 1970)].

မြ၊ ရဲဘော် နှင့်အပေါင်းအပါများ။ သုံးပါတီရှိသည်မှာ (ရန်ကုန်၊ မြယာပင်စာပေ၊ ၁၉၇၀) [Yebaw Mya and et al., *Three Parties Are* (Yangon: Myayarpin Sarpay, 1970)].

မြ၊ ရဲဘော် နှင့်အပေါင်းအပါများ။ သခင်သန်းထွန်း၏နောက်ဆုံးနေ့များ (ရန်ကုန်၊ မြယာပင်စာပေ၊ ၁၉၆၈) [Yebaw Mya and et al., *The Last Days of Thakin Than Tun* (Yangon: Myayarbin Sarpay, 1968)].

ဝန်ကြီးချုပ်ချိုအင်လိုင်းကြိုဆိုရေးတရုတ်အမျိုးသားများကော်မတီ။ တရုတ်မြန်မာချစ်ကြည်ရေးမှတ်တမ်း (ရန်ကုန်၊ ခေတ်မြန်မာပုံနှိပ်တိုက်၊ ၁၉၆၁) [Chinese Committee to Welcome Premier Zhao Enlai, *China-Myanmar Friendship Record — in Myanmar* (Yangon: Khit Myanmar Press, 1961).

သစ်မောင်၊ရဲဘော်။ ပြည်တွင်းသောင်းကျန်းမှုသမိုင်း (ရန်ကုန်၊ သတင်းနှင့်စာနယ်ဇင်းလုပ်ငန်း၊ ၁၉၉၀) [Yebaw Thit Maung. *History of Insurgency* (Yangon: News and Periodical Enterprise, 1990)].

သိန်းဖေမြင့်။ မော်စီတုံးတရုတ်ပြည်နှင့် မြန်မာ့အချုပ်အချာအာဏာ (ရန်ကုန်၊ နံ့သာတိုက်၊ ၁၉၆၇) Then Pe Myint. *Mao Zedong's China and Myanmar's Sovereignty* (Yangon: Nanthar Press, 1967), p. 57.

Unpublished Documents

ကာကကြည်း (သုတေသန)၊ တရုတ်-မြန်မာဆက်ဆံရေးအကျဉ်းချုပ် ၁၉၄၉-၁၉၈၄ (ပုံနှိပ်ခြင်းမရှိသောစာတမ်း) [Army (Research*). Sino-Myanmar Relations in Brief, 1949–1984* (unpublished paper)].

ကာကကြည်း (သုတေသန)၊ ပကပအရှေ့မြောက်စစ်ဒေသ သမိုင်းအကျဉ်းနှင့် အလားအလာသုံးသတ်ချက် (ပုံနှိပ်ခြင်း မရှိသောစာတမ်း) [Army (Research). *Brief History of the BCP Northeast Region and Assessment on its Future* (unpublished paper)].

ကာကကြည်း (သုတေသန)၊ အရှေ့ မြောက်တိုင်းစစ်ဌာနချုပ်နယ်မြေအတွင်းရှိ သောင်းကျန်းမှုသမိုင်း (ပုံနှိပ်ခြင်း မရှိသောစာတမ်း) [Army (research), *History of Insurgency in the Northeast Command* (unpublished paper)].

တပ်မတော်ထောက်လှမ်းရေး ညွှန်ကြားရေးမှူးရုံး၊ ပြည်တွင်းသောင်းကျန်းမှုသမိုင်း (ပုံနှိပ်ခြင်းမရှိသောစာတမ်း၊ ရက်စွဲမပါ) [Directorate of Defence Services Intelligence (DDSI), *History of Insurgency* (unpublished, no date)].

တပ်မတော်ထောက်လှမ်းရေး ညွှန်ကြားရေးမှူးရုံး၊ အရှေ့ မြောက်ဒေသ ပကပ (ပုံနှိပ်ခြင်းမရှိသောစာတမ်း၊

၁၉၈၃) [Directorate of Defence Services Intelligence (DDSI), *The BCP in Northeast Myanmar* (unpublished, 1983)].

CD 1017, *The Interrogation Report of Ex. KMT Major General Liu Shing Yie* (Date of surrender — 6 July 1956 and interrogated in August 1956, NBSD).

CD 1017, *The Interrogation Report of Ex. KMT Major General Liu Shing Yie.*

CD 1493, *Report on the Bangkok Meeting*, DSHMRI.

CD 28, *Report of Defence Services Goodwill Mission to China*, DSHMRI.

CD 5, *Report on the Operation Yein Nwe Par*, Vol. 1+2+3, DSHMRI.

CD 641, *Notes on the first session of the Chinese-Burmese Joint Committee*, DSHMRI.

CD 644, *Report of the Chinese-Burmese Joint Committee to the Permanent Secretary of Foreign Affairs*, DSHMRI.

CD 646, *Documents on the Operation Burma Boundary*, DSHMRI.

CD 648, *Boundary Treaty between the Union of Burma and People's Republic of China*, DSHMRI.

DR 9397, *Casualty Report on the Operation Burma Boundary — Mekong Operation*, DSHMRI.

DR 9398, *Report on the Operation Burma Boundary — Mekong Operation*, DSHMRI.

DR. 9453, *Interview with Colonel Chit Myaing.*

Newspapers and Magazines
Bangkok Post
Forward Magazine
Kyemon Newspaper
Min Bao Newspaper
Myanmar News Gazette Journal
New York Times
Peking Review
People's Daily [人民日报]
People's China
South China Morning Post
The Guardian (Myanmar)
The Living Color Magazine
The Mirror Newspaper (Myanmar)
The Myanmar Times (Journal)
The Nation (Myanmar)
Working People's Daily

INDEX

About the Author

Maung Aung Myoe received his B.A. in International Relations from University of Mandalay and M.A. in the same discipline from International University of Japan, and Ph.D in Political Science and International Relations from Australian National University. He was a visiting fellow at the Institute of Defence and Strategic Studies (IDSS), Nanyang Technological University (NTU) and a postdoctoral fellow at the Asia Research Institute (ARI), National University of Singapore. His research interests cover Myanmar politics and foreign relations as well as regionalism, security and strategy, and civil-military relations. He teaches Southeast Asian Politics and International Relations at the International University of Japan (IUJ).